THE LAST MIXTAPE

THE LAST MIXTAPE

Physical Media and Nostalgic Cycles

SETH LONG

The University of Chicago Press
Chicago and London

The University of Chicago Press, Chicago 60637
The University of Chicago Press, Ltd., London
© 2025 by The University of Chicago
All rights reserved. No part of this book may be used or reproduced in any manner whatsoever without written permission, except in the case of brief quotations in critical articles and reviews. For more information, contact the University of Chicago Press, 1427 E. 60th St., Chicago, IL 60637.
Published 2025

34 33 32 31 30 29 28 27 26 25   1 2 3 4 5

ISBN-13: 978-0-226-84046-8 (cloth)
ISBN-13: 978-0-226-84048-2 (paper)
ISBN-13: 978-0-226-84047-5 (e-book)
DOI: https://doi.org/10.7208/chicago/9780226840475.001.0001

Library of Congress Cataloging-in-Publication Data

Names: Long, Seth, author.
Title: The last mixtape : physical media and nostalgic cycles / Seth Long.
Description: Chicago : The University of Chicago Press, 2025. | Includes bibliographical references and index.
Identifiers: LCCN 2024059335 | ISBN 9780226840468 (cloth) | ISBN 9780226840482 (paperback) | ISBN 9780226840475 (ebook)
Subjects: LCSH: Mixtapes—History. | Sound recordings—History. | Sound recordings—Social aspects. | Nostalgia in music | Copyright—Music. | Computer file sharing.
Classification: LCC ML1055 .L65 2025 | DDC 781.49—dc23/eng/20241211
LC record available at https://lccn.loc.gov/2024059335

For Christina

> Music made with ribbons and magnets—
> what alchemy is this?
>
> HEID E. ERDRICH, "Autobiography as Mix Tape
> for Lady Mon de Green"

> Physical media is almost a *Fahrenheit 451* (where people memorized entire books and thus became the book they loved) level of responsibility. If you own a [disc] of a film or films you love[,] you are the custodian of those films for generations to come.
>
> GUILLERMO DEL TORO, in Sharf, "Christopher Nolan Says Streaming-Only Content Is a 'Danger'"

CONTENTS

Introduction *1*

1: The First Mixtapes: A Top 10 Countdown *14*

2: Hot Wax Pirates *42*

3: The Cassette Mixtape (Side A: Romantic Stuff) *60*

4: The Cassette Mixtape (Side B: Industrial Noise) *80*

5: A Rhetoric and Poetics of the Mixtape *102*

6: Music without a Medium *117*

7: The Infinite Playlist *140*

ACKNOWLEDGMENTS *165*
NOTES *167*
BIBLIOGRAPHY *179*
INDEX *191*

INTRODUCTION

Americans in the last century made two kinds of mixtape: public tapes and private tapes. This book is about the private ones. Public hip-hop tapes and private mixtapes aren't dissimilar, but from a rhetorical perspective, the contrasts override the similarities. The public mixtape was produced for a large audience; the private mixtape was dubbed for an audience of one. The public mixtape existed on multiple copies; the private mixtape lived on a single copy. The public mixtape was a published poem; the private mixtape was a hand-delivered note scribbled on a piece of paper. The public mixtape advertised; the private shared.

It's hard to pinpoint the moment the word *mixtape* was coined, which is odd, because it's a new coinage. Part of the problem is that *compilation tape*, *mixed tape*, *mix [space] tape*, and *DJ tape* are extant variations in the archives. Also, it is not always clear if a passing reference is to a public mixtape, a private mixtape, or some sort of promotional item. In 1982, for example, Kenwood Corporation offered "compilation tapes," such as *Hot Rock for the Road*, to anyone who purchased a Kenwood car stereo.[1] In 1974, Scandinavian record label Finnlevy released *Music in the Summer Night*, a "compilation tape" of bands whose full albums could be purchased on cassette.[2] Some of the earliest uses of *mix* or *mixed tape* in the Google Books corpus, based on Google Ngram results, reference master recordings (as in, a tape that has been mixed in a studio) or compilations of television clips stored on VHS tape. The term likely had a technical meaning before it had a pop-culture meaning. Even as late as 1995, Nick Hornby's cassette culture novel *High Fidelity* does not use the word *mixtape* at all. The protagonist, Rob Fleming, refers to them as "compilation tapes" or just "tapes." Most mentions of mixtapes in the eighties and early nineties point to self-promoted DJ or rap tapes. Using the word mixtape to refer to a custom playlist on cassette was not too popular until the first decade of the twenty-first century. The word's rise tracked the mixtape's death as an active youth ritual. That said, digital archives aren't history. I recall using the word in the nineties, so it was probably in circulation by the late eighties. However, the Google Books corpus, the *Billboard* archive, and a variety of audio archives verify that the signifier *mixtape* arrived long after consumers had learned to curate music playlists, for personal sharing, on magnetic tape cartridges, reel-to-reel tape, and lacquer discs.

Whatever the term, on a grand historical scale, not many people made or listened to mixtapes: just the twentieth century's most dedicated music fans, who knew how to connect turntables and rewind tape cartridges with a pencil. This book is written for those fortunate few. It is also written for anyone interested in the ephemera—like Kodachrome slides, PEZ dispensers, newspaper printing radios, public phones, rotary phones, POGs, pet rocks, mall Glamour Shots, cap guns, beepers, and the Pony Express—that litter America's cultural parade. And I'm writing for those who are curious about the relationship between technological turnover and generational cycles of nostalgia. "The medium is the message," wrote Marshall McLuhan. The blank cassette illustrates how a new technology coaxes tendencies from a generation and solidifies them into a cultural *thing*, just in time for technology to march on, for old media to give way to new media, leaving in their wake a dusty mixtape at the bottom of a box of CDs tossed into the garage next to a DVD player, a Discman, and a Compaq computer tower.

The mixtape was part of twentieth-century youth culture, and its history should be written down. But I'm interested in more than the cassette's melancholic pull for elder millennials and Generation X. Such is the topic in the documentary *Analog Love* (directed by Robert V. Galluzzo), Jehnie I. Burns's *Mixtape Nostalgia*, and other cassette retrospectives. Techno-nostalgia is not unimportant, but the mixtape also provides an allegory for the cycles of media obsolescence that produce nostalgia in the first place, and on whose crests and troughs cultures rise and fall. From saddle to internet, new technology has motivated cultural formation and practice, which in turn produces the demand for updated technologies to keep up with the culture's formation. Geoffrey Winthrop-Young notes how the literary culture of the nineteenth century "created a demand for media experiences that could only be met by post-print technologies."[3]

Whether motivated by new demands or new technologies, a cultural practice, in the short or long run, always risks being as fleeting as the novel technology with which it emerges. All technology is stamped with a sell-by date. Economic demands and the force of history stamped it at first, but Brooks Stevens and Vance Packard recognized half a century ago that engineers also build obsolescence into the technological environment. To the extent that media make culture, many cultures are destined to the same fate—obsolescence, at a quickening rate, especially as Packard's "obsolescence of desirability" and "obsolescence of function" collapse into each other in the digital century.⁴ Not every newfangled *thing*, be it a new medium or a cultural trend, gets to become what social critic Paul Skallas calls "Lindy," something whose long-term survival increases in proportion with its age.⁵

For media history, the mixtape is useful because it experienced one of history's most radical cycles of obsolescence: the analog-to-digital transition. From protomixtapes on 78 rpm discs to streaming playlists on Spotify, the mixtape is a test for how crucial the medium really is to the message. Did anyone create "mixtapes" before the cassette? What does mixtape culture evolve into without the cassette? This book looks forward and backward from the cassette to discover curious joints in history where other media produced similar but not identical encounters between technology and consumers. "Mixtapes cannot exist without cassettes" is a strong claim. "To what extent has American culture produced a mixtape without the cassette?" is a more valuable approach.

Our relationship with music is influenced by the way we listen to it. Since Edison, every generation has listened to music via a different medium. This book is therefore interested in media present and media future as much as in media past, recognizing that, for listeners if not for musicians,⁶ technological turnover and shifts in musical consumption habits are two versions of the same history. Teens did not listen to music on a lacquer disc the same way they listened to it on a Walkman. The rise and decline of music cultures, understood broadly, seems to track with these cycles of development and obsolescence. To reiterate Winthrop-Young's point, the expectations created by one generation's media experiences are often met by engineers who produce the media ecology enjoyed by the next generation, which destroys the previous experiences . . . and on and on.

For some media, their demise has meant a cultural *damnatio memoriae*—a total erasure from public memory. Shifting from music to film, we can ask, Who remembers the LaserDisc? Who recalls the social customs built up around that mammoth precursor to DVD? Ditto Betamax, 8-tracks, 4-tracks, the mimeograph, floppy disks, Sony MiniDiscs, wax cylinders, 9-track computer tapes, and MiniDV. The museum of obsolete media is cavernous.

Like the LaserDisc, many obsolete media are gone for good. Sadly, no one writes books about what we lose with the passing of truly dead media formats. For luckier media, obsolescence means not social amnesia but a lingering echo. Some musicians, for example, dream of a cassette revival; retro video game consoles are rereleased in miniature form decades after their initial production. More powerful than lingering echoes, the luckiest media become metaphorical touchstones or rhetorical commonplaces for societies that have otherwise discarded the medium: we still "hang up" our smartphones, measure things in "horsepower," "run out" of time, "cut" film, and "patch" computer code. In chapter 5, I explore how the mixtape may be turning into one of these unfortunately named dead metaphors—in this case, a metaphor for nostalgia, love, and the curation of memories.

But rhetorical traces are exactly that—traces, not the medium. No technology lasts forever. The Pony Express was the pinnacle of nineteenth-century American horse culture, taking center stage just in time for the railroads and telegraph lines to make it obsolete. The Pony Express lasted a year and a half. It existed at a "break boundary" or media reversal that, according to McLuhan, tends to occur just as a media infrastructure reaches peak intensity. Injured by the new steam extension of our feet, American horse culture dwindled in importance until another invention put it out of its misery.

The horse had a good run. The cassette had a comparatively short lifespan. Mixtape culture likewise rose and fell at a quick clip. Nonetheless, the mixtape seems to have attained a legitimate cross-generational metaphoric or imaginative potential, much like horse and saddle.

Attached to the book's media history is this interest in a tech-enabled culture's half-life and its longevity as a rhetorical commonplace. In the 2020s, it's an interesting dichotomy because it slams us directly into the strangeness of digital architecture, within which cycles of nostalgia and obsolescence have short-circuited. As it turns out, the mixtape's three decades of existence—roughly from the 1970s through the late 1990s—dwarfs the ephemerality of new cultural practices rising and falling online. The contrast between pre- and postmillennial cycles of media turnover suggests that digital media (especially digital media as consummated by the pocket-sized computer called a smartphone) have caused culture to speed up and to stop, simultaneously and paradoxically. The simplest way to put it is that digital/smartphone culture changes so rapidly with apps, updates, and viral trends that nothing solidifies into a mass cultural phenomenon. The result is what Skallas calls "stuck culture."[7]

"There just doesn't seem to be that much difference between 2002 and now," tweets journalist Holly A. Bell (@HollyBell8, February 1, 2022). "I wonder if our cycle of nostalgia has slowed," tweets Dr. James Joyner of the Marine Corps University Command and Staff College (@DrJJoyner, February 1, 2022). Social media and smartphones have exacerbated a trend that began with cable television. Presented with a hundred channels rather than five, we channel surfed until we ironically settled on five channels all over again, but with this distinction: now we were all watching five *different* channels. Cable TV struck a minor blow to the shared media environment enjoyed throughout the twentieth century. Social media and the smartphone have done the same thing to all content, with a more wholesale detonation of shared media. Culture has fractured into a thousand niche spaces, all of which change so rapidly that nothing congeals into a lasting moment perpetuated by shared media—a moment or experience or practice in which a critical mass of people participates and in later years reflects on.

The cassette, in contrast, was one of the last predigital items to survive long enough, within a shared media environment, to turn a fleeting youth practice into a lasting *thing*: the mixtape. Viral challenges, TikTok dances, and GeoCities pages register as strongly on the historical timeline as the mixtape registers in comparison with horse and saddle. The mixtape thus exists at a turning point, standing near the center of the analog-to-digital revolution but also within the ever-quickening crescendo of media turnover. That in-betweenness makes the mixtape a valuable boundary between physical media and streaming media, between the electric world and the digital world, between content ownership and leased access.[8]

At its most abstract scale, this book explores what has happened to music, music consumption, and music culture within this present information architecture—a paradoxical creation that promises abundance, replicates old music trends, and condemns new music to the forgetfulness of the digital ether. In the 2020s, in the age of both Orwellian data collection and dead hyperlinks,[9] we are beginning to realize that even as data multiply, traces of culture (musical and otherwise) remain more ephemeral, less stable, and increasingly less accessible than ever before.[10] Compared to a Spotify or a YouTube playlist, a cassette and a battery-powered Walkman start to look more stable.

If I haven't made it clear enough, this book offers a defense of physical media—durable, permanent ownership—against the current ecology's emphasis on perpetual renting. Music was freed on MP3 only to find itself locked behind monthly subscription fees or lost in an infinite stream of ad-driven "content." Consumers today are given a choice, in twentieth-century terms, between radio or jukebox.

To be fair, one possible argument against my case for physical music media is that, in the end, all music media are *reproductions*. Why value one medium over any other? Unlike cinema—which makes no pretense at replicating stage plays, and whose mediated existence is the "production"—music on LP, cassette, CD, or smartphone never meets the unmediated ideal of live music. All prerecorded music fails to live up to that ideal, so a defense of cassettes or compact discs against the smartphone, says the iPhone 20 owner, seems moot.

First, studio-recorded music, like film, is its own fine-tuned production, not a recording of live music (that would be called a bootleg if recorded illicitly or a live album if released). However, it is true that live music is culturally viewed, even now, as the purest rendering of a song or a symphony—and for good reason. There is a radical difference between the sensory "imprinting" of a flesh-space concert and listening to prerecorded music via headphones or speakers. The differences involve not only the type of sound encountered but also the material environment, the physical movement, and the social roles involved.

In *Representing Sound*, Jay Hodgson and Steve MacLeod define live musical performance as "the physical act of making air molecules vibrate." They continue, "However it is done, performing music is always vibrating (compressing and rarefying) air molecules into dynamic, undulating shapes. Sculpting air molecules, then, remains the substantive basis of every live musical communication—the very thing musicians do no matter how, where, when, or with whom."[11] Vibrating molecules hit more powerfully in person. Live instruments miked and amplified vibrate the air more violently than a prerecorded tape or CD—no matter how nice the stereo. The physical venue of the performance also plays a role, due to its acoustic effects. "Music evolves and adapts to resonate with material conditions and sonic spaces," writes Byron Hawk.

> Punk made at CBGB's, for example, fit that sonic space. The club was modeled on a small country and bluegrass venue in Nashville, but this low reverb environment was also perfect for noisy punk, which would sound like reverberating mush in a larger hall. The small space and tight acoustics meant that every sound would be heard.... African drums and complex polyrhythms work perfectly in open outdoor spaces ...; and the acoustic space of medieval cathedrals, which have sustained reverb of up to four seconds, made the slow, drawn out notes in a single key of the Gregorian chant almost a necessity.[12]

Onto live music's acoustic dimensions, we can add all the people gathered to hear it, whether in a church pew, an opera box, or a mosh pit. Concerts have *audiences*. No matter how many friends gather around a stereo, they do not form an audience; they are *listeners*. We *listened* to mixtapes; no mixtape ever had an *audience*. Live music is not just a shared experience but a public spectacle—often a rank and sweaty spectacle. So many bodies in motion; so many ears and vocal tracts in tune. Live music engages all five senses. In contrast, only the sense of hearing is engaged—although in a heightened state—when music is listened to on speakers or headphones.

Music is as old as humanity. Neanderthals could probably sing.[13] For millennia, the baseline experience of music was to listen to it in person. You came; you saw; you listened. You bopped your head; you moved your body; you joined with others in a dance. From an African village to an urban mosh pit, music for most of human history has been an embodied, communal experience. In a book on mixtapes and music media, there is no point denying live music's persistent primacy even in the age of digital abundance.

And yet the primacy of live music is no reason to lump together all music media under the same heading: "not live music." The book's argument is that consumers should value and retain physical, dedicated music media because the value of the music and the value of the delivery medium are intertwined. Not all music media are created equal. Cassettes and compact discs may have been cheap, but as industrially produced objects, they never reached a cost point of zero. Turning music into digital information, on the other hand, has allowed it to reach that cost point, as far as music's reproduction and circulation are concerned. That's why YouTube, Pandora, and other apps allow users to stream music for free if they don't mind the occasional advertisement. At best, streaming music reproduces radio. And I love radio—don't get me wrong—especially noncommercial regional or college radio, but it does not enable the intimate relationship with, or ownership of, music epitomized by rewinding a song on cassette or CD time after time.

Comparing music and linguistic media is helpful here. Like Plato in the *Phaedrus*, we can adopt a strong preference for live speech against any secondary impressions in books. From Plato's perspective, differences between the scroll, codex, printed book, and pdf are uninteresting because they're all *books* (a shorthand designation) that fail to reproduce flesh-space discourse and dialectic.[14] From a rhetorical perspective, however, that blunt distinction is wrongheaded. Unwinding a scroll is not like scrolling through a pdf file, and neither one is like reading a printed book. As Nicholas Carr famously argued, accessing written information on the internet short-circuits our attention spans in a manner not encountered when reading books in a library.[15] I can't click references in a book, after all, and books don't make noises at me. Even if all media are secondary reproductions of something best experienced in flesh-space (the example of film proves otherwise), not all secondary reproductions are the same sort of thing. Claiming that a cassette and a smartphone are alike because both produce pale imitations of live music means ignoring media effects. Considering the differences, listening to a cassette on headphones starts to seem more multisensory than I let on a couple paragraphs ago.

For starters, a tape is a dedicated music medium; a phone is a medium of media. One requires a playback device; the other is a self-sufficient device. One has a mechanical hum; the other offers cold perfection. One makes music spatial and tactile; the other makes music invisible. Like a book that grows heavier in the left hand while the right hand gets lighter, the cassette tape reveals its own time signature and journey toward completion. On a smartphone, the multisensory impact of music is flattened into two dimensions. These are the distinctions that media historians and rhetorical theorists are interested in—distinctions in perception or experience when content remains ostensibly the same.

From the sound archives of wax cylinders and lacquer discs, through reel-to-reel and cassette tape, to the transformation of music and all content into digital ones and zeros, this book anchors itself to the cassette mixtape while navigating the complexities of technological obsolescence, media ownership, nostalgic cycles, and the speed of cultural change during the analog-to-digital transition—a transition whose effects still reverberate in the 2020s. The first chapters of this book provide the history; the later chapters explore the present and future of digital music consumption. The book ends as a quiet polemic in favor of the media ecology the mixtape enjoyed: cheap and abundant but also tactile, limited in scope, and therefore owned, crafted, and meaningfully engaged with: the ultimate *cool* medium, in McLuhan's sense.

Chapter 1 investigates audio and magazine archives to discover, if not the first mixtape, at least the technological and cultural environment in which the first mixtapes exchanged hands. I define what a mixtape is—a mechanically copied, customized album for an individual recipient—then explore what mixtape-making looked like before it became a culturally recognized activity in the 1980s. People did indeed make "mixtapes" in the decades of reel-to-reel formats and long-play (LP) records; however, they lacked an abundant, portable, easily copied medium that could turn music curation into a widespread youth ritual. Audio letters, home recordings, opera bootlegs on wax cylinders, and a 1949 78 rpm disc all prove that the desire to capture, curate, and customize musical experiences arose alongside the technology of mechanically reproduced sound. That the ethos of the mixtape attached itself to the cassette tape in the eighties and nineties, I argue, has nothing to do with earlier media's inability to produce a mixtape and more to do with economic conditions, consumer inertia, and the long-standing distinction between consumers and prosumers, the former dictating what does and does not become a culturally recognized *thing*. Chapter 1 also transcribes what may be the earliest (certainly one of the earliest) extant mixtapes to turn up in the American audio archive. It's a mix-disc, a 78 rpm dubbed in 1949, located with the help of Grammy-nominated sound archivist Patrick Feaster. The disc contains a proper mix compiled from multiple LPs and manually dubbed, song by song, onto a blank disc. Crafted by a hardcore jazz hound, the mix-disc suggests an idea developed in the next chapter—that prior to the Compact Cassette (introduced in 1964), protomixtapes would have only been compiled by the most committed of music fans and audiophiles, who set the stage for cassette mixtape culture but never cut mixtapes in great enough numbers to gain cultural attention.

Chapter 2 lingers in the precassette decades, arguing that early and midcentury music pirates and bootleggers may have been the most specialized of audiophiles who possessed the technology and know-how to create customized albums on LPs and reel-to-reel tape. Integrated dual cassette decks made it easy to cut a mixtape in the eighties and nineties; before then, however, only music pirates would have been familiar enough with dubbing LPs to create anything like a full-fledged mixtape culture: a culture in which the technology's novelty had worn off, allowing interpersonal motives to take center stage. Dealing with music piracy, this chapter also introduces the book's recurrent theme of music ownership, as understood by musicians, publishers, distributors, media companies, and consumers. The legal and cultural history of who owns music—and in what form—runs alongside the mixtape's story. The chapter provides an overview of that history, from the original eighteenth-century frameworks for music "copy"-rights to early composer angst about piano player rolls, a failed lawsuit on behalf of Glenn Miller, and the perennial lag between technological development and the state's ability to regulate it.

Drawing on the Google Books corpus, personal interviews, and secondary retrospectives—such as John Z. Komurki and Luca Bendandi's *Cassette Cultures*, Thurston Moore's *Mix Tape: The Art of Cassette Culture*, and Jehnie I. Burns's *Mixtape Nostalgia*—chapters 3 and 4 dive into the cassette decades in all their analog glory. From the 1970s through the 1990s, Gen X and elder millennials had the techno-generational luck to possess a consumer machine that allowed them to dub music from multiple sources onto a single source; a practice difficult on LPs but too easy on digital playlists. Chapter 3 provides the nostalgic angle, describing cassettes as a happy medium of sound reproduction: cheap and convenient enough that most people could create a mixtape on their own but labor intensive enough that the hours of creation crystallized into lasting memories as well as material artifacts—the mixtapes themselves, complete with handwritten art and liner notes on the J-card (the paper insert in the cassette case). With the help of Jason Luther and other rhetorical theorists, I define the mixtape as an example of DIY culture—an object that co-opted the content of mass media and capitalist production and put it to use for interpersonal, noncommercial ends. I also emphasize in this chapter the *tactility* of twentieth-century music media and why it matters for our relationship to music. The tactility of the cassette (as with the LP) was ultimately more important to music fans than perfect audio quality. Music we can touch, after all, provides a powerful connection not only to the music but to the past with which we come to associate the item. Musical or even media nostalgia, I argue, is not a bad thing when we are the ones who own the mnemonic devices; it's a different matter, of course, when we swap old cassettes for algorithmic streams accessed on heavily monitored smartphones.

If chapter 3 leans into the nostalgia, chapter 4 counteracts it with the cassette era's industrial backdrop. America's offshoring of industry, the radical economies of scale unleashed by East Asian manufacturing, the Schelling effect by which consumers glom onto a new medium without any public discourse about its adoption, and the consequences of planned obsolescence are all intertwined in this chapter, with the mixtape caught somewhere in the middle. I argue that mixtape culture relied on exploitative processes that created an abundance of cheap magnetic tape cartridges and their playback devices. Indeed, the cheaper they got, the better they sounded, and the more suitable they became for sharing music.

Chapter 4 also draws on journalist Addison Del Mastro's and others' reporting on current trends in industrial obsolescence, recounting the story of how cassettes and tape players almost went extinct alongside VCRs and VHS tapes. The cassette was kept alive thanks in part to a stubborn manufacturer in Missouri and unlicensed Chinese clones of defunct Japanese patents. However, the cassette's continued manufacture is not guaranteed. Comparing the tenuous existence of cassette manufacturing with the rebirth of LP records, I argue that all tactile music media face an uncertain industrial future if the consumer market continues to gravitate toward the streaming playlist. At some point, if a niche but healthy market exists for almost obsolete technology, the cost to revive its manufacturing base nonetheless outweighs potential profits. Even with worthwhile demand, the medium risks permanent obsolescence. I end chapter 4 on an optimistic note, however, asking what *obsolescence* means for old music media amid a nascent discontent with cloud-based music consumption.

Chapter 5 provides a rhetorical pause between analog and digital music. It begins with a close, tongue-in-cheek reading of *High Fidelity*—both the novel and the film—as the pinnacle of mixtape culture's popularity. Beginning with the fact that the film version, released in 2000, was already a nostalgic portrayal of a dying practice rather than a living representation of youth culture, my close reading drains even more nostalgia from the mixtape by highlighting the racial and class connotations of personalized mixtapes (as opposed to hip-hop mixtapes). It uncovers the latent narcissism and self-indulgence involved in mixtape-making. As a counterstatement to previous chapters' nostalgia and optimism, it suggests that mixtape culture itself, far from being an interpersonal co-option of capitalist production, in fact embodied America's atomized individualism. "Mix tapes are like matchmaker forms," writes Thurston Moore. "But why must your match have to be so like yourself—do you just pretty much love yourself? Is there a desire to convert your lover into you?"[16]

The chapter then follows the mixtape's path from youth ritual to rhetorical commonplace. With the help of the Google Books corpus and music journalist Rob Sheffield's bestselling memoir, *Love Is a Mix Tape*, I look at the mixtape's growth as a productive metaphor even as the cassette itself was outpaced by compact disc and internet music sharing. This rhetorical evolution lies at the heart of the book's interest in mixtapes as an inflection point between analog and digital music—a point at which analog nostalgia already began to swell, turning the mixtape into a nostalgic touchstone, or a life raft, for a generation about to experience a Gutenberg-scale media revolution.

Chapters 6 and 7 confront the revolution. I begin with the compact disc's conversion of music into ones and zeros—a monumental event recounted in Stephen Witt's *How Music Got Free*, Jonathan Sterne's *MP3: The Meaning of a Format*, and Charles C. Mann's longform essay "The Heavenly Jukebox." CDs seemed, briefly, like an "end of history" storage medium. However, in twenty-twenty hindsight, the CD turned out to be, like all media, transitory—in this case, a medium caught between digital storage and *cloud* storage. The CD contained the means of its own obsolescence; as soon as music was converted into ones and zeros, it was only a matter of time before music freed itself from physical media altogether. Chapter 6 surveys mixtape culture's remnants in the days of compact disc and peer-to-peer (P2P) music sharing—the early 2000s, more or less—and how those remnants interacted with the embryonic advance of streaming music. There was a moment (not so long ago) when personal music curation—in the form of CD burning and ripping—emerged as the worst monetary threat the music industry had ever faced. Shocking as it may seem now, there was a short time in the early 2000s when the entire legacy content industry, from music publishers to film studios, had not yet figured out how to monetize the internet. The Digital Millennium Copyright Act provides the implicit backdrop for these naive years of CD burning, Napster downloading, and Kazaa lawsuits: a period when mixtapes (or mix CDs) not only retained a cultural *thing*-ness but even embraced a piratical ethos that had always existed below the mixtape's surface.

Before long, however, the music industry learned how to make money off the internet. CDs slowly began to drown in the digital stream. Chapter 6 settles on a spiritless listicle in a 2006 edition of *Elle Girl*—six months before Apple announced the first iPhone—as the final beat of the mixtape's heart.

Chapter 7 picks up the chronological thread with the release of the first smartphones in 2007. Making the smartphone my foil, I explore the music consumption models that have emerged within the smartphone economy: the pay-per-song model, the subscription model, and the ad-driven model. The first model (e.g., Bandcamp or iTunes) allows consumers to download digitally compressed audio files to their hard drives. The latter two models ask consumers to rent access to a "heavenly" infinite jukebox (e.g., Apple

Music) or to listen to endless music in between paid advertisements, à la radio (e.g., YouTube). The pay-per-song model, which at least secures a file, represented only 3% of music industry revenue in 2022.[17] Unlike in 2007, today few consumers bother to download songs or albums, so digital radios and digital jukeboxes have become the default music access modes. Drawing on Kate Eichhorn's *Content*, I argue that the rented jukebox and streaming radio models have cheapened music itself—once owned, displayed, and cherished—into disembodied, undifferentiated audio matter. The disappearance of albums, in favor of record singles, is an obvious consequence of the cloud's inability to meaningfully group song compilations into discrete objects. I speculate about why the jukebox and the radio models have become the default listening modes: Why have music lovers, young and old alike, universally agreed to offshore music ownership to the cloud, and how has this unexpected shift affected music culture and subjective listening experiences?

My attempt to answer those questions connects threads introduced in earlier chapters: music ownership and attachment; "stuck culture," Paul Skallas's idea that even as new music explodes online, we nevertheless seem uninterested in finding or cultivating it; and the consequent disappearance of mixtape culture in the shift to streaming.

The streaming music infrastructure, I suggest, offers the enticement of limitless musical experience while delimiting the music we in fact consume. The algorithm shuts off the potential for new discovery. In addition, when music is disembodied into omnipresent data, consumers free themselves from the need to own a dedicated object, which in turn frees them from the responsibility to retain and preserve the music they would otherwise hold dear. Novel technologies that enabled the mechanical reproduction of sound miraculously allowed us to experience a performance whenever we wanted—for whatever purposes desired. An attachment to physical media symbolized the twentieth century's media monoculture as well as mixtape culture in all its forms, from LP to CD. However, *cloud* reproduction is not compatible with that outdated sense of music attachment and ownership. "Sharing" cloud-based music loses its physical dimension and thus loses the pathos that once fueled the anticipation of purchasing a new album as well as the ritual of swapping mixtapes. At the same time, shared media, as such, have disappeared.

This is not an exercise in nostalgia. It's an argument grounded in industrial logic and media theory. In the streaming era, music becomes data and therefore not "shared" in the material sense. Taking cues from Marshall McLuhan, Friedrich Kittler, Kate Eichhorn, and other media historians, the final chapter argues that the shift from mechanical to cloud reproduction changes music's role in our personal and even civic lives (a point that applies to every other art reprocessed not so much by the digital as by the streaming revolution). Reprocessed by the cloud, music becomes ubiquitous yet invisible, cutting edge yet stagnant, accessible yet siloed, democratic yet controlled by algorithm, decentralized on the front end yet radically centralized on the back end. The old analog infrastructure—and the shared media it enabled—ironically provided a more robust and democratic access to new music than the algorithm provides. The contrast between cassette mixtape and streaming jukebox ends up being another object lesson in the paradoxes of digital abundance currently affecting the experience of culture as well as our collective cycles of obsolescence and nostalgia.

I end this introduction with a question: If you were stranded on a desert island, would you rather have a smartphone or a cassette player with some batteries and a dozen of your favorite tapes? It's a contrived scenario, but it illustrates the bargain the entire globe seems to have made regarding music—exchanging physical media for potentially limitless content that is yet so easily made inaccessible.

1: THE FIRST MIXTAPES

A TOP 10 COUNTDOWN

Jehnie I. Burns defines the mixtape as "a compilation of carefully chosen songs, often by various artists, primarily recorded onto a cassette by an individual."[1] In *Mix Tape: The Art of Cassette Culture*, Pat Griffin says it's an "[arbitration] of mood through the sequential playing of organized sound."[2] In the same book, Sonic Youth frontman Moore declares the mixtape's defining feature to be that it is given to a friend.[3] Proving the point, the recollections in *Mix Tape* revisit playlists made for friends, boyfriends, girlfriends, ex-boyfriends, ex-girlfriends, bandmates, and ex-bandmates. "Here's a tape I did for an ex-band member," writes musician Karen Lollypop. "I never gave her it because I had a fight with her boyfriend 'cause he's an asshole. Then she sent a note saying we can't be friends anymore. So she didn't get the tape. She's a loser anyway."[4]

Mix Tape, edited by Moore, is a collection of mixtape memories recalled by artists and musicians who came of age in the late twentieth century. It has a cassette on the cover. With one exception, the book is filled with cassette playlists and images of tapes: black tapes, white tapes, transparent tapes, Maxell tapes, Sony tapes, tapes with labels, tapes without labels, and tape J-cards adorned with personalized art. Burns's definition, interestingly, waivers on the medium—with that adverb, "*primarily* recorded onto cassette"—and Moore does allow a reel-to-reel mixtape into his collection: a playlist recorded on a BASF Magnetophonband, standard tape, 1,200 feet. If they're honest, children of the seventies and eighties will recall the smooth transition from mixtapes to mix CDs in the early 2000s, when the words *rip* and *burn* entered the lexicon (as in, *I gotta rip these songs and burn them onto a blank CD*).

I'm a rhetorician by training, fascinated by effects and practices more than objects and products, so, for this book, I adopt an ecumenical definition: a mixtape is a custom compilation of songs, duplicated mechanically from multiple sources onto a physical storage medium, delivered to an individual or a small group, and intended to create a mood or to share a musical emotion. The last two phrases keep the spotlight on the private mixtape rather than the public or DJ mixtape. The key, first phrase—duplicated onto a physical storage medium—is strategic. If I get too ecumenical, digital playlists sneak in through the back door. As Plato and Aristotle taught, one must define a thing with care before conjuring up an argument about it.

"DEAR HELOISE"

As near as I can tell, the *Kingsport Times* contains the first print reference to a private mixtape (figure 1.1). "Hints from Heloise" was the Tennessee paper's life advice column, and on May 16, 1973, the column published some advice from a reader named Margie B. Olsen. She does not use the word *mixtape* because it had not been invented, but that is the anniversary gift she made her husband.

> *Dear Heloise:*
>
> We recently celebrated our seventh wedding anniversary and it was so special I wanted to share my idea with you and others.
>
> A few days before our anniversary I came across some old records, our favorite love songs. I went out and purchased a high-quality cassette tape, and carefully hid it.
>
> When I had the opportunity, I recorded a brief reminder of how we celebrated each anniversary. Then I recorded twelve songs arranged to tell "Our Love Story."
>
> Some of the records were slightly scratched, but that added to the sentiment. It all began with a lonely boy and girl whose wishes came true on their wedding day, and continued with a devoted couple who feel that even their bad times have been good.
>
> On the card that came with the cassette I put the date, "seventh Wedding Anniversary." On the front of the cassette I put a list of the songs.
>
> I also cut tiny pictures representing the four seasons from gummed address labels and stuck them down the side of the song list. Then, on our anniversary date I presented my man with "Our Love Story."[5]

Reel-to-reel tape formats trace their ancestry to the 1928 Blattnerphone and the 1935 Magnetophone—both German inventions—but Olsen's "tape" is the user-friendly cassette. Developed by Philips in 1963 and released into the US market in 1964, the Compact Cassette (a trademarked name) beat out the RCA Sound Tape Cartridge, the DC-International, the Microcassette, and of course 8-tracks and 4-tracks as the dominant cartridge format

16 CHAPTER ONE

> ## *A Personal Love Story*
>
> **Dear Heloise:**
>
> We recently celebrated our seventh wedding anniversary and it was so special I wanted to share my idea with you and others.
>
> A few days before our anniversary I came across some old records, our favorite love songs. I went out and purchased a high-quality cassette tape, and carefully hid it. When I had the opportunity, I recorded a brief reminder of how we celebrated each anniversary. Then I recorded twelve songs arranged to tell "Our Love Story."
>
> Some of the records were slightly scratched, but that added to the sentiment. It all began with a lonely boy and girl whose wishes came true on their wedding day, and continued with a devoted couple who feel that even their bad times have been good.
>
> On the card that came with the cassette I put the date, "seventh Wedding Anniversary." On the front of the cassette I put a list of the songs.
>
> I also cut tiny pictures representing the four seasons from gummed address labels and stuck them down the side of the song list.
>
> Then, on our anniversary date I presented my man with "Our Love Story."
>
> — Margie B. Olsen
>
> Beautiful . . .
>
> And thanks a million for sharing your love story with us.
> — Heloise
>
> **Dear Heloise:**
>
> This is what I do when our family goes on camping trips. There are always a few things that need washing while we're camping.
>
> So I find it especially convenient to stop by the local laundromat before we leave home and get one or two of the vending machine boxes of detergent!
>
> One box seems to have enough to do the few things I wash out, and there are no extra jars or no large boxes to get damp (and the contents lumpy).
> — Marilynn Bevington
>
> **Dear Heloise:**
>
> I realize that many people buy several bars of soap at a time, especially when it is on sale. Then they remove the wrappers and tuck in the linen closet, stored luggage, etc., but I wonder if anyone ever thought of my idea?
>
> I always save one bar of soap for the guest room. I put the unwrapped one bar between the pillows on the bed so there is always a refreshing smell.
>
> You never have to worry about a musty odor in the guest bed, and my guests love it.
> — A Reader
>
> **Dear Heloise:**
>
> When drying children's tennis shoes, I find that by taking common draper hooks and hooking them through the top eyelet of the shoe, my hanging problem is solved.
>
> The shoes can be hung on the clothesline where the air can circulate through them.
> — Mrs. D. D.
>
> **Dear Heloise:**
>
> Lack space? Store extra blankets and pillows in decorator pillow cases to enhance divans, day beds, and chairs.
>
> These are easily removed when needed.
> — Dorothy Bonner
>
> THIS COLUMN is written for you . . . the housewife and homemaker. If you have a hint or a problem write to Heloise in care of this newspaper.

FIGURE 1.1. Early print reference to mixtape-making in a relationship column in the *Kingsport Times*, May 16, 1973.

for magnetic tape. Norelco, Philips's consumer brand name in America, released the first tape players/recorders the same year.

The "Hints from Heloise" column proves that within a decade of the cassette's development, *mixtape* was not a word but making mixtapes was a thing—right down to the romance and the customized artwork ("tiny pictures representing the four seasons from gummed address labels"). It wasn't a fad, at least not in Kingsport, Tennessee. Olsen wants to "share [her] idea," and Heloise and her editors thought the idea was novel enough to print in the paper. "Beautiful," responds Heloise. "Thanks a million for sharing your love story with us." If not a fad or a full-blown youth culture, the idea of a personalized mixtape—delivered to an audience of one—was in circulation by 1973.

EXCAVATING THE MIXTAPE ARCHIVE

So much for the print archive. Audio archives—in particular, archives of audio letters and home recordings—take us further back into mixtape history.

Audio letters have been recorded on nearly all audio media that predate cheap long-distance calls: wax cylinder, lacquer disc, reel-to-reel tape, and cassette tape. Historically, audio letters have circulated most widely in times of war. During Vietnam, the Red Cross headed the "Voices from Home" program.[6] The program supported reel-to-reel recording stations—staffed by specialists who knew how to operate the equipment—in which soldiers overseas and family members back home could record their voice on tape, more intimate than words on paper, and mail it to the other side of the world.[7] The 3M Company even provided special mailing boxes intended solely for the delicate receiving and delivery of reel-to-reel tape. The Red Cross program likely explains why Vietnam audio letter archives—particularly Texas Tech's excellent Sam Johnson Vietnam Archive—are packed with reel-to-reel tapes instead of cassette tapes. During World War II, though not on the same scale, the USO had provided similar recording booths housed with phonograph equipment.[8]

From the 1920s to the 1960s, in times of war or peace, the American public also had access to phonograph mail booths with names such as Vocamat or Voice-o-Graph in cities, tourist destinations, bus stops, military bases, and so on.[9] These were small recording cubicles in which out-of-town visitors, service members, or traveling salesmen could drop a quarter and cut a short (very short—just a minute or so) audio letter on a disc to be mailed home to Seward, Nebraska, or Dayton, Ohio. The earliest audio letter in the phono-post archive maintained by Thomas Levin is a 1909 wax cylinder recorded and sent to Thomas Edison by Mexican president Porfirio Diaz, who congratulates Edison on his innovations.[10] The next oldest is a 1931 78 rpm disc recorded in a Vocamat booth by a German tourist. He greets his Berliner recipients and sings a heartfelt rendition of Shubert's "Der Jüngling an der Quelle," or "The Youth by the Spring," before signing off.

Another early singing letter can be heard on an acetate disc (from a different archive) recorded by a sailor deployed overseas in May 1945.[11] Acetate discs—specialized discs used at the time for prerecorded radio broadcasts or master recordings—would not have been available in USO booths or Voice-o-Graph booths. This sailor, who was from Omaha, Nebraska, likely had access to Armed Forces Radio Network equipment. AFRN radio operators would have been the only personnel hauling recording equipment into the theater of war. "Hello, honey, how are you?" the young sailor begins. "Hello, Donny, what are you doing? Are you playing with Mommy?" He then repeats "Do you miss me?" multiple times, seemingly at a loss of what to do with this dictation machine. Promises of "lots of fishing" when he returns and "do you miss me?" sum it up nicely. He offers an "I love you," the disc goes silent for a second, then he returns as the lead vocalist, accompanied by three or four shipmates, on terrible but merry renditions of "You're in the Army Now," "Anchors Away (US Navy Song)," and, with a bit of naval disrespect, the Marines' Hymn:

> From the Halls of Montezuma,
> To the Shores of Tripoli,

We fight our country's battles
By air, on land, and sea!

They forget a few lyrics, and during the Marines' Hymn, a young woman's voice suddenly rises amid the cacophony of male sailors. Where was she before? I would pay a modest sum to know the circumstances behind this disc's production, but like so many discs and tapes in the vast audio letter archives, this one was purchased in the late twentieth century by an audiophile collector who had nothing more to go on than the packaging and the audio's contextual clues.

One of the sweetest singing letters I've come across—digitized, like many of my examples, by audio archivist Bob Purse—is a collection of nursery songs recorded on reel-to-reel tape and "presented to Jean Ellen by her grandpa" on Jean's first birthday.[12] In what I take to be a Germanic or Scandinavian accent, grandpa, who resides in Florida, introduces one song as "The Dance of the Minikins, Using the Five Fingers of the Hand."

Dance, thumbkin, dance
Dance, thumbkin, dance
Thumbkin cannot dance alone
So dance ye minikins, every one
Every one, every one!
Dance, ye minikins, every one!

He pauses to explain that the song continues in a recursive fashion with the other four fingers: "And this is to be repeated for the foreman, the first finger, middleman, ringman, and little man." A variety of familiar and unfamiliar lullabies fill up the rest of the tape. He ends his granddaughter's audio gift with a big kiss: "One like this—*pcha!*—did you hear that?"

Sweet as grandpa sounds, a disc recorded in the early 1950s captures a more common style of singing on audio letters and home recordings: drunken revelry.[13] "My Wild Irish Rose," accompanied by piano, is the first song attempted by the inebriated group on this home recording (there is no evidence on the disc, at least, that it was meant to be mailed to anyone). "Hail, Hail, the Gang's All Here" brings up the rear of the disc. In between, a young woman screams indistinctly at someone off mic before concluding, "Aw, hell with you. Got the dishes all washed, Max? Jeepers, you sure had your hands full with that sink." Someone, presumably Max, enters twenty seconds later to say, "Goddamn, I work all day and I have to warsh all the dishes." Confirming that people did once say *jeepers* and *warsh* without affect is one of the joys of old home recordings and audio letters.

I can offer a more precise year, 1941, with an all-singing home recording on a disc from the Fisher residence.[14] "A little bit of everything in the Fisher home tonight," it begins. "Mr. Miliwicki playing the harmonica and Mrs. Fisher playing the guitar." Some poorly executed blues ensues before a male voice cuts it all off with a guitar-accompanied solo performance of "Old Folks at Home" (a.k.a. "Sewanee River"): "Way down upon the Swanee River, / Far, far away." And that's as far as it gets before Mrs. Fisher cuts *him* off: "That's enough!" It's like a dueling pianos bit. It ends, in the last twenty seconds, with a collective singing of a song I can't place. All this is crammed onto side 1 of the disc—just 1:26 long. Side 2 contains congenial conversation without the singing.

These examples confirm that from the earliest days of amateur audio letters and home recordings, people knew that blank sound media demanded music as much as talking and general audio capture. Would these examples be mixtapes? No. Recall the definition: songs must be mechanically duplicated—that is, recorded or dubbed, not sung. Audio letters are a very old medium of communication, and people liked to sing on them, as much as they liked to sing on home phonograph and home tape recordings. The *oldest* home recordings—on wax cylinders made from the 1890s through the 1920s—contain plenty of singing as well. On these earliest of audio inscriptions, one can hear, for example, a mixed chorus performing the Old 100th Doxology, recorded on an 1894 cylinder,[15] as well as renditions of songs completely unknown to written history.[16] However, I would not describe any of these—neither the 1894 Doxology singers nor the sweet *opa* humming lullabies to his baby granddaughter sometime in the middle twentieth century—as mixtapes.

Such audio letters do meet one requirement of my mixtape definition: they are often addressed to a single individual. Even when addressing a family unit, as the choral sailor did, senders tend to speak to recipients one by one. ("Hello, Donny. Are you playing with Mommy?") This also was Sergeant Henry Tinkcom's manner on a phonograph made at a USO booth on Thursday, June 10, 1943.[17]

> How is the garden coming along, Mother? I hope you have good growing weather and that your flowers are more beautiful than ever before. Don't stay out in that hot sun too long.
>
> Dad, I hope your operation is a great success and that you completely recover from your present illness. Although I'm many miles away, I'll be rooting for you every minute....
>
> Now to air-minded Nancy [a little sister]. No, B-24s are not Flying Fortresses. The B-17 is a Flying Fortress, made by Boeing Company. The B-24 is a much bigger ship and of course you know the fellas who fly in 'em think

they're better than the Flying Fortress. Whether they are or not is just a, uh, a matter of opinion.

Demonstrating the audio letter's propensity to address recipients individually, Sergeant Tinkcom's transcript also exhibits two audio letter delivery styles: reading from a prewritten letter and speaking extemporaneously. Sergeant Tinkcom shifts from the former to the latter at "and of course you know the fellas who fly in 'em." His diction becomes less formal; he starts clipping his words and dropping his g's.

When I decided to write a book on mixtapes, it wasn't long before audio letters and home recordings appeared as the earliest and most likely sources for personally curated, mechanically dubbed playlists. It must have been an easy pivot, I assumed, from audio messages mingled with singing to messages interspersed with songs dubbed from LP disc or radio. I understood the technical difficulties involved in dubbing music onto a blank disc or reel-to-reel (R2R) tape, prior to the consumer-friendly Compact Cassette, but surely *some* people knew how to do it—to transfer songs from disc or radio onto a blank phonograph or R2R tape, mailed back home to loved ones.

A safe assumption. Collections of audio letters and home recordings searchable online are generous and contain examples of early mixtapes that predate the word's invention, the Compact Cassette's release, and the arrival of any sort of widespread youth mixtape culture. Stretching back to the 1920s, these archives contain lacquer discs of various sizes and speeds (lots of 78 rpm discs) and reel-to-reel formats in addition to cassettes.

Not being a historian of sound, I was surprised how productive reel-to-reel archives ended up being in my search for early mixtapes. I'd assumed R2R tape was a tool for professional recording studios and such—a not entirely wrong assumption. R2R tape manufacturers were indeed slow to advertise the technology as a consumer's music medium. According to media historian Karin Bijsterveld, Scotch and Philips executives in the early 1950s unequivocally did not want to compete with records and radios as another music playback device. Their marketing departments touted reel-to-reel recorders as either professional data storage and recording tools or as media for what Bijsterveld calls "acoustic family albums": devices for the creative upper-middle-class family wanting to capture baby's first sounds, Christmas carols, evidence of father's snoring, and so on. "Treasure her songs in front of the chimney," proclaimed an early Dutch ad.[18] I stipulate "upper-middle-class family" because midcentury R2R tape recorders were not cheap. One 1956 RCA Victor advertisement promotes a new high-fidelity recorder "for only $199.99,"[19] which translates to a two-thousand-dollar toy in today's reckoning. The ad promotes the toy mostly as a dictation or sound recording device, with the musical angle tacked on as an afterthought. Larger, nonportable R2R recorders sold for even more and were manufactured explicitly as machines for sound engineers and other audio professionals: "Standard of the Great Radio Shows" was Ampex's motto, for example. (As a historical aside, Bing Crosby was an early adopter and promoter of reel-to-reel tape. In October 1947, Crosby's show became the first live radio performance captured on tape instead of acetate disc. He personally invested $50,000 into Ampex, the tape recorder manufacturer, to ensure it had funds to finish developing its most cutting-edge devices.)[20]

However, despite the intentions of media companies to sell reel-to-reel technology as a professional tool or (for the savvy prosumer) an aural memory machine, the reel-to-reel format fell into the hands of music aficionados who recognized its potential for amateur music curation and song copying. Bing Crosby invested in the medium in 1947. Magnetic tape at that time was backed with paper, so paper-lined R2R tape indicates an early provenance. Collector Bob Purse, who has kindly digitized his R2R collection, owns two music compilations on this earliest magnetic tape. One, from 1948, was recorded onto a Soundmirror Magnetic Recording Tape and features church hymns played live at the Rader Memorial Methodist Church in Little River, Florida: "Dr. Messner is trying out a recording of the pipe organ," says a voice, "and Mrs. Gibbs is playing the pipe organ."[21] The second one, circa 1949–50, contains songs and duets dubbed from several LPs featuring Mario Lanza and Kathryn Grayson.[22] However, no contextual evidence indicates that this mix was intended for an audience of one.

Via email correspondence, Purse provided an example of a Scotch five-inch reel, from 1951, that likewise contains a custom playlist dubbed from multiple LPs. Jimmy Dorsey, Glenn Miller, the Andrews Sisters, and Hoagy Carmichael all made it onto this compilation tape, which looks like a good one (figure 1.2). Purse once had a large collection of similar compilation R2R tapes, he says, but again, they contained no hints that they'd been dubbed for a specific recipient. They were likely made as a playlist for a party or for personal use and are thus not mixtapes according to my definition.

Another early R2R tape in Purse's collection contains a recording of a July 1950 radio broadcast of the Lucky Strike (the cigarette brand) "Your Hit Parade," a Top 20 countdown show that ran from 1935 to 1953.[23] The number 1 spot with a bullet on this tape went to "Mona Lisa," an Academy Award–winning song from the 1950 film *Captain Carey, USA*. The song was given several renditions that year, Nat King Cole's the most popular. It's not a mixtape, but it is comforting to learn from this reel that as early as 1950 someone was sitting by the radio, waiting to hit *record* as soon as their favorite songs came on air. (Earlier radio-phonographs, such as the Wilcox-Gay

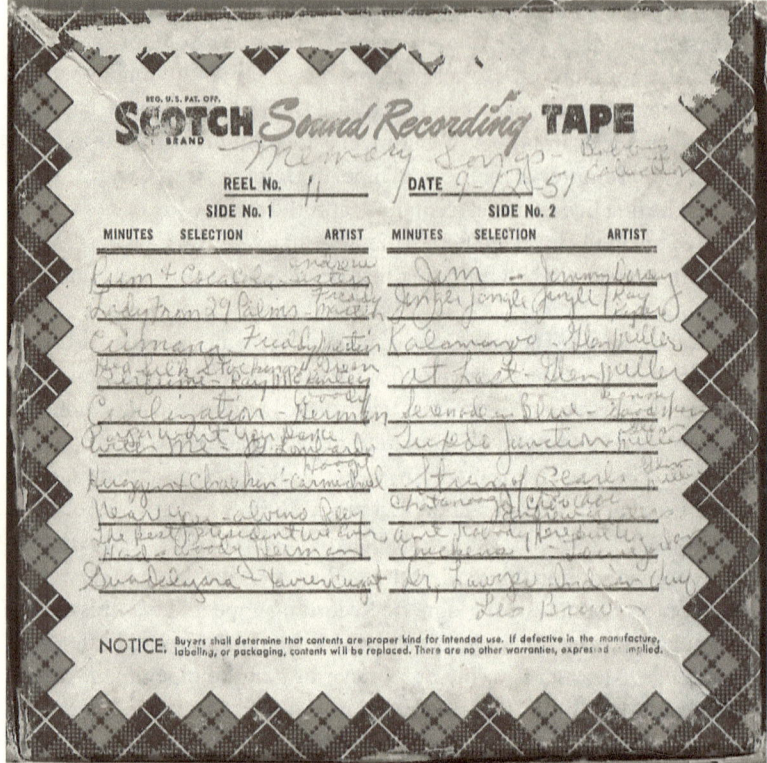

FIGURE 1.2. A Scotch reel-to-reel (R2R) mixtape from 1951, most likely created for a party or personal use. Bob Purse collection. Courtesy Bob Purse.

Recordio, made it possible to do the same on a 78, though I have not come across a home radio recording on a disc.)

These and many other R2R tapes in America's audio archives demonstrate that early adopters of the medium turned reel-to-reel into something its manufacturers had no interest in producing: a consumer, or at least a prosumer, music medium, now in competition with radio and LP. By the late fifties, writes Bijsterveld, instructional guides for reel-to-reel recorders had leaned into this market, suggesting that creating a custom playlist of songs, by recording from the radio or dubbing from LP discs, was a sanctioned use for the device: "As a way to ensure several hours of nonstop musical background during a dance party at home."[24] (Personal mixtapes had not yet suggested themselves to the suits at Philips or Scotch.)

Thanks to the efforts of reel-to-reel audiophiles, musical curations dubbed onto R2R tape are not too rare. In addition to Bob Purse's collection,

Internet Archive user Oldradios90 has digitized tapes from the 1950s containing, for example, compilations of Handel's *Messiah*, the Mormon Tabernacle Choir, and an opera from *The Voices of Firestone*, a midcentury variety show that aired on ABC.[25] From the prosumer's point of view, it must not have been a huge stretch from capturing the sounds of everyday life—the original R2R activity advertised by the media manufacturers—to dubbing the music that accompanied life: a little from this record, a little from that record, some radio, some television. The idea to dub a custom R2R mix not just for a special occasion but for a special recipient was surely in someone's head in the 1950s, even if the clunky medium kept it from being a widespread activity.

Audio archives are abundant, then, especially R2R archives. I soon realized the problem was not finding mixtapes but deciding how to define *mixtape* when compiling "early" exemplars of the thing. Most mixtape retrospectives—including Wikipedia's entry on the subject—exclude anything prior to the Compact Cassette. Such a strict definition, along with the reality that few cassettes survived their first decade, dumps most retrospectives into the late 1970s, deterring a deeper dive into the history of personal music curation. To discover earlier mixtapes, I needed to adopt the ecumenical definition laid out at the beginning of the chapter, ignoring the precise medium to locate noteworthy recordings that match the spirit if not the letter of the word *mixtape*.

1964–65: THE LOST MIXTAPES

Anyone who wants to scour the countryside for early mixtapes—strict definition, on cassette tape—must know this ahead of time: the material context of the cassette's first decade will work against their efforts. Like any new medium, the cassette took a while to catch on. In the 1960s and 1970s, the Compact Cassette was not as cheap and abundant as it would become in the 1980s, when cassette sales finally surpassed LP sales. Not abundant, the cassette in its earliest decade was nevertheless an industrially produced novelty—something most consumers didn't think to save for posterity. Both facts explain why cassettes in general and mixtapes in particular did not survive their first decade.

A third reason explaining the disappearance of 1960s cassette mixtapes is that the cassette's release was timed a little too perfectly with a more important historical event: the Vietnam War.

To reiterate, most magnetic tape in Vietnam audio letter archives is on reel-to-reel tape, on various inches-per-second formats (the R2R medium was never standardized). Also, a general observation about Vietnam audio letters, such as those housed in the Sam Johnson Archive, is that sharing news and capturing sounds were the primary motives for their creation—which is why these audio letters have gained a reputation as excellent primary sources for Vietnam's squad-scale realities. What music is to be found often involves songs in Vietnamese captured live at Saigon clubs or elsewhere.[26] Wanting to record wartime sound makes sense. For boys brought up on World War II movies, recording the real-life noises of military life and mechanized battle would have been a novelty. In 1967, Michael Baronowski took his reel-to-reel recorder with him to the front lines of Da Nang to tape mortar explosions, rainfall, and nervous foxhole banter:

[Boom]
    Those were heat rounds, high explosives. It's dark now. We're waiting for the illumination to go off. There goes the illumination. [laughs] That's the heaviest thing, a heavy feeling, sitting here in the dark with all that stuff going on. Sounds of the Enchanted Forest.
    [boom, boom, etc.]
    [machine gunfire]
    There they go. Jesus! Whoa, that was too close [boom]. Air strike [boom, boom, boom].
    They wiped napalm all over that place. Look at that.
    [big boom]
    [singing]
    You're in the Pepsi generation.[27]

Baronowski wanted to work in radio after being discharged. He figured his reel-to-reel demos from the field would be a nice calling card. He was killed in action at Da Nang. In 2000, his tapes fittingly ended up as the centerpiece of an award-winning NPR radio show.

Also in 1967, an unnamed sailor on luckier duty recorded ship sounds for his young son.[28] Porting into Naples and Rome, the sailor—a fair-minded man who offers kind words about "the church in Rome" even as he contrasts it with the great Martin Luther—begins his audio letter amid a cacophony of background music, indistinct naval scuttlebutt, and mechanical tapping of some sort. He says, "Hello, Jim. Just trying out this tape, getting some of the sounds from ship, so you can hear the noise and so forth that Dad listens to all day. I'm trying a new microphone, and it sure seems to be picking up real well. I'll play this on through for a few more minutes, then I'll pick up some more sounds around the ship and put 'em on this tape." Sounds from home were also welcome. The sailor details how, despite the nine-hour difference, he and other sailors work diligently to set up a ham radio at midnight to pick up the early morning US signals.

In addition to being a good example of R2R tape used (as intended) as a sound-capture device in the mid-1960s, this tape also highlights the difficulties still involved in midcentury communication between deployed men and women and families back home. FaceTime chats were a long way away.

The earliest *cassette* audio letter I've found on the official record is a tape from 1966, a mere two years after the cassette's release; however, it doesn't contain music either, just news and sounds.[29] It's a Highlander brand cassette, manufactured by Scotch/3M, sent from Lieutenant Colonel Robert Nopp to his family in Salem, Oregon, in 1966. Nopp was a reconnaissance pilot with the Army's 131st Aviation Company. He was declared missing in action after a July 1966 mission over Laos, the same month he had sent this cassette audio letter. Although it contains no music, its existence is at least a good piece of evidence that consumers did use the cassette for audio letters during the earliest years of the Vietnam War. An iconic scene in the movie *Apocalypse Now* provides indirect evidence: the scene in which Clean (played by a young Laurence Fishburne) receives a tape player and cassette letter from his mother—both of which, like Clean, are lost in the fog of battle.

Even if cassettes had survived their first decade in large numbers, searching for 1960s cassette mixtapes would likely introduce you to a wealth of Vietnam-era sounds and audio messages but not much in the of way of shared music. That the cassettes didn't survive aggravates the search. Cassettes, after all, were far more portable than reel-to-reel tape. Soldiers could put them in a pocket, stuff them in a rucksack, or toss them across their bunks. Back home in the States, the cassette could be called more durable as well as more portable than R2R tape, but the cassette's durability met its limit overseas. Reel-to-reel equipment in Vietnam, like phonographic equipment in World War II, necessitated a pretense of care if it was to survive its deployment. (Note, again, that the Red Cross's "Voices from Home" program offered specially equipped reel-to-reel recording booths, and that 3M offered specialized R2R tape mailing boxes.) The cassette cartridge, in contrast, invited carelessness. Its advertised durability worked against its survival as a medium for audio letters sent to Vietnam. Teens in the 1990s weren't exactly careful with the things, so there's no reason to think teens in Vietnam would have cared for them any differently.

Philips released the Compact Cassette to the US market in 1964. The United States deployed the Marines to Da Nang Airbase in 1965. I find it easy to believe that the first true mixtapes, on cassette, were sent overseas to Devil Dog brothers and boyfriends during the war's first year but simply did not survive the trip (which, thankfully, says nothing about whether the brothers and boyfriends survived the trip).

THE COUNTDOWN

The following Top 10 countdown list—from 1970 to 1949—adopts my ecumenical definition of a mixtape, as motivated by the dearth of 1960s cassette mixtapes in audio archives but more crucially by the existence of protomixtapes on audio media released earlier than the Compact Cassette. The list presents early examples of music duplicated from multiple sources onto a blank storage medium, of any sort, to create a custom album for a special recipient. (Fair warning, I fudge the definition on number 10 to make room for an early cassette tape.) It is not a comprehensive list by any means; that list would require a book unto itself. However, the list offers (objectively) the earliest protomixtapes I've discovered in the archive and (subjectively) the most endearing or interesting ones. I invite the reader to visit thelastmixtape.substack.com to listen to the recordings. The site will be an open, eagerly updated repository of pre-1980s mixtapes, as they emerge from America's attics and closets.

10. A Cruise for Dan Kleven, Cassette Tape, 1970

This tape does not meet all the conditions of my mixtape definition. It's a playlist recorded for an individual very much in need of curated music from back home, but its songs were captured live from the radio via microphone instead of mechanically dubbed one by one. But it's an early cassette and comes with a great story, so it slides into the countdown at number 10.

As reported by Sasha Aslanian on Minnesota Public Radio, Dan Kleven did his eleven-month Vietnam tour in 1970. He had the two most dangerous jobs in Vietnam: tunnel rat and point walker. Nicknamed Rabbit, Kleven was small enough that he could crawl into the holes leading to the underground bunkers dug out by the Viet Cong irregulars. When he wasn't crawling through tunnels, Kleven's stature meant he walked point, at the front of the unit, when on patrol. During that dangerous year, Kleven exchanged cassette audio letters with friends and family back home. His mother would bring out the tape recorder during family dinners, telling people to "Talk to Danny!" She'd just let the recorder run, capturing the blessedly normal sounds of life back on a Minnesota cow ranch. "We would forget the tape was even on," recalls Dan's sister.[30] (Dan's father, recalling an earlier technology, calls them "reels," but they were in fact cassettes.)

Friends sent him tapes too: "A buddy takes the tape deck for a ride in his Oldsmobile," reports Aslanian, "and sings along to the hits on the radio so Dan can feel like he's been out cruising his home town again." This is one of the best pre-1980s images of cassette culture I've come across: a young man, tape deck in hand (or maybe on the console or the seat), driving across the back roads of Minnesota with radio blaring and tape recording, so that a friend drafted into Vietnam can have a taste of musical life back home, a reminder of what things will be like when he—*when* he—gets out. Kleven's buddy most likely recorded the tape using a portable recorder with an integrated microphone. It's not a mixtape in any strict sense, but capturing on cassette the feel of cruising the open road with the radio on is a good example of why anyone ever made a mixtape in the first place.

9. Fiancée to Fiancé, Reel-to-Reel Tape, 1968

This 4-track mono, three-inch R2R tape sits in the Sam Johnson Vietnam Archive.[31] From 1968, it meets all requirements of my mixtape definition: mechanically dubbed from multiple sources onto a physical medium *and* delivered to an individual recipient.[32] Ironically, given the gendered assumptions about mixtape-making that developed in the eighties and nineties, this mixtape (like Margie B. Olsen's) was made by a woman and sent to a man—a fiancée to a fiancé.

Kay Snead was still Kay Surber when she made this R2R tape in reply to a request from Gary Snead in a previous audio letter: "If you want to put some music on there, you get tired of talkin'—but I'd much rather listen to you talk than to music, but if you do have that record of that happy feeling, you might put it on one separate tape, with all music on it."[33]

I can provide only an artist and a partial track list for Kay Surber's resulting tape because not a single song on it contains lyrics—lyrics being the only way to track down song titles without the aid of serendipity and shared media. This is a purely instrumental mixtape. Upon first listen, it reminded me of soundtracks to midcentury Western films or TV shows: a cheerful cowboy riding high and free in the saddle against a cloudless sky. Other songs reminded me of low-key, midcentury lounge music, almost elevator music, not unlike the sonic backdrop to the party scenes in *Breakfast at Tiffany's*. I was on the right track with the Muzak vibe; the cowboy vibe was way off. It turns out that Gary Snead was a fan of Bert Kaempfert, a midcentury German orchestra leader popular for his easy listening jazz tunes. If any readers want to help with the full track list, check out the recording at thelastmixtape.substack.com and leave a comment; the two songs I can confirm are "A Swingin' Safari" and Kaempfert's version of "Wimoweh" (popularized, with lyrics, as "The Lion Sleeps Tonight" by doo-wop group the Tokens).

One point of a mixtape is to communicate a vibe. I can't imagine a better vibe to send to a fiancé stuck in Vietnam than the one communicated by Bert Kaempfert and His Orchestra. If the reverberating volatility of "The End" is the sonic embodiment of napalm dropped on jungle tree lines, then

Bert Kaempfert tunes embody the swinging sixties—upbeat, optimistic, carefree; a gin cocktail and Kay in a party dress. The tape's audio quality is excellent. No microphones held up to speakers; these Kaempfert tunes were properly dubbed by Kay (assisted by an unnamed audiophile friend) from LPs onto a quality reel-to-reel tape.[34] Her message at the end of side 2 is worth transcribing in full. It's an innocent voice from the past, amid a time of war, whose words portray the purest motive for making a mixtape: to gratify the recipient, rather than to aggrandize the impressive musical taste of the sender. Kay speaks with a Texan twang:

> Hi, Gary.... I sure hope you enjoyed the tape ... I think you'll really enjoy listening to it sometimes when you have a chance to rest and don't want to have to think about anything.... I know that, through your letters, things must be rough at times. I know that it's not easy. I just want you to know that you're in my prayers every day. I think about you so often. I know that if we just stay strong, our faith—and keep our faith strong—that it will keep us and give us all the encouragement that we need. Well, I'll write more later. The tape is nearly gone. So I'll see you soon. And I love you. Goodnight.[35]

8. A Homemade "Radio Show" for a Deployed Sailor, Reel-to-Reel Tape, 1968

A voice made for radio welcomes you to "the good sound of music on the Brian Nelson show" at the beginning of this creative R2R tape from 1968.[36] Nelson starts side 1 with the quick piano eighth notes of Ray Stevens's "Unwind" and finishes that side with a glib awareness of his chosen medium: "We're almost out of tape. How 'bout maybe you turn this thing over and you can hear us back on the other side, and I know it's just such a thrilling thought, to hear more of us—that's just about enough to say for you to rewind the whole wall! Bye-bye, we'll see you on the other side."

The tape is from Purse's collection, a 2,400-foot reel at seven and a half inches per second, meaning each side could record a solid hour of audio. It was given to Purse by an acquaintance who wanted to share it with a wider audience. It's not just a mixtape; it's a mixtape *production* that mimics a radio show complete with call-ins from Nelson's friends, live news reporting, comments from guests (Nelson's family members, who wander into the room while he was recording), lots of music, and a strong DJ personality to give the whole thing an auditory unity. However, Brian Nelson wasn't a pro. He was a broadcasting student having fun with his equipment. To my ears, this tape represents the innovative heights the mixtape genre could reach when made not just by a music fan but by a dedicated audiophile.

The whole thing was recorded for and sent to one of Nelson's closest friends, deployed at the time aboard the USS *Lawrence*, a guided-missile destroyer. Made in 1968, the tape was given to Bob Purse by the son of this deployed friend. "Brian Nelson was the ultimate audiophile," the son reports. "He built his own mixing consoles, modified the preamplifiers and amplifiers he used: 4 JBL L100's with 4 Ionovac tweeters powered by a modified Phase Linear 400 that produced a kilowatt total audio." Nelson made multiple practice-broadcast tapes like this one, honing his chops as a broadcaster while inadvertently creating a protomixtape on R2R: songs dubbed from multiple copies onto a single blank medium, delivered to an individual recipient.

I'll argue in the next chapter that early twentieth-century music pirates may have been the first *audiophiles* in the Brian Nelson sense, adjusted to and familiar with sound equipment to the point where mechanical dubbing ceased to be a novelty. Brian Nelson seems to have been the sort of midcentury audiophile who prefigured the 1980s' intimacy with the act of musical curation: making compilation tapes was just something he *did*.

7. A Gunship Band, Reel-to-Reel Tape, 1967

Back to Vietnam. This audio letter from the Ernie Miller collection dubs a taped recording of an ad hoc band formed by members of the Utility Tactical Transport (UTT) armed helicopter gunship group (that is, the crew of a helicopter designed for close cover of ground troops).[37]

Side 1 of the tape—seven and a half inches per second, Ernie informs us—is a typical audio letter. Side 2 contains the music. It opens with a Vietnamese song recorded from the radio; it's followed by Miller's salutation: "Hello, hello, hello, people back there in the United States of America, especially all the Owens's and all them, you know, Millers and descendants—aunts and uncles, cousins and nephews and nieces, sisters and brothers and ma and all you." Like many young men in Vietnam, Miller knows his whole family unit will listen to his audio letter, so he humorously dispenses with the typical approach of addressing folks individually. However, because this tape is addressed to Miller's family, and not literally to the United States of America, it can slip into our number 7 spot.

Not sure what to say on this side 2 (he has spoken his piece on side 1), Ernie Miller informs his listeners: "So, what I'm going to do is give you a special treat. There's a bunch of people over here, up in Saigon, that kinda composed themselves a bunch of songs and sang 'em a few times, you know, and one of the guys over here, in the crew chief hooch, who's got some, uh, a tape of this—so I'm going to go over and I'm going to tape some of the songs that they sang." Stated more neatly: soldiers in a helicopter gunship group have got together a band, recorded some songs, and cut a proper album on tape. Miller borrowed a copy of that tape and dubbed it onto side 2 of his R2R audio letter. Importantly, Miller did not dub the whole thing without intervention. He included only "the cleaner songs," he says, and couldn't dub them all because, "naw, that'd give you the wrong idea about your old son." Miller's selective dubbing makes side 2 of his audio letter a proper mixtape, crafted with intention.

Above and beyond my definition's requirements, it's important to include Vietnam tapes in this Top 10 countdown because the war looms heavily over early cassette and mixtape history. Vietnam was the historical backdrop against which Americans first communicated via magnetic tape, tape cartridge, and other post-WWII media advances. In my view, all cassette retrospectives should make room for tapes recorded, dubbed, and, in this case, performed by young men and women overseas.

While researching the songs on this tape, I learned that more than one unit in Vietnam formed an a cappella ensemble or guitar-supported band that performed and recorded their own tunes (figure 1.3).[38] Miller's side 2 includes an album cut by such a group. It is a fine mix, representing what General Edward Lansdale calls *wartime folk music*: songs made by American men and women, civilian and military, while they served overseas. All sorts of broadcast and playback equipment found its way into Vietnam: "Sony radios, Akai stereos, and Teac tape decks were easily available," writes Lydia Fish. "American music was performed live by the ubiquitous Filipino rock bands, AFVN Radio broadcast round the clock, and GI-operated underground radio stations [played] hard acid rock."[39] Surrounded by music whenever and wherever they could get it, Marines, soldiers, airmen, and sailors also found time to create their own musical cultures, influenced no doubt by the popular music they craved. They wrote, performed, and recorded their own songs, sometimes called *unit songs*. The typical approach was to take a pop song or traditional folk tune and invent new lyrics for it, better suited to the wartime situation. Miller's tape, for example, contains "The 12 Days of Christmas" tortured into "12 Months in Vietnam": "On my first month in Vietnam, my CO gave to me, / A country full of vicious VCs."

This remix tradition stretches back to at least World War II, if not earlier.[40] General Lansdale, a former CIA operative, collected Vietnam-era unit songs into two collections: *In the Midst of War* and *Songs by Americans in the Vietnam War*. Ernie Miller's tape is a living aural memory of this tradition, dubbed from a recording made by members of the UTT. Redesignated throughout the war as the 68th, the 197th, and finally the 334th Armed Helicopter Company, the group was always referred to as the UTT. The UTT's musical group included lead and backup vocals (with a deep baritone back there somewhere), a guitar, and some makeshift percussion

FIGURE 1.3. A Vietnam unit song book. "497th TFS Night Owl's Song Book," The Jack Horntip Collection, https://www.horntip.com.

at times. In a personal communication, a former member of this squadron, Jim Bodkin, confirmed that Miller's tape does indeed include a copy of the UTT's tape. (The guitarist, Mike Davis, was still alive as of this writing, Bodkin reports.)[41] To a twenty-first-century ear, the UTT group sounds like a folk-rock band with a country twang. While the lyrics convey a clear-eyed, cynical view of America's involvement in Vietnam, they rarely cross the line into protest songs.

The songs on Ernie Miller's R2R tape—dubbed, as Miller reports, from an original copy in "a crew chief hooch"—include "Letter Home" (sung to the tune of "Hello Muddah, Hello Fadduh!"), "Swing Low, Sweet 707" (sung to the tune of "Swing Low, Sweet Chariot"), "This Land Is Their Land" (sung to Woody Guthrie's "This Land Is Your Land"; despite the title inversion, the lyrics represent the crew's feelings about Vietnam and the Viet Cong more than any antiwar sentiment), and "Airsick ARVN" (sung to the tune of "Drunken Sailor" and dedicated to the Vietnam army regulars who rode with the gunship group and regularly vomited all over the copilots in the back; ARVN is pronounced *ar-vin*, matching syllabically with "sailor" in the line "What shall we do with a drunken sailor?"). My personal favorite, however, is the song that opens Miller's side 2: a version of Marty Robbins's 1959 gunslinger ballad "Big Iron"; as a Vietnam folk song or unit song, it was often called "The Test":

> It was early in the morning and the crew chief wore a frown
> He didn't know if this new replacement could get his chopper off the ground
> He knew this was a deadly business, and there couldn't be a slip
> And he knew a fledgling pilot could bring troubles to his ship, troubles to his ship
> Soon this pilot learned his lesson, while flying all around
> He received his first baptism from the VC on the ground
> Many rounds came through the cockpit, and they struck the rotor head
> And he looked around behind him, thinking everyone was dead, everyone was dead
> He could see the gunner shooting, he could hear the crew chief shout
> I can see them bastards running, God, that marking smoke is out
> Before the Viet Cong reached cover, his bullets fairly ripped
> And the wingman's aim was deadly, with the weapons on his ship, weapons on his ship
>
> It was over in a moment, there was silence all around
> And the bodies of the VC lie before him on the ground
> He'd survived his first encounter, and just like all the rest
> Now he was a combat pilot who had passed the crucial test, passed the crucial test

6, 5, 4. A Three-Way Tie: Audio Pen Pals, Reel-to-Reel Tape, 1960–1968

These curiosities are from Bob Purse's collection again. According to Purse, some of the most dedicated reel-to-reel audiophiles in the fifties and sixties became audio pen pals, sending tapes back and forth with messages and, unsurprisingly, music dubbed from LPs or recorded from the radio. Some pen pals were international. Three R2R letters, from 1960, 1963, and 1968, were sent from the same German man to two American pen pals, a man named Larry in Lewiston, Maine (the 1960 and 1963 tapes), and a man named Pat in New Oxford, Pennsylvania (the 1968 tape).[42] Audio letters to friends and family are well documented, but audio letters sent between strangers, as aural pen pals, are few and far between. (Searching "audio letter" and "pen pal" in Google Scholar turns up only two results—including one relevant to a murder case[43]—and searching both terms with Google doesn't return much either. It must have been, and still seems to be, a niche pursuit among committed audiophiles.) On Purse's audio letters, the German is excitable about his hobby. His name is Roland, I think—the accent makes it difficult to tell—and he sure enjoys giving Larry from Maine the technical details about his R2R setup.

Roland was living in Stuttgart when he sent the tapes to Larry, and in Frankfurt when he sent the tape to Pat. On the Larry tapes, Roland seems to have had a taste for classical music and Germanic folk tunes rather than pop music. (And why not? No point sharing the same Beatles songs Larry can listen to in America.) The 1960 tape includes two orchestral numbers, one at the beginning and one at the end. The 1963 tape opens with first calming and then rousing central European folk numbers—*oompah-oompah* music, beer hall material, the aural incarnation of lederhosen and dirndls. "I hope you enjoyed this little bit of music I put on the tape in the beginning," says Roland, in his accented but fluent English. "It is music from the Bavarian Alps, and I think this kind of music, you like." The middle of the tape contains a range of pen pal divulgences, and at the end of it, Roland reminds Larry that he had asked about a song from a shortwave radio program he had heard—a song "about a little train." Roland tells Larry he may have found the song in question: "I shall dub it now for you. Listen please." Roland then dubs what I believe to be a piano-and-tuba rendition of "Die Kleine Bimmelbahn" ("The Little Train"), a song in German by Marianne Vasel and Erich Storz that had climbed the American Billboard Charts in 1958. *Oompah-oompah!*

On Roland's 1968 audio letter, his tastes and his recipient have changed dramatically. He dictates this audio letter to the president of the Charlie Louvin Fan Club, one Pat Sullivan, residing in New Oxford, Pennsylvania. Charlie Louvin was one half of the Louvin Brothers, a popular country and western act from the fifties and sixties. The duo appeared regularly on the Grand Ole Opry, made it into the Country Music Hall of Fame in 2001, and ranked fourth in a *Rolling Stone* Top 20 list of best duos of all time.[44] It seems their fame stretched all the way to Germany.

"On a tape, you can send a word—ah—on—a message in words," our Teutonic audiophile says at the beginning of this R2R tape, "but you can also send music, and this is what I want to start here, right now." He then dubs the Louvin Brothers' twanging melody "Take Me Back into Your Heart." There follows a rambling sprawl of pen pal messaging—relevant, I'm sure, to a different book on midcentury history—followed as expected by more Louvin Brothers material. Before he gets to the tunes, however, Roland praises country music in what must be one of the earliest extant pronouncements on American country music by a German: "I think I've talked about a lot of things, so I think we'd better make some more music. How about that? Here's Charlie Louvin! . . . I'll tell you one thing, country music is the best music in whole wide world, and I tell you I enjoy life much more with country music. Country music is part of my life, and it's part of Trudy's life too." Trudy is Roland's wife. He informs Pat that she loves country music as much as he does, even though she can't understand the words. Then a quick pause on the tape, followed by a needle drop, and here comes more Louvin twang: "Show Me the Way Back to Your Heart," so unlike the *oompah-oompah* stuff on the previous tapes to Larry. The rest of the tape contains the Louvin Brothers singing Roy Acuff numbers, about which Roland says: "This is my personal opinion, when the Louvin Brothers sing Roy Acuff songs, is just—it just has to be good, there is no other way, because it's a combination that you can't beat, and here's one of my favorite songs, 'The Great Speckled Bird.'"

The flat-picking kicks in just as Roland says, "here's one of my favorites." He must have had a good microphone integrated into a setup that included two reel-to-reel recorders and a turntable, all three connected via RCA cables—not a common setup in the 1960s. The Red Cross's "Voices from Home Program," which ran from 1966 onward, staffed its booths with recording specialists, realizing that soldiers and American families needed help to tape audio letters; Kay Surber likewise required help from an audiophile friend. But here, from the same era, a German and two American audiophiles used their own hobbyist knowledge to expertly record R2R mixtapes of music and messages. These tapes—to Larry and Pat—don't include large song selections, but they meet my requirements of a mixtape and, more importantly, just like the Bob Nelson radio show, they anticipate the joy of sharing music that mixtape culture would come to exemplify.

3. A Musical Letter to Darlene, Reel-to-Reel Tape, Circa 1961–62

In the eighties and nineties, the mixtape acquired a romantic subtext.[45] It was understood to be, in its most essential function, a compilation dubbed and delivered as a teenage courtship ritual. If I had included that romantic intention in my mixtape definition, this gem from the early sixties would still make the cut.[46] It's a flirtation, a musical love letter, sent by the midcentury version of John Cusack in *High Fidelity*.

"That's a very beautiful number—don't you think?—by Jaye P. Morgan and 'I Miss You,'" the suave narrator cuts in after the second song, on what sounds like a quality microphone. He cuts in after every song, a masculine baritone praising the beauty and aptness of his song selections. The man, Talmadge, is in Vicksburg, Mississippi, and Darlene, the darling recipient, is in California somewhere. He hopes she is having "a great big ball out there" and hopes she enjoys this tape "just half as much I enjoyed making it for you." (Already on display in 1961 is the latent self-indulgence of the romantic mixtape—its desire signifying the maker as much as the recipient, a point I'll explore in chapter 5.) The playlist opens with a Henry Mancini orchestration but otherwise includes love ballads: "I'm Walking the Floor over You" by Georgia Gibbs, "I Love Paris" by the Four Aces, "If I" by Jimmy Clanton, "Angry" by Gale Storm (a roadhouse blues version of the Perry Como song), "If You Like-a Me" by Teresa Brewer, "Is It Really Love?" by Lloyd Price ("the words are the thing that makes the song," Talmadge opines here), "There Must Be a Way" by Joni James, and "Bring Us Together" by Patti Page. Just after the opening notes of Joni James's "There Must Be a Way," Talmadge cuts in: "I'm working on it." The lyrical context suggests Talmadge and Darlene may have been separated by fate or economic necessity, and that Darlene is more finished with the relationship than Talmadge: "I look for a way to be happy, happy with somebody new / Oh, there must be a way but I can't find a way without you." Maybe Talmadge was gathering funds to purchase a bus ticket and first month's rent on a California apartment. Maybe the whole tape was a last-ditch effort to stay in Darlene's life. The mixtape ends on a melancholic note, with Guy Lombardo's 1953 "There's Always Someone That You Can't Forget": "There's something about a new love / That reminds you of your first true love."

Talmadge turns down the volume before the song has finished, proclaiming, "I hope you enjoyed this little tape, Darlene, I've certainly enjoyed making it for you.... I oughta be expectin' a tape from ya'll real soon, okay? And a letter too. Until then, goodnight." The valediction indicates that the relationship is on surer ground than the earlier lyrics suggest. For this couple, sending mixtapes back and forth across the country was perhaps something of a ritual. Or not. Maybe Darlene hasn't sent anything at all to Talmadge, and his sign off is a guilt trip of some sort. Who knows. Either way, this R2R tape is one of the earliest and purest examples of a romantic playlist curated as a love letter, which would become a defining mark of cassette culture three decades later.

2. *An Early Eclectic Mix, Reel-to-Reel Tape, Circa 1947–1951*

After our interview, speaking about his public collection, Bob Purse kindly stayed on alert for anything that met my definition of a mixtape. In May 2024, he stumbled across a noteworthy mix dubbed from records and radio, and he put it on his website.[47] What makes this mix special is that, according to Purse, it's dubbed onto what must be one of the earliest—if not *the* earliest—magnetic tape reels made available to American consumers. The recording appears on a Soundmirror paper-backed tape, and as I mentioned in an earlier chapter, R2R magnetic tape was lined with paper from its earliest consumer release circa 1947 until about 1951. This is a very early tape mix, and unlike the other early tapes in Purse's collection (the organ music from Rader Memorial Methodist Church and the collection of tunes from Mario Lanza and Kathryn Grayson), the music on this tape was dubbed from records and radio and sent or given to someone as a novelty.

As on the other tapes in this countdown, the added voice message provides evidence that it's a protomixtape. It's not nearly as interesting a message as the one to Darlene or the jazz-hound banter in number 1, below, but it's enough to conclude that the music mix was intended for a specific recipient. A male voice introduces most of the songs with their titles: "Now we'll give you the 'Field Artillery March.' Here we go!" or "The next number is—uh—hold on now—'The Spanish Waltz.' And then after that, the 'Ripple,' and another one by Henry Ford's Old-Time Dance Orchestra." Filling out the rest of the tape are Stephen Foster's "O Susanna," a recording of a nineteenth-century antislavery ballad called "Nelly Gray," some Scottish highland music, and a rendition of the "Hokey Pokey" (called "Hokey Cokey" in this version and spelled that way on the scribbled track list). It's an eclectic mix, not themed by genre or lyrics, and whatever interpersonal purpose the sender and recipient tacitly cued into is lost to time. But the final message on the tape suggests that this Soundmirror R2R tape is, in fact, as Bob Purse writes, "one of the earliest mixtapes you're ever going to hear . . . more interesting for what it is than for what it contains."[48]

"All right, that's all," says the voice at the end of the tape. "Change the reel or turn it back. Hurry up!"

1. *"Cornhusker Special," 78 rpm Disc, 1949*

Below is a full transcript of the earliest mixtape I've stumbled across in the vast wilderness of the American audio archive. It adheres to the definition set down at the beginning of the chapter and sits in the collection of Grammy-nominated sound archivist Patrick Feaster, who was generous enough to share it with me (figure 1.4).

Earlier, I wrote that phonograph audio letters and home recordings from the 1940s contain plenty of live singing. This 78 rpm disc is special because it contains a custom playlist mechanically dubbed, or "cut," as the maker says, from multiple records onto a blank 78 and sent to an individual recipient. The audio quality is good enough that the unnamed mix-disc maker was not just holding a microphone up to a speaker. "He would have needed two turntables," Feaster says. "There were double turntable machines back then, but that is something a radio station would have had."[49] Lacquer discs had shorter runtimes than what R2R tapes and cassettes would one day possess, so dual turntable machines were useful for archiving a long radio broadcast, for example. "Right as the first disc was running out," Feaster explains, "you'd start the second disc, and then swap out discs so that you wouldn't lose any content." As described by media historian Emily Thompson, multiturntable units originated in movie theaters leading up to and after the advent of sound pictures in 1927. These units allowed an operator to sync recorded music and sound effects with the film, fading in or out from one disc to the next at the right second. Some of these units integrated up to six turntables. With names like Orchestraphone, Theatrephone, Mell-O-Tone, and Bell-O-Tone, these units gave movie audiences their first taste of a film soundtrack.[50]

However, Feaster thinks it's unlikely a consumer or even a hobbyist prosumer would have owned such a machine in 1949. The disc-cutter mentions that he is a salesman, and that he will soon start work as a stock clerk at a night club—not a wealthy man, in other words. More likely, he simply connected two turntables with RCA cables, screw terminals, pin connectors, or some other proprietary connector (by 1949, standard RCA cables would be the most plausible means of connecting two record players). The output of one machine hooked to the input of the other—one spinning the music, and the other spinning a blank disc—the setup and operation would have been conceptually like but more involved than the integrated dual cassette decks that made dubbing frictionless in the eighties and nineties.

The voice on the "Cornhusker Special" 78 is, expectedly, an obsessive music fan, a jazz hound, who refers casually and intimately to BG, TD, Bunny, and Lena—that is, Benny Goodman, Tommy Dorsey, Bunny Berigan, and Lena Horne (all jazz and big band legends). His recipient must have shared the enthusiasm because the voice never clarifies the references, only pausing to do so when he name-drops more obscure artists, such as Howard Smith, a member of Dorsey's orchestra.

At one point between the songs, the sender says, "Got your letter today, so this is why you're getting more of the same." As with Talmadge and Darlene in the number 3 spot, it seems that sending or receiving song compilations was becoming something of a ritual for these two jazz aficionados (one or both were Nebraskans, presumably). One of them requested songs; the other delivered. But it still would have been a novel ritual at this point. For example, my favorite part of the recording is when the sender declares: "Drop me a line. Always love to hear from you. I love saying that." Maybe I'm overthinking the words, but it seems like he's enamored with this voice message technology, which allows him to "hear from" his recipient in the literal and not the metaphorical sense. The long-distance phone call transcended space, but the audio letter transcended space and time, connecting a voice recorded two weeks ago with an ear here and now.

For posterity, here is the full playlist and transcript of the 1949 78 rpm mixtape from Feaster's collection. The sender never mentions his name. The recipient is either Gene or Jean, a distinction with a difference. I think it's Gene because the sender also calls him "boy" and "pop." Gene/Jean also gets called a "doll," but it sounds like a bit of fun, playing on the 1940s' vernacular "you're a living doll" (as in, a nice person). The vocal messages between the songs, to my subjective ear, give off a familiar vibe—brothers or cousins, a particularly close father and son, old schoolyard chums, or maybe even a love interest. It's impossible to know for sure. All I can claim is that it's a proper mixtape from 1949. Out there, somewhere, earlier ones exist, but 1949 sets a pretty good benchmark.

The mechanical reproduction of sound enabled the capture of music and singing. The idea to dub and share bespoke song mixes probably began to spread across America by 1940. Feaster sets Christmas of that year as the moment when media companies began to heavily advertise devices for home disc-recording, such as the Wilcox-Gay Recordio, which made it affordable(ish), for example, to record radio broadcasts onto blank discs. However, prior to the release of consumer machines that enabled mixtape-making, the desire to customize a music experience was already in the public's mind. In the 1920s, phonograph "albums" were literal books with blank labels: collections of empty sleeves for whatever discs the consumer wanted to curate into them. Advertisements in the 1920s—"The Perfect Plan"—demonstrate that these albums were indeed curated for small group settings, so it's not hard to imagine someone in the Jazz Age gifting an album collection to a friend or lover (figure 1.5).[51] Even in the earliest days of wax cylinders, at the advent of the twentieth century, Edison sold portable boxes for storing and transporting multiple cylinders. Someone out there, someday, will find textual or physical evidence that an Edison box contains the earliest protomixtape: a personalized set of wax cylinders given as a romantic gesture.

It's hard to know if the idea of the mixtape came before or after technology's capacity to generate such a thing. Portable wax cylinder boxes, 1920s blank album labels, and the mechanically dubbed mix-disc and mixtapes in this countdown signify a tight connection between mechanically reproduced music and the impulse to personalize that music experience. Either way, the examples referenced in this countdown represent just a small sample of the full mixtape archive, which, if we were to march forward from 1971 into the cassette era proper, would become nothing less unwieldy than an audio version of Borges's Library of Babel.

"Cornhusker Special" 78 rpm Disc Playlist
Side 1

    [0:00-3:11] "Love" (Judy Garland)
    [3:20-6:13] "A Lover Is Blue" (Tommy Dorsey and Jack Leonard)
    [6:22-8:46] "Am I Proud" (Tommy Dorsey and Anita Boyer)
    [9:54-11:03] portion of "I'm Nobody's Baby" (Judy Garland)

Side 2

    [0:00-2:55] "Love Is Never Out of Season" (Tommy Dorsey and Jack Leonard, Howard Smith on piano)
    [3:09-5:51] "You Brought a New Kind of Love to Me" (Benny Goodman and Jane Harvey)
    [6:14-8:57] "You Must Have Been a Beautiful Baby" (Tommy Dorsey and Edythe Wright)
    [9:20-10:35] Selections from *Bunny Berigan and His Orchestra* (Bunny Berigan)

"Cornhusker Special" 78 rpm Disc Voice Messages
Side 1

    [3:11-3:20] If you remember correctly, Lena sang that in the Ziegfeld Follies of '46. Judy on that one. Hang on!
    [6:14-6:21] Yeah, man, that was your boy. My boy too. One of 'em. Here's some more.
    [8:47-9:53] Yes, sirree-bob, that was it, boy. That was Anita Boyer on the vocal. Hey, you been a good boy? Got your letter today, so this is why you're getting more of the same. Better talk into the mic, hadn't I? Local news: there is none. I've been peddling a paper dust cloth called the Luster Duster. What they are, they're seconds on diaper liners. And we got a sewed-up deal on it. Sell them for polishing cloths for cars and whatnot. And we sold forty-seven and a half thousand of them. First of the month, I start to work for Cabana Lincoln as a stock clerk, you know, keeping track of sheets and towels and whiskey and food and whatnot. Then I work on up to where I get the patio; now, they're gonna put a glass roof on the patio and bring in live talent on the weekends and have it all year round. It's gonna be a good deal. Hear you've been real good; I'll give you a surprise right here at the end. Hang on.
    [10:22 *over a Bunny Berigan solo*] Get it there, get in there!
    [11:03-end] Man, I'm still shakin'. Check back down there, and I'll see you on the other side, boy. This is Saturday the twelfth of March. When I cut the other side of this, heaven only knows! Hope you like it, Gene, and hope you enjoy it as much as I do. I know you get a kick out

of hearing it, and you know I get a big kick out of cutting it. Enough said. See ya, doll. You're a livin' doll! Bye, pop.

Side 2

[2:56–3:08] Knew you'd really go mad for that piano. That's, incidentally, Howard Smith. That's the boy that cut "Boogie Woogie." Coming up, a good Benny number you'll love.

[5:51–6:11] Yes siree bob. That was old BG. Got some nice TD coming up, when he used to work, you know? This is the old Clambake now. Edythe Wright now. And—hey, they'll probably think I'm queer as a three-dollar bill with all this doll stuff. I'm just on a doll kick. Hang on.

[8:58–9:17] Yes siree. I'm done up now. You know. Isn't it fun? I got about an inch left on here and I'm gonna—well, it really isn't that much, it's about half inch. I'm gonna turn it off for a minute, put on something that'll put you to sleep, you know. Something you can dream about. Hang on.

[10:36–end] There's just a couple to tease you along, Gene. Hope you enjoy it and hope you sleep peacefully. Somethin' to dream about. I got this Firestone Philharmonic. It says here Air Chief. It's a album of Bunny. I think I played it once for you before.... It was '42 ... so it came out after he died ... and uh, thought you'd enjoy it. I'll cut the whole thing for you sometime. I'll see ya. Drop me a line. Always love to hear from you. I love saying that. Bye now. Hey, any favorites you want, let me know. I'll cut it for you. Just give me the word. You know? Bye. For good.... Go on, shut it off, shut it off ... [disc skipping] ... shut it off ... shut it off ... shut it off ...

FIGURE 1.4. A 1949 mix-disc. Can you find an earlier one? Courtesy Patrick Feaster.

FIGURE 1.5. "The Perfect Plan": A 1920s advertisement for a self-curated "album." "An Important Accessory—Albums for Filing Disc Records," *The Talking Machine World*, February 15, 1920, 6.

2: HOT WAX PIRATES

A year after Margie B. Olsen penned her "anniversary tape" missive to the *Kingsport Times* and eight years after Kay Surber sent an easy listening R2R mixtape to her fiancé in Vietnam, the word *mixtape* still hadn't been invented, but the earliest reference to a public, DJ mixtape dropped in *Billboard* magazine. The reporter calls them "'Illegit' Disco Tapes" in the headline, writing on October 12, 1974:

> The tapes are dubbed from records by disk jockeys active in the growing number of disco clubs in the metropolitan area. One to three-hour programs bring anywhere from $30 to $75 per tape, mostly reel-to-reel, but increasingly on cartridge and cassette. They are not only sold to individuals, but also to commercial non-dance locations. Some, in addition, are sold to foreign buyers. One observer reports he is personally aware of a dozen disk jockeys, each of whom makes and sells from "10 to 30 tapes a month at an average price of $50 a program." But more are engaging in the trade every day, he adds.[1]

Discotheque jockeys, in short, were recording their sets for resale to individuals and businesses alike. Their tapes made it possible to take the club home with you. The disco tape offered an extended playlist with the right background vibe for a party or a shop. A California company named, literally, Discotapes "placed full-page ads in such publications as *New Times*, *Playgirl*, and the *Village Voice*, for the mail order purchase of a $9.95 disco tape," about fifty dollars in 2020 currency.[2] The custom DJ tape was a valuable item in the midseventies. And the fact that DJs recorded their sets onto R2R tape in addition to 8-tracks and cassettes suggests public mixtapes may have been available as early as the 1950s, tracking the rise of the discotheque itself. Given the abundance of R2R audio letters, it's reasonable to assume an audiophile market existed for R2R club music in Swinging London.

Outside the Anglosphere, Russian youth were also pirating music in the fifties and sixties. Stephen Coates has documented the trafficking of "bone music," *roentgenizdat*—improvised gramophone recordings made on X-ray films.[3] With Western music banned in Soviet Russia, teens and young adults went to extreme lengths to listen to the Stones or Ray Charles: they'd purchase or pilfer medical X-rays from hospitals, cut them into circular shapes, burn a hole in the center with a cigarette butt, and then cut 78 rpm grooves onto them. These bone record grooves were produced with the help of old phonographs and, presumably, nearly-as-old audiophiles who had no truck with the Soviet regime and its censorious ways. Onto these cut and grooved bone records, a smuggled 78 could be duplicated, sold, and traded. The bone records—music "deep on the ribs" as the Soviet kids said—only lasted five to ten turns on the phonograph, however, so the trend didn't last long.[4]

Bone records, disco tapes, or rap mixtapes are not the subject of the book, but they do provide an excuse to address music piracy, copyright law, and the legal and industrial backdrops of the personalized mixtape. Attentive to the nostalgia, many cassette retrospectives skip over the legal and economic forces that allowed mixtape culture to thrive in the first place. The first-sale doctrine had always made it permissible to sell or give away a copy of a legally purchased object; however, manufacturing *copies* of the object, on blank media, was at best a legal gray area and at worst actionable, especially when copies were sold for profit or distributed in large numbers (as would one day be the case via MP3 sharing).

In most European countries, blank media were and still are taxed with a "private copying levy," whose proceeds (in theory) compensate copyright holders "for the losses suffered as a result of others making copies of their music and films for their private use."[5] In 2018 alone, the European Union netted $1.2 billion in private copy royalties.[6] In the United States, the Recording Industry Association of America (RIAA) adopted a more litigious strategy against the existence of blank audio formats. In the 1980s, it tilted against the windmill of blank cassette tapes[7] and threatened legal action against the release of the first digital audio media, Sony's Digital Audio Tape (circa 1987) and Philips's Digital Compact Cassette (circa 1992). Legal maneuvering between media companies like Sony and Philips and the music industry resulted in the Home Audio Recording Act of 1992, a byzantine piece of legislation that, in general, legalized the noncommercial duplication of music for personal use, established America's version of a private copying tax, and created the first state-mandated tech standard in copyright history: the Serial Copy Management System (SCMS), designed to prevent consumers from making copies of an officially released digital copy of a master recording. (In the long run, the SCMS worked out as well as you'd expect.)

However, the Home Audio Recording Act of 1992 did not apply its levying fees to the Compact Cassette and other magnetic tape formats—which technically kept mixtapes in the same legal gray area they'd always existed in. Whether a custom compilation of songs dubbed for a friend or lover constituted fair use was left in the ear of the beholder. In 1980, as reported in the *Washington Post*, the music industry was dead set against the whole idea of the blank cassette: "Polygram, one of the world's largest record conglomerates, informed retailers that it 'will not pay for any advertisement which includes blank recording tape on the same page or in the same radio or television copy.' Arista Records joined in last week, and other companies are expected to follow along."[8]

From this amusing volley against "blank tape" ads in 1980 to the 1992 Home Recording Act, no compromise was ever reached regarding the legal status of copyrighted recordings dubbed onto a blank cassette. The act simply represents the reality that, throughout the cassette era and, in fact, the entire history of sound reproduction, music producers and manufacturers of audio media—from player pianos and jukeboxes to cassettes, digital audio tapes, and compact discs—vacillated between being uneasy allies and mortal enemies, with young adults sharing music caught somewhere in between.

While private mixtapes were not released from culpability in these legal matters, the DJ mixtape, dubbed and distributed for profit, obviously and explicitly violated copyright protections. And yet, despite appearances, I want to suggest that pirate DJs and early LP bandits may have been the first groups among whom a private mixtape culture took shape, a culture distinct from the scattered, one-off musical audio letters and home recordings profiled in the last chapter.

Audio archives contain personal mixtapes in the strict and loose senses, but even as late as the "Dear Heloise" letter, in 1973, individually curated mixes had not evolved into a *thing*. The practice lacked a name, a cheap medium, and a cultural milieu in which one could share a mixtape without any technological novelty attached to it. Cassette sales did not surpass LP sales until 1982,[9] so although the Compact Cassette hit the market in 1964, it was not a cheap and abundant item until the eighties. And a medium must become cheap and abundant before a youth culture can grow on its heels. In addition to being cheap, the medium must also become user-friendly. Reel-to-reel copying and lacquer disc dubbing required not only excess cash but hobbyist skill. It wasn't as easy as pressing *play/record* on a dual tape deck.

In 1974, when the term *disco tape* made its debut in *Billboard*, teens and young adults were not yet creating private mixtapes at a critical mass. But there seems to have been a critical mass of DJs—the epitome of dedicated, savvy music fans—making money from their public mixes. These

DJ pirates, I suggest, may have been the latest in a long line of copyright flouters who, despite their economic intentions, may have slipped personal mixtapes from hand to hand as a normal cultural practice. Like Bob Nelson in the last chapter's countdown, they would have owned the equipment and possessed the requisite know-how to produce a custom playlist in the days of phonograph disc and R2R tape. Accustomed to such mechanical dubbing, they would have taken the whole process for granted and made mixes as a matter of course. Music pirates would have been familiar with the practice, in other words, and media familiarity is a prerequisite for a widespread media culture.

It'd be nice to imagine a history in which the romantic, private mixtape came first and later was bastardized into an item for self-promotion and mass consumption. But this is an American story as much as a media history. In the American context, dubbing music onto a blank disc or tape was first motivated by profit through illicit sales as much as by love and friendship.

That chronology, however, is part of the mixtape's allure. The history of capitalist critique is a history of disappointment. Every ground of critical appraisal ends up annexed by the genius of commodification. Alexander Galloway writes, "Desire and identity are part of the core economic base and thus woven into the value chain, 'normalized' into the mode of production."[10] Miraculously, the mixtape seems to have worked in the opposite direction. The blank cassette and the tape player were products of capital allocation, items mass-produced as cheaply as possible to sell as many units as possible. But a glitch in the system—someone was asleep at the wheel—meant these new media systems enabled easy reproduction of copyrighted material for whatever noncommercial purposes the consumer had in mind. To repeat: *easy reproduction for noncommercial purposes.* The whole thing sounds suspicious to capitalist ears. This book is not a piece of Marxist or socialist critique, but I want to emphasize the piratical ethos of mixtape culture from the start because, with no ethical intention whatsoever, mixtapes showed the world what it looked like for culture to co-opt capitalism for a change rather than the other way around.[11]

"YOU CAN'T ALWAYS CATCH THEM"

The bought-and-sold disco tape—a curation of songs dubbed from various copyrighted records onto a single tape source—was the latest example of music piracy or bootlegging, a practice that emerged in tandem with recording technology itself. (For the audiophiles, I'll specify that *piracy* refers to copying studio-recorded music onto a blank storage medium while *bootlegging* refers to recording a live performance.) Edison invented the phonograph in 1877. One of the first chronicled instances of bootlegging occurred in 1901, when Lionel Mapleson, the librarian at New York's Metropolitan Opera House, began recording opera performances with an Edison phonograph fitted with a Bettini Micro-Recorder and Micro-Reproducer. The setup allowed Mapleson to record performances on wax cylinders, the earliest and standard recording medium at the time. Mapleson recorded first from the prompter's box in front of the stage and later from the catwalks above the stage. There is no evidence that Mapleson sold his wax recordings—these cylinders could capture only two minutes of sound—and most of them were donated at his death to the International Record Collectors' Club. However, in 1939 and 1957, small private collections of Mapleson cylinders emerged, suggesting that a small trade existed for his opera bootlegs. The cylinders ultimately landed in the New York Public Library's Rodgers and Hammerstein Archives of Recorded Sound, where they remain to this day.[12]

No one would have called Mapleson's cylinders *bootlegs* when he recorded them at the Met in 1901. That word didn't enter the lexicon until Prohibition, when *bootlegging* became a catchall term for things illicitly produced and profited from. By the 1930s, however, the *Billboard* archive is replete with references to bootlegged music.[13]

There were complaints about bootlegged sheet music, specifically in East Asia and the Philippines, where it was popular to "slap native lyrics" onto American pop tunes recorded from secondhand sheet music.[14] There were demands for "bootleg royalties" from film companies and sound equipment manufacturers when copyrighted music began to appear in the talkies.[15] There were references to radio stations forced to bootleg music after refusing to agree to licensing terms demanded by the American Federation of Musicians (AFM),[16] and subsequent references to "bootlegging musical recordings [for] the stick outlets"; that is, copying records for rural radio stations that didn't want to abide by the AFM's terms for broadcast royalties.[17] (*Bootlegging* at this point seems to have referenced music piracy in all its forms, from copying sheet music to dubbing records.)

Who should get paid every time a song gets played? That question motivates the entire history of musical copyright. The question didn't formulate itself until the late 1700s because, until then, music was by default a live, embodied experience that couldn't be reproduced elsewhere. (Ditto most other arts.) Music notation is a technology that in some sense could "reproduce" a song or score, and music notation is over a thousand years old. However, to become embroiled in legal disputes over ownership and royalties, music notation needed help from the Gutenberg device—it needed, in other words, to become commercially viable, mass printed *sheet music*. By the late eighteenth century, sheet music had indeed developed a robust consumer base, from the young Marianne Dashwoods of the world on pianofortes to music hall owners wishing to stage a concert. Printing and selling licensed sheet music was a respectable business in Jane Austen's era. A bit less respectable was the business of printing and selling unlicensed copies of sheet music. Alongside these illicit printings emerged a reactive, litigious culture of music "owners" who wanted the illicit printers hauled into court. In 1777, Johann Christian Bach—lesser-known son of JS—sued a London music publisher who had printed unauthorized copies of two of J. C. Bach's sonatas. Deciding in Bach's favor, one Lord Mansfield determined that copyright statute protected not only "books and other writings" but also musical notation. "Music is a science," wrote Mansfield. "It may be written; and the mode of conveying the ideas, is by signs and marks."[18] This judgment established the legal precedent, adopted in America in 1831, that music could in fact be copyrighted, not in the aural abstract but *as a piece of printed sheet music* (we'll return to this legal reality in a few paragraphs, but the loophole exploited by LP and tape pirates should be obvious).

Copyright lawsuits over unauthorized sheet music printings and street-level sales were not uncommon in the late eighteenth century and into the nineteenth century. One of the most litigious composers was Arthur Sullivan, of Gilbert and Sullivan fame. Sullivan's operettas had the misfortune of being popular and, from a technical standpoint, easy enough to play that amateur performers could replicate them with sheet music. To copyright their operettas at all, Gilbert and Sullivan needed to print the sheet music. Having printed the sheet music, however, they could only stand by and watch as unauthorized copies flooded every conceivable market from Sebastopol to Schenectady. Wising up, the duo published *The Mikado* not as a complete orchestral score but as a piano and vocals score only. In 1894, however, an American entrepreneur named James Duff found someone to turn that copyrighted piano score into a fully recreated orchestral score, from which he staged performances of *The Mikado* in New York to much acclaim and good box office receipts. Sullivan sued. American courts found in James Duff's favor because Sullivan had never published and had therefore never *copyrighted* the entire *Mikado* orchestra. Best laid plans! Gilbert and Sullivan never attained any sort of royalties from or control over amateur or otherwise unauthorized performance of their work in America.[19] Decades before the common adoption of phonograph and radio, their plight laid bare the problem with musical copyright, as originally formulated: that it must appeal to the eye, not the ear, in the form of a precise music-and-lyrics sheet.

The music ownership dilemma was not settled in the nineteenth century. Edison's invention of mechanically reproduced sound aggravated the problem. Who should get paid whenever a song gets played? In the 1930s, the debate still raged, and the stakes had become much higher than Arthur Sullivan could have imagined. Music ownership and music piracy were still in the eye of the beholder in the days of radio and phonograph. One can imagine a rural radio proprietor thinking he'd paid good money for a record and by God he had every right to broadcast it as often as he wanted on the local frequencies, between paid advertisements. At the other extreme, the protagonist in the book *About a Boy*—written by Nick Hornby, author of the mixtape bellwether *High Fidelity*—lives off royalties from a popular Christmas song penned by his late father. "Do the carol singers have to pay you ten percent?" asks a skeptical friend. "They should do," he replies. "But you can't always catch them."[20]

Your average music enjoyers imagine a clean, logistic line between the money they pay for music and the musicians and sound engineers who wrote and recorded it. That may have been true for a few fortunate acts, those with the business savvy to write, record, and publish their own songs within the framework of a self-owned publishing house (and even in those cases—as with Lennon and McCartney's Northern Songs Ltd.—the artists themselves often received a small stake in the business compared to the producers),[21] but for most early twentieth-century and midcentury artists, the music profit funnel looked grim. Charles Portis describes it in his essay on midcentury country music: "A record can make the top five in the country charts and not sell more than 15,000 copies. At a wholesale price of 50 cents per record the company gross on a 15,000 seller would be $7,500. Take at least $700 off the top for the cost of the recording session and that leaves $6,800. The singer would then get about four percent of that or a $272 check for his 'hit.'"[22] Portis goes on to explain that musicians received so little for hit records "because of a curious interpretation of the copyright law" and the curious definition of a hit. A record became a hit not through physical LP sales but through repeated airplay.

> Jukebox operators, who buy most of the country singles, pay no royalties to anybody, and radio stations pay no royalties to the "artist" or the singer. The stations do, however, pay royalties to the publisher and composer. So almost every singer seems to be a music "publisher" these days. The word actually is a misnomer, a holdover from the days when sheet music was a substantial part of the business, but few [publishers] print anything. If you went to a small "publisher" and tried to buy a sheet copy of something, the chances of getting it would be slim, unless you had a subpoena.[23]

In other words, singers and songwriters had to incorporate themselves as "publishers" if they wanted any chance at collecting royalties from repeated radio airplay. (In the case of repeated jukebox play, they were out of luck.) Yet the average starry-eyed young artist relied on savvy industry executives to do the incorporating, which tended to result in the Lennon and McCartney situation. Even if the artists gained a decent stake in the royalties, it was no easy task, as *Billboard* headlines demonstrate, to be an AM and FM hall monitor, patrolling the great American hinterlands to ensure that every call sign from Buffalo County, Nebraska, to Inyo County, California, paid what was owed. Even today, most musicians make their money from concert sales rather than record sales, radio airplay, or digital downloads. The latter three are just too easy to reproduce without money flowing in the copyright owners' direction.

As its name suggests, and as Gilbert and Sullivan learned in the days before radio, *copyright* is a legal protection cooked up for the print era, for printed things. As soon as Edison figured out how to mechanically reproduce not just a music-and-lyrics sheet but the music itself, copyright law was destined to become obsolete (indeed, it was already obsolete in the days of sheet music and player piano rolls). Never mind enforcement, how does one *copyright* something that floats through the air or imprints almost invisibly on a lacquer disc or magnetic tape? In the early twentieth century, no one had a good answer to that question. A legal conundrum.

Trafficking in flat discs, bootleggers during and after World War II earned the short-lived moniker *disklegger*: "Disklegger, Riding High, Floods Phony Label Widely," reads a headline in the September 1, 1951, issue of *Billboard*: "Almost every diskery with a hit record on its list is being plagued by the industry's newest form of record bootlegger or pirate. Latest unscrupulous and illegal move is to dub a pop hit disk and press it on platters bearing counterfeit copies of the original label. Such bootlegged platters have been flooding the market, some territories recently at 25 cents per disk to retailers willing to take the chance of handling the pirated wax."[24] One New York diskelegging operation, according to the same report, "presse[ed] 50,000 disks a week but [was] foxy enough to escape sleuths."[25] This bootleg operation did not, à la Mapleson, record live music for resale or broadcast but rather dubbed a professional recording onto a blank disc for illicit resale (which we would now call *piracy*). The practice ensured that music revenue flowed nowhere near publishers, songwriters, singers, or anyone else involved in the original recording. (Contra the *Billboard* article, such an operation was not illegal at the federal level, though some state and municipal legislators had enacted more stringent copyright protections.)

In the 1960s, *pirate* and *piracy* replaced *bootleggers*, *bootlegging*, and *disklegging* in the popular press and in legal complaints. However, a case from 1956 that involved both bootlegging and piratical reproduction is worth mentioning. It is an interesting anecdote in mixtape history because it suggests that music pirates were perhaps the first individuals with enough technological savvy not only to make a private mixtape (or mix-record) but, as I said at the beginning of the chapter, to be so familiar with the process that mixtape-making became something like a ritual. The case is also a good example of how technology outpaces the state's or society's ability to regulate it. As soon as, in the 1870s, Edison took sound out of the air, put it on a cylinder, and replayed it back into the air, all the Copyright Acts from 1831 onward became outdated. This technological tension came to a head in the infamous *Miller v. Goody* case of 1956.

"TO THE EYE, NOT THE EAR"

The *Miller v. Goody* case involved a live radio performance by Glenn Miller broadcasted on the Armed Forces Radio Network during Miller's storied run in bombed-out London, 1942 to 1944. Following the war, a recording of this radio performance—the case never mentions an exact origin—was dubbed onto blank records and sold en masse without the proceeds flowing to Miller's estate or to the music publishers who owned the tunes. A 1952 edition of *Billboard* reported on the situation in its cease-and-desist phase, before it reached the courtroom:

> In an attempt to stop the sale of two LP disks containing Armed Forces Radio Network performances of the Army band conducted by Glenn Miller, the Miller estate this week sent written notification to a long list of distributors, pressing plants and record manufacturers and to every disk dealer in New York that failure to comply with a request to stop handling the records would result in naming the violators as co-defendants in any legal actions to come up.... [S]everal distributors and dealers have admitted selling or distributing the pirated LP disks and two pressing plants also admitted that they had been approached by an unknown individual to press the disks. One of the latter plants had on hand LP jackets left by the pirate.[26]

The "unknown individual" and "pirate" was a man named Joseph Krug, a record salesperson who "[had come] into possession of certain acetate disks" containing propaganda radio broadcasts made by Glenn Miller and orchestra when Mr. Miller was a major in the United States Army.[27] The Miller performance Krug somehow stumbled across must have been pretty good for it to sell in large enough numbers to attract the attention of the Miller estate. It took a few years to play out, but Mrs. Miller's threatened "legal action" finally landed in 1956. The court's decision on the case provides the technical audio details: "Krug tape-recorded the selections on those acetate disks, and made the matrices, plates, molds, stamps, etc., necessary for the manufacture of records; then, doing business as the A.F.N. Record

Company, he commenced to manufacture and sell two ten inch long-play records of the Miller performance. The jackets in which the records were sold carried a picture of Glenn Miller in his army uniform and the captions, 'Major Glenn Miller and His A.E.F. Orchestra,' 'An AFN Presentation.' The labels on the records themselves were similarly captioned."[28] As described in the previous chapter, acetate discs are specialized, higher-quality discs used in the forties to capture master recordings of studio sessions or to archive radio broadcasts. The Armed Forces Radio Network did exist, and it did use acetate discs to archive live broadcasts and to play back the broadcasts for troops abroad. The Miller acetate discs—wherever they came from—would have been legal recordings themselves. Krug, however, tested the legal waters doing what he did with them next: dubbing those discs onto reel-to-reel tape, then transferring the tape recordings to LPs, which he mass-produced and sold for his own profit.

To contemporary eyes, Krug's case looks like a blatant copyright violation, right down to the diminutive variation in his record company name (from AFRN to AFN). But in 1956, Krug's actions were not technically in violation of any federal copyright protections. Sympathetic to the Miller estate's suit, the court nonetheless denied its case on the basis that it had no legal precedents to which it could appeal, for the same reason mentioned by Charles Portis—a "curious interpretation of music copyright law" that privileged sheet music over recorded music. The court in the suit proclaimed: "In the present case, the best that can be said for plaintiffs' position is that Congress has not considered this problem and the worst, that Congress has considered this problem and has decided against the plaintiffs' position. Under either interpretation of legislative history, the hands of the judiciary are tied. The plaintiffs' motion for summary judgment in the sum of $250 per infringement . . . must, therefore, be denied."[29] Here, in 1956, we see lawmakers moving like a tortoise to music technology's hare: *Miller v. Goody* involved the use of acetate discs, mass-produced vinyl LPs, and even tape in a bootlegging operation (the "tape" in question would have been a reel-to-reel format, not a cassette cartridge). Half a century of audio recording developments, and jurisprudence had not caught up to the realities involved. The crux of the issue, as portrayed by Portis, was that existing copyright law was written in an era when sheet music, not mechanical recordings or audio reproductions, epitomized the "song" or the "performance" as far as legal ownership was concerned. At the time of the Miller lawsuit, the Copyright Act of 1909 reigned supreme, and the wisdom of Congress had not extended the definition of a musical "copy" to include a mechanical reproduction of sound. Congress had not foreseen the rapidly approaching future in which people would consume songs on a record or a radio far more often than at a live performance. (Even in 1909, litigious artists like Arthur

Sullivan decried the fact that sheet music printers and piano-roll makers could make a profit without paying royalties.) The 1909 law protected a *song* not as an aural abstraction but as a literal piece of paper—notes and lyrics. "The appeal of a copy must be to the eye, not the ear," wrote the judge in the *Miller v. Goody* case. Like today, a band couldn't learn to play a Glenn Miller tune, claim it as their own, and record it for profit; however, it was not strictly unlawful to copy a legitimate Glenn Miller performance onto a blank storage medium and resell it with proper attribution.

There are two takeaways from the case:

First, new media move faster than state regulations. The economic pursuits and social habits that new media encourage will always be two or three steps ahead of the government's attempt to regulate media-enabled behaviors and their second-order effects (when the state and corporate lobbyists catch up, however, they do so with a vengeance). In 2019, nearly three decades after the internet's popular adoption, Facebook CEO Mark Zuckerberg famously asked—*begged*—Congress to step in and provide a regulatory framework for decisions regarding information sharing and content censorship. Similarly, it took Congress until 1973 to finally update copyright law for the era of mechanically reproduced art.

Second, through the character of Joseph Krug, *Miller v. Goody* gives a peek into the technological milieu in which an early mixtape culture possibly arose: the culture of the industrial pirate, within which dubbing music would have become a naturalized activity rather than a novel act. The last chapter detailed how consumers and prosumers shared individual mixtapes on 78s and various R2R formats long before the Compact Cassette's introduction. However, that term, *mixtape*, or *compilation tape*, was not coined until the 1980s. As retrospectives like Thurston Moore's *Mix Tape* confirm, the idea remained a novelty as late as 1978; nearly all the cassettes and mixtape memories shared in that book are from the eighties and nineties, when mixtape *culture* had become a recognized *thing*. Prior to the 1980s, big-time music pirates would have been the only people comfortable and familiar enough with dubbing technology to make compilation tapes a *thing*.

When I made and received tapes in the midnineties, the blank cassette was a common object, taken for granted, and the tape deck didn't call any more attention to itself than my mother's coffeepot did. For most of us, the technology of the cassette had become so ubiquitous and familiar, tied so closely to our enjoyment of sharing music, that it disappeared as an autonomous object. Dylan B. Dryer explains how all technologies, at some point, "become invisible through use" as people "naturalize their relationship with technological arrays." He continues, "Keyboards and other tools of inscription—pens, pencils, chalk, dryerase markers, software for computers and cellphones—fade from consciousness through use."[30] I'd argue that for secondhand youth cultures to emerge because of a new medium, the medium must first become cheap and abundant, until it merges with and disappears into the rituals of the culture. I'll return in a later chapter to the concept of economies of scale, but that's essentially what I'm referring to here when I say that a medium or technology needs to become ordinary before it becomes a thing utilized in a DIY culture like mixtape-making.

In the 1940s, phono-post booths were still novelties; ditto reel-to-reel tape in the 1950s to 1960s and the cassette tape in the 1970s. However, the pirate's recording bay may have been one place where the mechanical reproduction of sound had attained a later-twentieth-century degree of ordinariness. The *Miller v. Goody* case gives us a pirate, Joseph Krug, who knew how to dub music from medium to medium. His expert working environment represents the sort of place in which someone may have alighted upon the bright idea to curate a mixtape (or mix-record) not for resale but for personal devotion to a friend, a family member, or a lover. The proficiency to dub audio recordings would have allowed the adept to take songs from multiple records and put them onto a new, personally curated album of his own design. More importantly, however, a professional music pirate, like Krug, operating at scale, would have become far more accustomed to the machinery and the process than our friends from the previous chapter, Talmadge or the singing grandpa. For someone like Krug, the whole process of dubbing music onto a blank tape or disc would have been ordinary. Hence my suggestion that music pirates may have been the first people who made mixtapes, not as a novelty, but as a matter of course—*this is just a thing we do*. That's the shift from the 78 rpm disc that ended the last chapter (recall the voice: "Drop me a line. Always love to hear from you. I love saying that.") to a culture of making, wherein dubbing tapes is not only possible but regularly done.

Whether diskleggers like Krug enjoyed creating personalized mix-records in the thirties and forties is a question lost to audio history. Maybe the profit motive overruled the romantic or relational potential of the pirate's trade; there is, as far as I have discovered, not much archival evidence for mix-records dubbed en masse. (But then, Krug's pirated Glenn Miller records aren't easy to come by either.) Nevertheless, I find it a reasonable hypothetical that wax pirates may have created an early form of not just mixtapes but of what would eventually become a full-fledged mixtape culture.

COPYRIGHT CATCHES UP

There *is* plenty of evidence, however, that record pirates in the fifties and sixties had become a long-standing thorn in the record labels' side. Rushing the piracy narrative forward, the piratical dubbing and pressing of discs—always a financial hit—became a much greater threat when the media companies unveiled their upgrade from LP disc and R2R tape to magnetic tape cartridges, especially the small, durable one known as the Compact Cassette.

It took know-how and equipment to pirate lacquer discs. The disklegger was a thorn in the side but not an existential threat to labels and artists because not just anyone could be a disklegger. The same was true, to a lesser degree, of reel-to-reel formats. The fact that R2R tape was never standardized likely created too much friction for widespread piracy; plus, R2R equipment never became cheap enough for widespread adoption. The rise of the cassette, however, changed the technological landscape. With a blank cassette and a dual tape deck, anyone could dub music. Cassette cartridge technology leveled not only the learning curve but the cost curve when it came to copying songs from a studio-released album onto a blank medium. Economies of scale eventually made the equipment and the blank cassette accessible for nearly everyone. That scaled production hadn't ramped up yet in the medium's first decade of existence, but the recording industry already recognized the threat of the consumer-friendly cassette tape. They attempted to get out in front of its popularity by lobbying Congress for federal action on the musical copyright issue, once and for all. In 1971, the Recording Industry Association of America went before Congress and laid out the existential threat:

> Stated simply, a typical illicit tape duplicator will take a conventional commercial record or tape cartridge and on very simple, inexpensive equipment will copy the recordings onto blank tape cartridges or cassettes. He will then sell this product on a retail or wholesale basis to customers of his own, thus displacing business that might normally be ours. In this process, the duplicator pays no record company; he pays no artist; he pays no musician; he usually pays no music publisher; he merely appropriates the creative and commercial property of others for his own gain. For these reasons, he is known within our industry as a tape pirate. He is known as a thief.[31]

The little tape cartridge known as a cassette was the greatest threat the music industry had yet faced—much greater than pirated discs had ever been—due to the "greater susceptibility of tape to piracy which can be accomplished at little cost, and with relatively simple facilities as compared to those needed for reproduction of records."[32] Attendees at the 1970 meeting of the National Association of Recording Merchandisers had come to the same conclusion: "In the late fifties and early sixties," reports *Billboard*, transcribing a speech made at the event, "the industry flushed record counterfeiters, who were bilking the music industry of about $20 million a year, out of existence. But our problem is more complex with tape pirates. . . . Today, the sophisticated duplicator has turned to tape pirating [because] it is easier to illegally duplicate."[33] Reading through *Billboard* reports and congressional hearings on the matter, it's hard not to notice the RIAA's and the music industry's increasingly shrill tone in the 1970s, as the consumer market shifted away from the LP to the cassette as its preferred medium for music consumption. A cassette album peddled on the same market as a blank cassette was a financially dangerous combination.

The law always plays catch-up to techno-social advancement. The gold miner always precedes the sheriff. However, when the law shows up, it can show up with a vengeance. State and city jurisdictions had already begun to craft their own versions of updated copyright protections when, in 1976, compelled by the powerful RIAA, the feds finally normalized the legal landscape via a congressional act. The Copyright Act of 1976 appeared amid *Billboard* headlines already brimming with reports on nationwide crackdowns on record and tape piracy: "FBI Raids Tape Assembler," "N.C. Bust Naps Alleged Pirate," and "2 N.J. Men Plead Guilty to Piracy" proclaimed three headlines from the same May 31, 1975, *Billboard* edition. The new, media-savvy copyright laws had finally caught up to the reality of mechanically reproduced sound, and the reality of the mechanical reproduction of artistic property in general. The Copyright Act extended protection to "original works of authorship fixed in any tangible medium of expression, now known or later developed, from which they can be perceived, reproduced, or otherwise communicated, either directly or with the aid of a machine or device." Also, alongside "musical works," one could now find "sound recordings" officially protected, defined as "works that result from the fixation of a series of musical, spoken, or other sounds [on objects], . . . regardless of the nature of the material objects, such as disks, tapes, or other phonorecords, in which they are embodied."[34]

It's a fun exercise to imagine how this definition does and does not anticipate the first kid who uploaded an MP3 file to Napster, but we'll save the internet and cloud for later chapters. For now, the 1976 act solved the problem met by the analog world and the Glenn Miller estate: that the old copyright law had hitherto protected music-and-lyrics sheets but not officially licensed copies of legally recorded music. After 1976, at last, dubbing copyrighted music onto blank storage media for resale, without official license, made one liable for civil damages.

Unlicensed copying was now actionable whether done in the back rooms of an office building or at a discotheque downtown; however, the recording industry was initially concerned with the former circumstance: industrial piracy. In 1975, an FBI raid on a Los Angeles "tape assembler," for example, seized eighteen thousand pirated tapes "from three locations involved in a single alleged tape pirate operation."[35] These scaled operators were the primary threat the RIAA needed to neutralize. Lone DJs copying their sets onto "disco tapes" were not, at first, targets for litigation—which may be why DJs in the midseventies began to hustle disco tapes under the radar in increasing numbers, just as large-scale tape and continued LP piracy came under pressure leading up to and after the federal Copyright Act of 1976.

Recall the first archival reference to a disco tape, in 1974: "'Illegit' Disco Tapes Peddled by Jockeys." Right when the legal hammer landed on the large-scale pirates and bootleggers, local DJs realized that sets spun at local clubs could easily be recorded on tape, reproduced, and sold for profit. And back in Kingsport, Tennessee, Margie B. Olsen was letting the world know that you could make little custom mixes on a blank cassette tape as a romantic gesture. A *Village Voice* column announced the same basic idea to a much larger and hipper audience in 1978.[36] And in 1982, electronics manufacturer Amstrad began to advertise its dual cassette decks with the catchphrase: "It tapes tapes!" (see next chapter, figure 3.1). The commercial pirate may have been put under pressure in the midseventies, but at the same moment, the blank cassette was about to turn not only every DJ but every consumer into a potential pirate. Pandora had opened her jar, and no army of RIAA attorneys could put the curse back in.

NOSTALGIC CYCLE 1.0

The terms *nostalgic cycles* and *cycle(s) of nostalgia* pop up in the Google Books corpus in the eighties and nineties. (Earlier references are to symphonic movements). The basic idea is that, at a certain point in their lives, people become nostalgic for a time in their past. The typical cycle involves a midlife longing for the simplest moments of adolescence, which of course did not seem so simple then.

Regarding media nostalgia, a peer group comes of age with a given technology, new at the time. As the peer group grows into middle age, the technology becomes outdated or obsolete, but the peer group begins to reminisce and discourse eloquently about those media recalled from youth, even if the purposes they served (the "content") are served as well or better by more recent technology. The American car industry provides an example of the typical cycle. Ten years after its production, a car starts to show its age; twenty years after its production, a car is a jalopy; thirty years after its production, a car gains strange new respect; forty years after its production, a car sells for more than its original asking price, refurbished by a mechanical artisan and purchased by a middle-aged man who longs not for the car but for the youth he associates with it. Middle-aged men in the 2020s have lived long enough to see nostalgia recycle the Toyota Supra into a desirable vehicle,[37] as desirable to Generation X as 1960s Mustangs were to the baby boomers. More recently still, *Road and Track* reports "The Sport Compact Nostalgia Cycle is Finally Here," referencing the resurgence of 1990s design styles in the latest electric cars offered by Japanese manufacturers.[38]

It's a basic observation, described in different ways in different periods. But this metaphor—nostalgia as *cyclic*—seems to be a recent entry into the American lexicon, used to diagnose the strange feeling that the traditional experience of nostalgia (as displayed by the car example) has been short-circuited by digital technology.

Social media and its handmaiden, the pocket computer, are likely culprits; however, social media and smartphones are also easy scapegoats. A more sober view will admit that, for 120 years or more, growing up in America has meant growing up with what Marshall McLuhan called "the electric media," an ever-more-present influence on our "psychic and social" lives because electric media extend nothing less than our souls—the electrical pulses of our central nervous systems—just as horse, chariot, and train extended our feet. "We have extended our central nervous system itself in a global embrace,"[39] McLuhan wrote in 1964, when computers still filled an entire wall, "abolishing both space and time as far as our planet is concerned." Social media and smartphones are easy scapegoats because they consummate, rather than inaugurate, the psychic and social path dependencies of electrified media.

There's nothing new under the electric lights, but Ryan Lizardi, in *Mediated Nostalgia*, writes that the globe's mediated embrace—the extension of our central nervous systems ever more deeply into the network—has made it ever easier for commercial and propagandistic interests to sync with the hearts and minds of everyone connecting into the network. In the deep past, appealing to someone's youthful memories required intimate knowledge of the person's coming-of-age experiences: young hopes, fears, and encounters. However, as C. S. Lewis says about mass taste in literature—"tell me the date of your birth and I can make a shrewd guess whether you prefer Hopkins or Housman, Hardy or Lawrence"[40]—it is possible in the age of mass media to know what nostalgic chords to strike simply by knowing when someone was born. Knowing that I came of age in the 1990s, without being given any other demographic input, a company can predict with precision the dead media and old content that will likely grab my attention.

For Lizardi, as for all media historians, media architecture is the primary driver of nostalgia production, not content as such. "The particulars of the past, the content of the media representations," he writes, "are . . . of secondary importance to the fact that the viewer or player is constructed as a past-centered consumer unwilling to relinquish lost media objects."[41] Rhetoricians Jeff Pruchnic and Kim Lacey likewise distinguish between the "content" of memory and the external "programs" consumers use to imprint memories in the age of digital reproduction.[42] Humans have always converted memory into external, material forms. Some are public or communal—war memorials, statues, museums—while others are familial, such as a family Bible or a photo album. On social media, however, Pruchnic and Lacey argue, the "affective dispositions" of private memory bleed outward into public displays. There is no longer a clean cut between public and private memory. The memories of social media users become public content, allowing corporate and state forces to exert influence not only on public memory—which has always been the case—but on private, idiosyncratic memory.

We own our natural memories; we do not own the new mnemonic programs or devices. And we are not the only ones with access. This welding of private and public memory on social media is the logical endgame of the nostalgic cycles felt by earlier generations for mass-produced objects, such as muscle cars, turntables, cassettes, and Polaroid cameras. From the standpoint of the 2020s, it is possible to appreciate that creating nostalgia for technology was capital's first, analog intrusion into private memory, an intrusion now completed by digital technology.

This distinction between nostalgia for media and nostalgia for content is important, to be sure, and I'll emphasize it in the next chapter. However, in the 2020s, even the content industry has succumbed to a backward-looking obsession built into the new media architecture. More remakes, reboots, and sequels flood movie theaters than ever before in film history.[43] Old music dominates new music on Spotify, Pandora, and Apple Music. As reported in *The Atlantic*, 70% of music sales in 2022 came from songs released earlier than 2020.[44] Given contextual data, most of that music was likely released not two years earlier but twenty, thirty, or forty years earlier. Music labels' largest investments in recent years have been into legacy catalogs owned by twentieth-century artists and their publishers, from Bob Dylan to the Beatles to Stevie Nicks to Shakira.[45] With hundreds of millions sunk into back catalog music, the industry has retreated from recruiting and promoting new talent.

The music industry has always been overly reliant on the permanence of the latest music medium, but the industry seems to be correct about the smartphone's stability compared to magnetic tape or compact disc. The smartphone is nearing its twentieth birthday without any competitors lurking in the wings, a situation unlike previous cycles of obsolescence. The cassette surpassed LP sales in 1984, but the compact disc had already been released in the United States in 1983.[46] Today, in contrast, both content producers and media manufacturers—now economically aligned—orient consumers toward an eternal past instead of the future or even the present. Apple has just released the iPhone *15*. Imagine Apple in the last century releasing Apple Computer 15 instead of a Macintosh, a Power Mac, an iMac. We have entered a media cycle that puts us "face-to-face with our own mirror of nostalgic desire," Lizardi says. The media companies have invented a time machine that only travels backward.

However, putting my cards on the table face-up, I don't think nostalgia is *bad*, either individually or socially. C. S. Lewis said, "When I became a man, I put away childish things, including the fear of childishness and the desire to be very grown up."[47] Mixtape nostalgia looks backward to a beautiful moment of shared culture as much as to a period of neoliberal economic policy. The mixtape, in fact, showed that industrially manufactured objects can be co-opted and converted back into personalized objects exchanged without GDP accountability. Socioeconomic conditions are not always a good representation of life's navigation at street level, as Michel de Certeau once observed.

Nevertheless, nostalgia today is admittedly a different thing than it was in 1923 or even 1993. Our nostalgic "cycles" (a novel metaphor, to reiterate) seem to have both sped up and slowed down at the same time. On one hand, the time-space of social media forces more and more of these cycles into existence, at a quickening rate, until our sense of history becomes "shallow," says Michael Washington, or "thinner"—the "cycle of nostalgia gets shorter, the wheels of change spin on ice."[48] Apps and memes and viral trends turn over more quickly than ever before, making consumers nostalgic, not about thirty years ago but about three years ago, three months ago, three days ago, with TikTok threatening to make us nostalgic about three seconds ago. On the other hand—as evidenced by old music statistics and the never-ending reboots and remakes at the movie theater—certain cycles aren't allowed to emerge in the first place because old content is continuously recycled. Fashion trends stuck in the aughts could be added to backward-looking trends in film and music to demonstrate that cycles of cultural obsolescence and nostalgia have ground to a halt as they have sped up online.

I'll try to square that circle in the final chapter. For now, the point is that the whole idea of a nostalgic "cycle" represents an economic incursion into the deepest crevices of personal memory by mechanically and then digitally reproduced culture. Media nostalgia (over and above content nostalgia) is the outcome of America's fusion of private and public memory on cutting-edge mnemonic devices. In defense of nostalgia, capital's influence does not create but simply exploits the appeal of "lost time" that every human experiences. We can condemn capitalism for exploiting nostalgic desire without condemning the yearning itself. Learning to control our mnemonic trances is a basic act of maturity, so I think it's more ethical to condemn capital, not for making money off nostalgia, but for ruining our collective ability to exert a mature control over it.

3: THE CASSETTE MIXTAPE

(SIDE A: ROMANTIC STUFF)

Audio archives reveal forerunners on vinyl and reel-to-reel tape, but the mixtape—both the word itself along with its cultural associations—awaited the Compact Cassette for its arrival on the American and global stage. From 1964 until the 1990s, teens and young adults had the techno-generational luck to possess consumer gear that duplicated music, on the cheap and without hobbyist training, from multiple sources onto a single source: an involved activity on reel-to-reel and lacquer disc but too uninvolved on digital devices. Because most cassette decks sported a microphone jack, this nonexpert machinery even allowed youth to experiment with multiple tracks by overlaying songs with voices and sounds.

Tape players were as important to mixtape culture as the cassettes themselves. Radio-phonographs existed on the consumer market by the late thirties and early forties, but they could only capture music from the radio, not dub one disc to another. (I don't mean to sound glib about the radio capture. Like I said in chapter 1, it's comforting to know that someone in 1940 sat for hours by the radio, waiting to record a favorite new song on a disc, just as I did in 1995 with a Compact Cassette.) Dual cassette decks, however, were not only cheaper than radio-phonographs had ever been, but they also allowed users to record radio broadcasts *and* copy an album onto a blank tape. Dual cassette decks all but incited kids to pirate music. "It tapes tapes!" exclaims an early 1980s advertisement from the British electronics company Amstrad (figure 3.1). The ad contains a picture of soccer (a.k.a. football) star Terry Venables, a diagram of two cassettes with an arrow between them—"Magic! Record from one tape to another!"—and lawyered-up fine print at the bottom ensuring Amstrad could not be sued if a user tried to record from one tape to another: "The recording and playback of certain material may only be possible by permission. Please refer to the Copyright Act 1956." (The year references British jurisprudence, quicker on the draw than the American legal system.)

FIGURE 3.1. 1980s ad for Amstrad electronics highlighting the piracy potential of cassette technology.

Not many companies were as bold as Amstrad to advertise the piracy angle outright, and most kids in the eighties and nineties did not understand copyright law. The difference between the first-sale doctrine and making copies was lost on them. Youth simply did what technology allowed them to do. Press *eject*, pop a Madonna cassette behind tape door one, and close the door. Press *eject* on the other door, pop in a blank Maxell cassette, and close the door. Hit *play* on Madonna, *play/record* on the blank cassette, and let the machine do its thing. When equipped with an FM dial as well as recording button, a cassette deck allowed teens to continue that time-honored tradition of waiting by the radio to capture a specific song on tape (too often interrupted by radio host blather). Media companies made the whole business frictionless with their cassette-deck integrations, as though they had made an intentional decision to turn the American teenager into a copyright flouter. "Home tape is killing music!" was a slogan cooked up in 1980 by the British Phonographic Industry, part of a larger antipiracy campaign that circulated in America as well. On its heel, the punk band Dead Kennedys released a cassette album with a blank side 2: "Home taping is killing big time entertainment industry profits; therefore Side Two of this tape has been left blank for your convenience."[1]

Tape players like the Walkman and the boombox conjured new social roles for the music listener. The portability of the cassette, matched by the portability of its playback devices, could turn you into an impromptu party host (the boombox) or an introvert withdrawn from your surroundings (the Walkman). The Walkman, in fact, introduced the world to an experience impossible until 1979: the ability to listen to music *privately* in public. The headphones announced you were not to be bothered, just as the boombox—volume up—broadcasted a bit of aural defiance and announced a spatial autonomy for kids growing up in a harsh environment. In *Cassette Cultures*, John Z. Komurki and Luca Bendandi put it this way: "The boombox embodies a mode of sociability that is different, even opposed, to the individualistic values typical of contemporary global capitalism. It is all about the street, coexistence, communal culture. Its opposite is the Walkman. If the cliched vision of the boombox is of a group of brightly dressed kids breakdancing on a New York street corner, the Walkman evokes a 1980s salaryman gazing blankly at his own reflection in the window of a crowded metro carriage, orange earphones clamped to his head."[2] To balance the metaphor, I'd add that a Walkman also evokes a grimly dressed white kid walking home alone on a suburban sidewalk. The point is, in a nice parallel to the duality of DJ mixtape and private mixtape, the boombox and the Walkman quickly amassed racial and cultural connotations due to the social station of the listeners themselves, and due to the different types of listening they invited—one communal, the other individualistic.

The Walkman sold fifty thousand units in its first two months and would eventually sell 220 million units during its production lifetime.[3] It had always been possible to listen to music in private, but why would you? The Walkman turned private music listening into a socially recognized activity, just as print novels turned reading into a private rather than an oratorical activity. Marshall McLuhan wrote, "Print created the portable book, which men could read in privacy and in isolation from others. . . . The printed book added much to the new cult of individualism. The private, fixed point-of-view became possible and literacy conferred the power of detachment, non-involvement."[4] McLuhan's description applies to the Walkman and to all future portable media devices, portability being the ideal toward which all media moved in the twentieth century. Made portable, music (as one day video) was no longer anchored to a specific corner of a specific room. In the mid-twentieth century, consumers still understood the phonograph to be a communal device, like a television, placed in a room where all might enjoy it—and fight over who controlled it for the evening. A 1948 Westinghouse ad by Albert Dorne, for example, portrays a father slouched resignedly against the wall as his daughter listens to pop tunes and his son waits next in line to use the phonograph (figure 3.2). Dorne's ad portrays the default music media experience for most of the twentieth century: music was something people gathered around, not something hidden away into private headphones. (Another late 1940s Westinghouse ad, however, already sells privatized media to the upper-middle classes with the slogan: "Mother has a Westinghouse table model in the kitchen for her very own. Buy more than one Westinghouse!") Bob Purse tells me that reel-to-reel owners also typically placed their equipment in a common room rather than a private room.[5]

As the cassette and its playback devices became cheaper and smaller, however, music receded from the communal space of the living room to the private space of the bedroom. At the same time, in the eighties and nineties, the American middle class had smaller families and larger homes than ever before. Every teen having their own room was a novelty restricted to the rich until very recently in America's history. Just in time for that novelty to expand across the country, the cheap cassette and the cheap tape player also made music a private bedroom affair. But the Walkman went even further: it made privacy portable, ubiquitous, on demand. If offered

FIGURE 3.2. 1948 Westinghouse advertisement in *Collier's* magazine, art by Albert Dorne.

instant "detachment, non-involvement" in any space, private or communal. It soon became normal to see people, especially young people, wearing headphones in public spaces. For the youth themselves, it became normal to walk through halls, into malls, and along sidewalks without hearing any ambient sound or natural noise. With a Walkman, there was no noise in their world at all, just music (though parents likely thought it was noise).

Shuhei Hosokawa compares the Walkman to the Polaroid. Both offered "speed of act, immediacy of effect, ... ease of operation.... The Walkman is to the auditory domain what the Polaroid is to the visual domain."[6] Both are "often taken as frivolous" by those who use them, even though both objects radically deterritorialize the user: the Walkman because it switches off the world's sounds, the Polaroid because it entices users to perceive their immediate reality as an object to duplicate. Unlike the traditional camera, the Polaroid's appeal was its quick-snap immediacy in both ordinary and special settings; it could capture life in motion. No one "posed" for a Polaroid shot. It's a stretch, but not much, to say the Polaroid and the Walkman were the world's first smartphones, the first always-with-you gadgets that rearranged sensory relationships with the physical world, "evok[ing] in us unique ratios of sense perceptions," as McLuhan puts it.[7] The Walkman hyperengaged our aural sense and thus disengaged us from the other senses, while the Polaroid heightened our visual perception at the expense of all the other senses. So-called disposable cameras—popularly left scattered around tables at weddings and birthday parties in the 1990s—were a similar pre-smartphone device that turned users into perpetual media producers whose sense of vision was overtly and overly engaged (the pictures themselves, at least, remained safely within private analog circulation).[8]

Portable audio's capacity to detach and to objectify was latent even in the first portable cassette player/recorders, like the Norelco Carry-Corder, released in 1964 alongside the cassette itself. One early adopter, Andy Warhol, took his tape recorder with him everywhere he went, reportedly calling it "my wife."[9] He enjoyed recording every conversation, no matter how mundane, because it turned his interpersonal communication into a literal object capable of reproduction, commodification, and even erasure. Far from frivolous, portable tape recorders and, later, the Walkman and the Polaroid were analog steps toward the hyperreality of social media, with their ability to commodify and detach us from private daily life.

THE MIXTAPE AS AMERICAN FOLK ART

At the time, no one thought of the Walkman as any sort of sense-rearranging device, and no one remembers it now with anything but nostalgia. All those hours locked up in our heads, music blaring—we weren't detaching ourselves from our surroundings so much as heightening our sonic receptivity, entering a Zen musical state, and letting the music shred our anxieties. That sounds like taking drugs, but music injected directly into our ears was a kind of drug—one without any negative side effects as far as we could tell.

Heartstrings plucked by nostalgia, I am tempted now to dedicate huge paragraphs in this chapter to the dream of the eighties and nineties. Instead, I'll remember that my theme is mixtape culture within media history, not the cassette or the cassette decades as such. Author and artist Matias Viegener describes how the cassette galvanized mixtape culture and secured the mixtape's place in music history: "The mixtape is a form of American folk art. Predigested cultural artifacts combined with homespun technology and magic markers turn the mixtape to a message in a bottle. I am no mere consumer of pop culture, it says, but also a producer of it. Mixtapes mark the moment of consumer culture in which listeners attained control over what they heard, in what order and at what cost."[10] Feeling like you controlled your music experience and that you could share the experience with others characterized the cassette era. The album purchased at the store, the thing recorded by musicians and promoted by labels, could also be duplicated, or even recorded over with stuff from the radio if you wanted. Blank cassettes and recording buttons embody the era as much as cassette albums.

However, if Viegener's "folk art" label is too stodgy, "DIY culture" might be a better one for mixtape makers in the late twentieth century, a designation also applied to amateur zine publications from the same era. Zines were, and still are, small, self-published periodicals containing original work but also repurposed (read: copyrighted) text and images, all designed to circulate among a specific fandom, enthusiasts of a pop-culture phenomenon, whether punk rock or comic books. DIY culture represents what Jason Luther and others have called "the extracurriculum," the place where education and cultural production arise without any sort of official sanction. Luther writes that DIY culture arises from "obsessive consumption practices" (compare Viegener's "predigested cultural artifacts") but also from "countercultures and leftist politics" because although pop culture is its reason for being, DIY culture circulates—along with copyrighted material in the form of pictures and quotes and, in the case of mixtapes, songs—outside the purview of official, money-making markets.[11] DIY culture works with the stuff of a capitalist system that, in one sense, has fractured our spirits and communities; however, DIY culture offers what William C. Kurlinkus calls a "human-centered design," or redesign, of mass-produced items for new, unsanctioned, noncommercial purposes.[12] If that doesn't describe a mixtape, I don't know what does.

The cassette—especially the blank cassette—tempted the consumer to become, if not a pirate, at least an audio manipulator or even an audio creator. For example, a popular gag from the 1950s and 1960s was the break-in record, a novelty comedy compilation that used song and television clips for humorous effects, typically in the form of a fake interview. Dickie Goodman and Bill Buchanan pioneered the technique, starting with 1956's "The Flying Saucer" (a droll rendition of Orson Welles's famous radio play). Dickie Goodman's 1975 "Mr. Jaws" is one of the funniest:

NEWS ANNOUNCER: We are here at the beach, where a giant shark has just eaten a girl swimmer. Well, Mr. Jaws, how was it?
JIMMIE WALKER: Dyn-o-mite!
NEWS ANNOUNCER: What did you think when you took that first bite?
MARVIN GAYE: How sweeeeet it is . . .[13]

This continued to be a popular radio gag in the 1980s and 1990s. I recall an exchange that went something like this:

RADIO HOST: Mr. Clinton, do you have anything to say about the allegations regarding Monica Lewinsky?
FINE YOUNG CANNIBALS: She drives me crazy, and I can't help myself, ooh! ooh!

Goodman and Buchanan were professional studio producers. In the days of LP disc and reel-to-reel tape, it would have taken their expert knowledge to produce a break-in record, a sort of comedic spin on the mixtape. But in the eighties and nineties, blank cassettes and tape decks made it possible—fun and easy, even—for anyone to do it. I remember making these things in fifth or sixth grade with an older neighbor kid.[14] We'd crouch over the radio for hours, waiting to record that one song we needed. Or we'd scour the parents' cassette collection for verses and choruses that held comedic potential. I recall my greatest contribution one Saturday afternoon was using INXS's "Need You Tonight" chorus as an interview response. I can't recall the exact setup, luckily, as it was a twelve-year-old boy's humor.

Returning to the point, the fact that anyone in the cassette era could make their own break-in record is a concrete example of how cassettes in the late twentieth century became a medium for what Viegener calls American folk art or what Luther describes as DIY culture. The blank cassette was a blank canvas, an industrially produced item to craft, not consume. You no longer needed to be an audiophile hobbyist to create your own personalized song collection taken from this, that, or the other source. You no longer needed to be a studio engineer to take dozens of three-second clips from proprietary records and splice them together into a mock interview or comedic gag reel. The mixtape, as well as the amateur break-in cassette—created on a Saturday afternoon by two kids surrounded by a cassette deck, microphone, tapes, and empty cases scattered everywhere—represent the cassette's impact not only on musical history but on American youth culture.

"BECAUSE IT'S A PHYSICAL THING"

The MP3 player was the last physical object the American public consumed music on. Apple discontinued the iPod in 2022. It is still possible to purchase cheap and not-so-cheap MP3/MP4 players, but most consumers in the 2020s listen to music on a computer or smartphone, neither of which is a dedicated music medium. Songs now float passively into our ears from a background app that selects music for us, hour after hour, until the app demands to know: *Are you still listening?* LP disc, radio, R2R tape, magnetic tape cartridge, compact disc, and even MP3 player in contrast were dedicated, sole-purpose devices that required regular, active input from the listener. (With its ability to hold hundreds of songs, the MP3 player admittedly introduced America to the never-ending playlist. Similarly, in midcentury, professional-grade reel-to-reel players had been advertised to DJs, "Muzak franchises," and other professionals as machines capable of offering multiple hours of music without an operator.)[15]

That said, a physical storage medium and a playback device dedicated to one purpose—listening to audio and music—provided the media infrastructure that kept music a tactile activity, a physical experience, throughout the twentieth century. If you wanted to control the songs, you needed to apply a little effort (even on a radio): turning the dial, flipping the disc, lifting the needle, swapping out the CD, twisting the cassette to the other side, fast-forwarding, rewinding, pausing. Listening to music was both a physical and an aural undertaking, as it had always been in the context of live music. Music was something you touched. It took up space, required physical storage. "Holding a tangible item allow[ed] people to cherish and collect music," writes Burns.[16]

Until the invention of MP3 and other digital formats, the history of mechanically reproduced sound was a history of making sound three-dimensional. Music in flesh-space sets molecules vibrating, but only the ear can receive the vibrations, and when they're gone, they're gone. The goal of Wilhelm Weber, Édouard-Léon Scott, Thomas Edison, and other nineteenth-century inventors was to snatch those waveforms and frequencies out of the air and transcribe them onto a material surface. Like a photograph, a physical sound transcription would capture a moment in time as a permanent object. Charles Cros, a Parisian inventor who developed the idea of a phonograph at the same time as Edison, later wrote a poem called "Inscription," a "belated monument," as Friedrich Kittler puts it, to his inventions, particularly the phonograph:[17]

> Like the faces in cameos
> I wanted beloved voices
> To be a fortune which one keeps forever,
> And which can repeat the musical
> Dream of that too short hour;
> Time would flee, I subdue it.[18]

The inventors of mechanically reproduced sound, like Cros, understood the radical reorientation of the senses their inventions entailed. They "transferred [the] functions of the ear to [the] sense of touch . . . ; [they] made visible what, up to this point, had only been audible. . . . All the whispered or screamed noises people emitted from their larynxes appeared on paper."[19] What was once measured in time could now be measured in space—rotations per minute, inches per second, and so on.

As waveform transcriptions go, audiophiles have long debated which material surface offers the highest fidelity transcription or the most tender sound. The wax cylinder is right out. Hi-fi idealists argue that compact discs provide the purest representation of the master recording: "Perfect Sound Forever" was the CD's advertised slogan. LP collectors prefer the warmth of lacquer disc. And what of magnetic tape? My view, both now and when I was thirteen, is that America fell in love with the cassette because it was portable and durable. Audio quality was a distant third-place consideration. Vinyl may be warm, but you can't play it in a car or slip it into your pocket.[20] The compactness of the cassette also made it easy to handle multiple tapes all at once in a small space when making mixtapes or confronted with storage limits. The cassette case felt nice in the palm of the hand; the cassette sat nicely between thumb and forefingers when slid behind a tape door or kindly pushed into a car stereo. No diddling about with sleeves, no "don't scratch it!" frilliness. It could be slid and pushed but also tossed, dropped, jostled, and handled carelessly without breaking it or ruining the magnetic strip sealed inside. Few consumers cared that it did not sound as warm as an LP.

The cassette also outperformed the LP when it came to total playing time. The standard time for a disc is twenty to twenty-five minutes per side; cassettes managed to fit thirty to sixty minutes onto each side without affecting sound quality. A similar runtime dispute played out in the home-video format wars between Sony's Betamax and JVC's VHS tape. Economic historians have concluded that a longer play capacity was the key feature ensuring VHS's success over Betamax. Sony thought consumers would prefer a more compact "paperback size" tape, while JVC prioritized a longer recording and playback time. It turned out that consumers wanted the longer recording time even if it meant a somewhat bulkier item to store.[21] By the end of the century, of course, engineers would solve the competing requirements of size, portability, and runtime by inventing a digital compression algorithm, but in the eighties and nineties, portability, durability, and longer running times were the features that drove the cassette tape to pole position in the magnetic tape cartridge wars.

Rumors of a cassette revival have circulated since the aughts. Thurston Moore's *Mix Tape* collection was released in 2004 and contains more than one reference to (then) current mixtape makers and the CD's potential, or lack thereof, to continue the analog tradition. After the book's release, Moore sat down for an interview with NPR's *Talk of the Nation*, receiving enthusiastic call-ins about the cassette mixtape and its nostalgic pull. NPR host Neil Conan concluded: "If you hang on to the tape, I think you'll appreciate it as time goes down."[22] However, the reality was that, by 2004, music aficionados had converged on the vinyl LP as *the* vintage medium for experiencing a warm, analog glow amid the cold, surgical precision of the digital music universe. What need for the cassette? Magnetic tape's hissy audio is a known problem, and it's not hard to find a contemporary audiophile who hates cassettes on principle and casts aspersion on the whole idea of a "cassette revival." *What Hi-Fi?* is a British consumer electronics magazine published since 1976. Here is a sampling of the magazine's online forum, from an April 2023 thread labeled "First a viny revival, now a cassette comeback":[23]

> **12th Monkey**: Vinyl has tactility and a sound that appeals to some—cassettes were rubbish—poor fidelity, wear out. Ugh.
>
> **podknocker**: I listen to well recorded music on CD and now similar quality streaming. The sound quality is great and there's no surface noise, or clicks and the levels of distortion are negligible. The vinyl revival and the current cassette fad are happening because people want to rebel against modern things, for whatever reason and they want to stand out and be different. That's fine, but they are listening to old, low resolution and poorer quality formats. Fact.
>
> **Sixtyten**: You realise that it's not to do with the quality and all to do with "quirkiness." "Look at us, we're releasing a "cassette" (is that how you pronounce it?)." Now? You can buy stuff on 8 track, and DCC, and MD. Well

I'll show you "quirkly," as my next release its on CED and V2000, with a special Zoetrope and Steam Organ version coming in the Autumn.

The most you can expect from this group is a backhanded compliment:

> **manicm**: Actually cassettes could sound excellent. We had a Technics double deck, and I copied the well recorded Pink Floyd AMLOR, onto a decent TDK blank, and the copy sounded better than the original! This often happened with vinyl copies onto tape as well. But as you say, the sound quality was ultimately negated by the inherent unreliability of tapes and players. Good riddance.

And yet, despite the judgment of these high-fidelity purists, the niche recesses in which cassette nostalgia has been stewing—populated by aging punk and New Wave fans—are finally seeing a glimmer of hope. According to the National Association of Musicians, cassette sales hit a twenty-year high in 2023, following a trend that had started five years earlier. Two hundred thousand cassette albums sold in 2020 and over four hundred thousand sold in 2022.[24] "Cassette tapes are making a comeback," proclaims the *Los Angeles Times*.[25] "Cassette tapes are making a comeback, but can production keep up?" asks the industrial-minded *Billboard* magazine.[26] "Who the hell is buying cassettes in 2020?" ponders UK pop-culture magazine *NME*.[27] One answer is Gen X and elder millennials, now middle-aged and rediscovering the medium of their youth. However, signs indicate that younger generations—the kids of Gen X and millennials, in other words—have rummaged through Mom and Dad's cassette collection and dubbed it cool. Lacking their own nostalgic tape memories, the digital natives are having an epiphany about music and tactile media, apprehending at last that a physical thing to touch and arrange on a shelf provides a deeper connection to music than a streaming subscription.

I'll repeat, for the anticassette crowd, that audio quality has nothing to do with the cassette's (very slowly) rising popularity. The cassette just happens to hit a sweet spot of tactility, durability, and portability. It's nice to hold; it takes up space but not *too* much space. Some younger listeners have begun to invent arguments on the sound quality front—a Medium post declares, in an encomium to the cassette, "The sound tape gives is warm. Saturated. It promotes a degree of imperfection, and creates an underflow of infamous tape hiss that leaves the format feeling nakedly honest, which is gold dust for the sincere-inclined musician"[28]—but no child of the seventies or eighties would have claimed any such thing about the cassette. The LP record, whose sales and manufacturing base dwarf the cassette revival, such as it is, can claim a bit of legitimacy when it comes to unique sound qualities and the warmth of analog music. But no teens in the twentieth century would have talked like that about cassettes. The cassette was our preferred medium because—it can't be repeated enough—we could play it in the car or in a Walkman at school. Portability trumped sound quality as far as we and the rest of the world were concerned. Who doesn't want a soundtrack for life?

It is impossible to argue against the power of digital music—music on compact disc, in particular—to preserve the quality of the "master recording," the Holy Grail of the audio purist. However, high-tech audiophiles who gaze at fans of LP or cassette and declare "it's not to do with the quality and all to do with quirkiness" are only half correct. They are right that current interest in old media is "not to do with the quality," but they are wrong that it has "all to do with quirkiness."

Aubrey Wood, author of the Medium post—"tape hiss leaves the format feeling nakedly honest"—hits closer to the truth: the cassette's imperfections *do* appeal to the middle-aged cassette enjoyer and, through secondhand nostalgia, to young cassette enthusiasts. "Our relationship with music is much more complicated than audio enjoyment," writes journalist Leonid Bershidsky. "It can't be described in terms of dynamic range."[29] The purist whose relationship with music depends on high fidelity is a marginal character. Most listeners in the twentieth century developed emotional connections to music not despite but due to the imperfect media through which they experienced it, whether on LP, R2R, or cassette. In fact, those defects, along with the old tactility, characterize the music for anyone who grew up with them. The loss of the defects on digital remasters is what seems like a loss of fidelity. (The loss of something to hold is a deeper loss still.) A song without clicks or magnetic hiss is not the same song we fell in love with. "Analog has the mystery arc where cosmos exist," writes Thurston Moore. "We used to listen to records over and over and each time they would offer something new because the ear-heart would respond to new resonations not previously detected."[30] Or, as Margie B. Olsen put it, a little more simply, in her letter to the *Kingsport Times* about making a mixtape for her husband on their anniversary: "Some of the records were slightly scratched, but that added to the sentiment."[31]

For many, the object itself—the cassette, the cracked case, the tape that comes unwound—was just as important as the songs, which, after all, could be heard on the radio or at a club or wherever else (today, they can be pulled up on a phone with a few taps). About her favorite mixtapes, Lili Dwight writes, "The tapes are stretched to the point that the original beats droop and hop in odd syncopations, but when they're on the box I am back ... in those halcyon cyclonic days."[32] A song as such can become mere "content," but a song on a particular cassette or LP is a private heirloom. Theorists of sound say that music is a series of vibrations impressed on our sensorium, a physical imprinting of vibrating molecules on ears and bodies, and from thence to hearts and minds. It is therefore a humble suggestion that the music media we touch, make, collect, and share likewise imprint on us. "Music affects the body—literally—as soundwaves permeate and resonate with flesh," writes Ben Harley, riffing on the sonic rhetorical theory of Diane Davis. "Our relationship to sound is embodied."[33]

Some cassettes or LPs, the important ones, become mnemonic devices, taking us back to those "halcyon cyclonic days." There are several reasons the cassette is still alive, but an important one is that Americans who came of age in the seventies, eighties, and nineties suffered through an adolescence accompanied by a cassette soundtrack, just as their parents had come of age to an LP and radio soundtrack. First pecks on the cheek, make out sessions in the backseat, first dances, heartbreaks, sleepovers, all-night hangouts, weekend cruising, porch chilling. Bad things too. Screaming parents, divorcing parents, shattering dishes, trips to the hospital. A song in any medium conjures up those Proustian madeleine moments, to be sure, but if it still exists, the actual cassette or record we played over and over in those years conjures the past with intensity. (Worth noting—playing a song over and over on a cassette was not done instantaneously, as on a CD; it required thirty seconds of rewinding, and those seconds of anticipation made the process sweeter and more memorable.)

Anyone complaining about the fidelity of cassette tape misses the point. Cassettes are more than a quirky retro medium, and their appeal has more to do with memory than fidelity to a master recording. The dusty cassette allows the mind to time travel. In the 2020s, listeners value cassettes (and LPs) not for their sound quality but for their potential to reconnect them to an aesthetic, nostalgic cultural moment. Music quality has nothing to do with it.

"Yes, yes, indeed... I can remember everything very clearly. I can even hear this particular song," says a member of the 1959–1966 generational cohort in a 2014 study of media memory.[34] Göran Bolin, a media studies professor in Sweden, conducted interviews with a focus group of Swedish and Estonian individuals born during the 1940s and a group of individuals born in the late 1950s and early 1960s. It's an interesting study to cite because Bolin's Scandinavian and Baltic participants sound exactly like Americans when it comes to the nostalgic pull of cassettes and vinyl in the age of digital abundance.

MARIE (Swedish, born 1962–1964): But, it's like this has to do with quantity. I mean, sometimes you lose the value in... As I see it, today you lose the value in it, because when I went and bought a vinyl record with a cover.

You do remember the covers of certain records still, don't you? And you remember the feeling when you bought it, and what it stood for. Today, they just sit online, and I get totally confused, because I'm there myself, and I think ... God, I can download anything and listen to it. ... It has to do with quantity, and you somehow lose the value in it.[35]

Later, during the same interview, the topic of mixtapes comes up:

MARIE: Yes, but you've recorded them yourself. Mixed music ... mix tapes. I think it has to do with ... that it means ... It's nostalgic, and has a stronger meaning because it's a physical thing.
MATS (Swedish, born 1962-1964): Yes, it [making mixtapes] was something you put an effort into making.[36]

The 1940s generation in the study has similar things to say about radio, the radio itself, as an object that conjures both social and individual memories, memories of putting effort into music, especially for Bolin's Estonian subjects. Nostalgia for the radio, as a family object, was particularly pronounced among that group because radios in Estonia were confiscated during World War II; families had to hide them if they wanted to keep them. The key takeaway is that all the participants, when talking about music memories, emphasized the *medium*, not the *content* as such. Nostalgia was triggered by memories of objects—the radios, records, and cassettes—not by songs. That is the power of physical media.

Whether a radio alive with static, a record that skips in a specific place, or a crinkled cassette, the nostalgic pull of old, tactile media is more vital than high fidelity. Bolin writes, "This nostalgia is seldom connected to content itself, since content lives on and can appear on many platforms of consumption. ... Old media are not thrown away, however, but rather stored away in attics and cellars as an archive of bygone events and feelings. It is not just any version of a certain song or album, but the specific copy of a certain record (the vinyl copy with its original cover) that is the trigger of memories and emotional states. And you simply do not throw these things away."[37] If you do throw them out—worse, if a parent or a spouse throws them out behind your back—you'll find yourself dreaming about those objects, not the songs of course but *that* cassette, record, radio, or tape deck, those industrially manufactured talismans that once connected you to past time more imaginatively than remastered content on Spotify. Reflecting on the sadly disposable nature of the cassette in its heyday—recall that 1960s Compact Cassettes are a rare item today—Thurston Moore confesses, in his introduction to *Mix Tape*, "While preparing this book, almost every person I solicited had a tale to tell about the mix tapes they had made.... And almost every person bemoaned the fact that their beloved tapes had vanished."[38]

Ditto. A transparent, light blue cassette containing a mix of New Wave hits—dubbed in spring 1999—survived in my possession until 2015. At some point in that year, roughly calculated, the tape was taken by the Babadook or an overzealous spring cleaner. I still know the song list. Listening to the songs on YouTube or Spotify is always edifying. Hearing one become popular all over again (thanks to its inclusion on the *Stranger Things* soundtrack) has been a pleasant, increasingly rare moment of shared media. But picking up and playing that transparent cassette delivered a more powerful mnemonic shock that no digital simulacrum can replicate. Mere content fails to invoke memory as strongly as a tactile object that survives the decades with us. Beyond personal memory, tactile music media—LP, cassette, and even CD—also helped create what Josh Sheppard calls "affective historical continuities." A media historian and director of the Library of Congress's Radio Preservation Taskforce, Sheppard says that, in the old physical media infrastructure, music could have something like a genealogy. "Everyone could track the micro-lineages of rock or jazz history; you knew where the influences had come from."[39] Because we'd listened to old blues records, we knew where Led Zeppelin got its sound from. An old Joy Division cassette could sit poignantly next to a remastered New Order CD in our collection. At a corner record store, the audiophile behind the counter could point you to Green Day's or Nirvana's immediate influences. Now, of course, Sheppard says, cloud-listening has "fragmented" that sense of a well-ordered, trackable music history. Music's ability to connect past with present relied, like so many other things we took for granted, on a physical media environment.

"HOURS TO MAKE A MIXTAPE"

The physicality and potential longevity of the cassette tape played a part in the aesthetic appeal of making, sharing, and keeping mixtapes. The blank cassette was a mass-produced consumer item, but it invited young Americans to craft it into something unique, to stamp it with their personalities before sharing it with a friend, a lover, or a would-be lover. Andy Warhol sought the dissolution of identity and personal relationships in the sameness of mechanical reproduction.[40] The mixtape sought their consummation.

Viegener calls the mixtape American folk art. Like traditional folk art, the mixtape utilizes an industrially supplied and logistically abundant material but is itself a one-off production serving both artistic and functional ends (musical delight and relationship building being the functional ends in this case). Meeting another requirement of traditional folk art, the mixtape reflects not only individual artistry but a communal aesthetic or sensibility. "The concept of group art," writes John Michael Vlach, "implies, indeed requires, that artists acquire their abilities, both manual and intellectual, at least in part from communication with others. The community has something, usually a great deal to say about what passes for acceptable folk art."[41] Replace "folk art" and "group art" with "mixtape" and Vlach still makes passable sense. A good mixtape was good, could in fact be art, because the creator, the recipient, and anyone overhearing it shared a certain taste in musical genre as well as a taste for tonal arrangement; that is, a taste for what sorts of songs might "hang together" in a custom playlist. The public, DJ mixtape would have likewise been deemed good or bad depending on, among other things, the beatmatching agility of the tracks included. The distinction between turntable beatmatching on public mixtapes and the lyrical, tonal, or personal associations on a private mixtape's playlist demonstrate that both mixtapes existed within a context of communal expectations. Barring Platonic ideals, these cultural or rhetorical expectations are what make art, art—especially folk art. In *Vinyl Princess*, the protagonist notes that a mixtape just gifted by a suitor "contains no song list." She wonders, "Maybe that's a test." She is subsequently "blown away" by the tape's sonic journey through rock history, from the initial bluesy numbers "dripping with the South" to the later blues/rock experimentations of Nick Cave.[42]

"Making a film is like making a mixtape," director Derek Cianfrance said in an interview. "You're collecting all this stuff and putting your favorite stuff into it."[43] Like a film or any piece of art, a mixtape took time to craft. My opening definition of mixtape had a key phrase—*duplicated mechanically from multiple sources onto a physical storage medium*—implying that a mixtape required physical as well as mental or emotional effort. It was not a quick process, gathering and dubbing all those songs onto a blank Maxell or TDK cassette, especially if the songs had first been recorded from the radio (hours of waiting!). All those moments spent making a mixtape—all the moments we knew someone had spent making a mixtape for us—have a lot to do with the mixtape's nostalgic power as well as its status as an American folk art.

"When you make a mixtape for somebody, it's special . . . you really have to sit there and create the tape, and it takes a long time," say Sean Bohrman and Lee Rickard, owners of Burger Records, a California label that still puts out cassettes for indie bands.[44] "It used to take her hours to make a mixtape," reflects the protagonist in Chelsey Johnson's *Stray City*. "That was the art of it—you had to measure your time so carefully, rationing those forty-five minutes per side, and sequence with precise intent since the order of the songs was fixed forever."[45] And recall the observation from Bolin's participants in the previous section: Making mixtapes "was something you put an effort into making." On the short end, making a mixtape took at least as long as it took to fill both sides of the tape—an hour or more—plus the time spent fast-forwarding and rewinding the tapes being duplicated to get to the right song. Including all the adolescent angst that went into curating a playlist beforehand, the process might take two or three or even five hours, depending on the occasion and the recipient. You would collect the cassettes needed, slide them behind the cassette door, one by one, hitting play on the cassette album and play/record on the blank cassette, then sit, wait, and listen to each song play through as it duplicated itself onto the blank tape.

Then there was the J-card. While waiting for songs to play through onto the blank tape, artistically inclined teens would doodle or draw on the insert that came in the blank tape's case. At a minimum, you'd write out the playlist in pen with your best handwriting—side A on one side of the J-card; side B on the other. Some were also inclined to write or draw on the cassette label itself. You hated to mess up the handwriting or art on a J-card, but if it was bad enough, you could throw it out, steal a J-card from another blank cassette, and start over. You really hated to mess up handwriting on a cassette *label*, because there was not much you could do to remedy the smudged ink. Cassette labels were factory adhered with industrial glue and did not easily peel off or re-adhere once removed. You had one and only one shot with the label artistry.

On display in Moore's *Mix Tape* are superb examples of mixtapes that adapted the J-card into an artistic canvas. One side contains the playlist, and the other side contains a full illustration—of flowers, for example, or a little rural cottage, or an oval-headed woman with thought-bubble ("Talking to my therapist makes me feel like an ugly cunt"[46]), or a lady in lingerie holding a whip. Other J-cards in the collection have been converted into mixed-media collages, with cut-out photographs and newspaper clippings adhered in creative fusions. Not a few were created on specialty paper, cut, and folded into a J-card shape. All the book's examples of cassette artistry come from the eighties and nineties, so it provides a sense of media continuity to remember that Margie B. Olsen also fashioned a collage on the mixtape made for her husband in 1973: "I cut tiny pictures representing the four seasons from gummed address labels and stuck them down the side of the song list."

During the cassette decades, teens and young adults "made" mixtapes; the verb denoted a prolonged set of activities. A mixtape was a handcrafted item, a piece of physical audio art that took time to come together. Youth in the 2020s "make" playlists on smartphones, but the verb denotes a barely tactile activity that takes no time at all and does not result in a customized, physical item. "Just as water, gas, and electricity are brought into our houses from far off to satisfy our needs in response to a minimal effort," wrote Paul Valéry in 1928, "so we shall be supplied with visual or auditory images, which will appear and disappear at a simple movement of the hand, hardly more than a sign."[47] Valéry's prophetic description of streaming media augurs Pandora, Apple Music, or the Spotify playlist. However, conjuring songs with "a simple movement of the hand" is the opposite of making mixtapes on cassette.

What about mix CDs, circa Y2K? My ecumenical definition of a mixtape allows CDs to sneak into the fold before it slams a metaphorical door on streaming playlists. CDs, after all, came with jewel cases, labels, and inserts that became canvases for handwriting, doodling, and collage. I personally do not recall mix CDs being as adorned as cassette mixtapes, but that could reflect the difference between being thirteen and being eighteen. I imagine junior high kids in 2001 enjoyed adorning mix CDs with the same handwritten flourishes that I had adorned cassettes with. Also, duplicating songs onto a CD retained a mechanical component: the disc tray on the computer, of course, but the laser etching that occurred within the desktop tower or laptop—"burning" the CD—required an electrical/mechanical machine. The same material impression of sound onto a physical storage medium that transpired on lacquer disc and magnetic tape also occurred, at a digital distance, on compact discs. (The distance will become greater by the end of the sixth chapter.)

Another fact in the mix CD's favor is that compiling songs from multiple sources onto a blank disc required the same gathering process the cassette mixtape had required: stacking a dozen or more CDs next to the computer tower, inserting them into a disc tray, one at a time, then "ripping" the desired tracks from the proprietary albums onto the hard drive, using some sort of CD-burning software. (At the turn of the millennium, it was common to find disc-burning software sitting on retail shelves across from copyrighted CD albums, an irony lost on young adults at the time.) Songs could also be downloaded via early versions of Apple iTunes or illegal peer-to-peer sharing sites, such as Napster or Kazaa. Downloading a song in the late nineties and early aughts took five minutes to an hour, depending on the download source and the speed of the internet connection: to include born-digital music on a mix CD announced itself as an act of love, devotion, and time.

At long last, once you had a song collection ripped onto the laptop's or tower's hard drive—visualized as MP3 icons on the desktop or in a file folder—you inserted the blank CD into the tray and then used the same burning software to tell the computer to laser etch those files onto the blank disc. When I think about it, I don't recall the mix CD taking less time to create than the mixtape. An hour at least. It remained a tactile affair, resulting in a physical object designed to be shared. The only difference—and it is significant—is that you no longer needed to play through an entire song to duplicate it onto the blank disc.

I am tempted to compare mixtape-making to the addict's famous reflection that the ritual of taking a drug becomes just as pleasurable as the drug's effects. I won't do that, but anyone who made mixtapes in the last century will recall that the time and tactile sensation involved in turning a blank cassette or a blank CD into a Sharpie-adorned compilation was as enjoyable as listening to the music at the heart of the whole endeavor. The pleasure arose, in part, from the anxiety of wondering whether the recipient would enjoy these songs, in this order, as much as you did. It was like the pleasure of wrapping a birthday present for a loved one: you were momentarily moved by the same emotion you hoped to provoke in them.

SNAP BACK TO REALITY

It is now time to pivot away from this nostalgic chapter. To provide a reality check about mixtapes and cassettes in the 2020s, consider once more the official sales count from 2022: 440,000 cassette albums were sold that year.[48] Sean Bohrman and Lee Rickard, co-owners of Burger Records, located in California's Orange County, claimed in 2019 that the company had released 500,000 cassettes between 2007 and 2018, roughly 50,000 cassettes per year. "People started doing stories on us," says Rickard, "and we started getting in the *New York Times* and the *L.A. Times* and the *Wall Street Journal* and stuff. Everybody was doing this cassette revival story, and they're still doing it."[49] A true observation. It is a great story, especially for aging Gen X and millennials who like to read and reminisce about the cassette era. But the actual numbers are not salutary. The cassette market remains bespoke, serving a small community of fans and pay-to-play local acts. Compare the 200,000–400,000 cassette albums sold annually in recent years to LP sales: 41 million units sold in 2022 alone (a number that exceeded CD sales for the first time since the 1980s, by the way).[50] Indeed, the popularity of vinyl records has made it difficult for lesser-known regional acts to cut their master recordings onto LP; their orders go to the end of the line when Taylor Swift or Adele decides to release a vinyl album.[51]

It's too early to tell if the cassette will someday match the LP's renewed popularity, finding its magnetic way into America's heart all over again—a far more diverse heart than in the 1980s. Nonetheless, it is a small miracle that the cassette can be purchased at all in the 2020s. The same cannot be said for the 8-track cartridge, the VHS tape, the LaserDisc, the MiniDV recorder, and so on. Increasing cassette sales indicate that the cassette at least has a healthier chance at long-term survival than all these and many other defunct media, raising the obvious question, Why the eleventh-hour stand for the cassette?

4: THE CASSETTE MIXTAPE

(SIDE B: INDUSTRIAL NOISE)

Figuring out why you can purchase a newly manufactured cassette today (but not a new 8-track or VHS tape) means swapping out the nostalgic lens for an industrial one. The mixtape's economic backdrop involved supply-side policy and a global pivot to East Asian manufacturing. Today, the phrase "supply-side economics" evokes Regan, Bush, Clinton, and debates about taxes. While lowering taxes was a feature of that economic approach, it also favored unrestricted global trade and the decoupling of capital investment from national markets—offshoring, in other words, or "onshoring," from the other countries' points of view. By the end of the twentieth century, Asian labor markets could manufacture consumer goods more cheaply and more efficiently than unionized American labor. (Asian markets also began to consolidate the machine shop expertise required to create the dies and molds needed to manufacture consumer goods in the first place.) Today, the "closed factory" in a "dying rustbelt town" is a trope, almost a cliché, in American literature and film; however, in 1978, this passage from Stephen King's *The Stand* portrayed a stateside reality: "In Arnette, it was hard times. In 1970, the town had two industries, a factory that made paper products . . . , and a plant that made electronic calculators. Now the paper factory was shut down and the calculator plant was ailing—they could make them a lot cheaper in Taiwan, it turned out, just like those little portable TVs and transmitter radios."[1] Moore's *Mix Tape*, Burns's *Mixtape Nostalgia*, the documentary *Analog Love*, and Komurki and Bendandi's *Cassette Cultures* make it easy to forget that mixtape culture developed in part thanks to an abundance of cheap electronic goods—cheap cassettes, cheap tape decks, cheap boomboxes, and cheap Walkmans. Like many twentieth-century youth rituals, mixtape culture developed on the back of globalized trade and economies of scale. It was an epiphenomenon produced by shifts in policy, market forces, and automation—all long-evolving trends that the old mercantile supplier of sugar and cotton would have envied.

SCHELLING POINTS AND ECONOMIES OF SCALE

I mentioned in a previous chapter that cassette sales did not surpass LP sales until 1982.[2] No wonder, then, that a protean version of mixtape culture is hard to come by in 1960s and 1970s audio archives. The cassette's scaled economic production had not kicked into high gear. And a medium must scale before it becomes cheap and abundant enough—which is the same thing—for secondary cultural practices to spread alongside its widespread adoption. ("Economy of scale" refers to the idea that as quantity of production increases, the average cost of each unit decreases.) Of course, cheapness and abundance cannot come at a total sacrifice of quality. Consumers still must *want* the thing. Future mixtape artists would never require high fidelity from their tapes, but without passable audio quality, compiling a tape would not be worth the effort.

One explanation for the cassette's slow pace of adoption—among consumers—was that magnetic tape had been developed and advertised as a voice dictation or sound-capture technology. R2R's musical aspirations were siloed in pro-grade machines not promoted on the consumer or prosumer market. Recording a radio show on R2R tape, Bing Crosby had access to higher-quality equipment than young men taping audio letters in Vietnam. Music of course found its way onto R2R audio letters and home recordings, but professional artists never released records or albums on R2R tape. Sound capture and dictation were its market intentions, so crisp audio quality was beside the point for consumer tape and consumer recorders. When Philips released the Compact Cassette in the United States in 1964, audio quality suitable to the signal highs and lows of music was likewise a secondary goal; professional albums released on cassette remained a novelty. To become a medium appropriate for music, the cassette needed to find a happy balance of affordability and quality. It didn't need to sound better than the LP, it just needed to sound not awful. And "not awful" needed to be affordable to consumers not named Bing Crosby. The cassette, after all, had portability and durability on its side, two ever-present advantages over the LP. It only needed to add a modicum of aural appeal.

Achieving that balance required some research and development. It required, for example, improvements to the type of magnetic tape put into the cassette's plastic shell. Magnetic tape is magnetic, meaning it contains little bits of iron that react to the transducer heads in the cassette player. For scientific reasons I'll happily gloss over, the nature of the iron coated onto the tape ribbon affects the tape's quality for both recording and playback. Ferric oxide coated the earliest and cheapest magnetic tapes, Type I. Later and more expensive tapes, Type IV, were coated with pure iron rather than oxides. Type III tapes, coated in ferrichrome, never caught on, especially after the development of the pure iron tapes. The sweet spot for most consumers was Type II, coated with chromium dioxide or "chrome equivalent" material. Type II tapes minimized the worst hiss associated with ferric oxide tapes. Also less prone to losing quality over time due to the stresses of bending around tape heads, they were ideal for tapes played repeatedly—stop, rewind, play, stop, rewind, play—or recorded over multiple times with different songs. In addition, Type II tapes were resistant to interference from nearby magnetic fields, such as those generated by televisions, speakers, or "the residual magnetism that accumulates in the metal parts of the tape deck itself."[3]

If you grew up in the eighties or nineties you might recall Maxell and Sony blank tapes advertising "high bias" on their plastic shrink-wrap—those were usually the Type II cassettes consumers purchased. Nowhere near as expensive or acoustically rich as the Type IV iron or "metal" tapes, Type II cassettes nonetheless offered quality improvements over the original ferric oxide tapes, whose magnetic hiss and low fidelity had stopped the cassette from becoming a popular music medium in its first iteration. As the Type II cassette caught on, the demand for cheap but quality-ish cassettes even pushed manufacturers to improve the ferric oxide Type I tapes. Maxell, for example, in the mideighties, developed their Ultra-Dynamic Type I series as "Ultra-dynamic. Ultra-clear. Ultra-quiet. But ultra-inexpensive."[4]

Tape decks and stereos also had to strike a balance of affordability and quality. What good was a superior cassette tape without a quality playback device? Improvements to tape heads, electronics, and especially noise-reduction systems were all part of the engineering mix that enabled tape decks to play a role in the cassette triumph over LPs. Writing for *Stereo Review* in a "Special Tape Issue" from 1984, Craig Stark confessed: "A dozen years ago, the cassette was the tape format that the 'experts' (myself among them) almost unanimously agreed could never become a true high-fidelity medium. Then, in 1972, came the Nakamichi 1000, the world's first three-head cassette deck, which featured dual-capstan drive, the Dolby-B noise-reduction system (then relatively new), solenoid operation, a manual head-alignment mechanism, and peak-reading meters. Its design showed the way for a whole industry."[5] The release of the Nakamichi 1000 in 1972 was nearly a decade after Philips had released the Compact Cassette and the first tape player, the Norelco EL-3300 (Norelco was Philips's brand name in America). Those were the early years when audio experts like Stark assumed the noisy disposition of magnetic recording and playback would always mar the cassette's fitness for music capture and consumption. However, some companies, like Nakamichi, recognized the medium's potential. I can picture a Japanese engineer convincing a corporate board that portability and durability would be the things in the future. Assuming tape manufacturers would overcome the hiss problem, Panasonic, too, put an early optimistic stake in the cassette's future when, in 1973, it developed the RS-296US, a twenty-cassette carousel foreshadowing the multidisc CD player. On the march toward the infinite playlist, the RS-296US may have been the first step. But what to do about the hiss?

"There's no way around it," writes David Ranada in the same *Stereo Review* issue. "Analog tape is a noisy recording medium. It *has* to be to work at all."[6] The signal on magnetic tape results from an averaging process, he explains, during which the "average" behaviors of the magnetic particles on the tape ribbon are captured by the recording head; in electronics, "every signal that is the result of an averaging process is noisy." If you took a blank tape, pressed play, and listened to it, you'd hear the quietest playback the tape could ever offer. Ranada invites the reader to conduct an experiment: press the recording button on a blank tape without plugging a microphone into the tape deck's mic jack. Let the tape record its soundless input for thirty seconds or so, then rewind it and listen to the recorded section. The unmistakable hiss would reveal itself, without anything having been "recorded" at all except the average behavior of magnetic particles. Improving systems to reduce this noise was one of the biggest hurdles for the cassette medium.

From Dolby-A in 1964 to Dolby-C in 1980, the development of better noise-reduction systems on tape decks helped to seal the LP's fate (along with that chromium-coated ribbon on Type II tapes). None of us could decipher all that technical jargon, of course, even though it was advertised prominently in commercials and on retail posters. All we knew was that "high bias" and "Type II" and "Dolby" and "noise reduction" meant better sound quality for musical enjoyment. Did many teens and young adults make mixtapes with expensive noise-reduction decks or pure iron Type IV tapes? Unlikely. However, before the cassette could become a cheap and abundant medium, media companies needed to persuade the American public that the cassette, rather than the LP, should be its go-to item for musical consumption. Persuading audiophiles with high-end offerings played a role in that inclusive rhetorical effort.

It took a while, but the effort paid off for Philips and other companies, who, after years of research and development, found a balance of cheapness and quality that appealed not only to the audiophile but to the average music fan. Ten to fifteen years after the Compact Cassette's release, with tape and tape-player improvements allowing companies to continuously upgrade their advertised features, and with more and more artists releasing albums on cassette, the American public was finally convinced. At some point in the late 1970s, both cassette and tape deck manufacturers had engineered themselves into a virtuous feedback cycle. Sound quality improved, more units were purchased, prices came down little by little, and sound quality improved even more. As with any consumer technology, cassettes and tape players always maintained a price-point hierarchy. "A $19 cassette is a difficult sale to make," an ad executive noted in 1982, referring to high-fidelity Type IV cassettes designed and manufactured to appeal to audiophiles rather than broke teens and average music fans.[7] However, when cassette sales surpassed LP sales in 1982, consumers had come to expect good-enough audio quality from the cheaper cassette types and the cheaper tape decks. "Many popular-priced tape decks offer adequate or even excellent performance and convenience features," wrote Stark in the 1984 *Stereo Review* article quoted above.[8]

Throughout the eighties and early nineties, with audio quality made good—or good enough—for music, the cassette's killer features of portability and durability quickly turned the cassette into America's favorite music medium. With each passing year, cassette prices dropped, cassette sales rose, and cassette prices dropped even further.[9] *Stereo Review*'s 1984 "Special Tape Issue" is a good anecdote for the larger economic trend: by 1984, the cassette had claimed its place as a Schelling point, the obvious go-to option for any consumer wanting to listen to or record music. The virtuous cycle of cost reduction had worked its magic. By 1984, when people wanted to buy an album, they purchased a cassette as a matter of course. A similar format transition, at about the same time, had occurred in the home-video market. By the end of the eighties, if consumers wanted to watch a movie in their living room or make home videos, they purchased a VCR and a VHS tape, not a Betamax, a VHS-C, a U-matic, or a V2000. Much later, from 2006 to 2008, the same process unfolded again in the high-def digital video format wars: Sony's Blu-ray eventually triumphed over Toshiba's HD DVD, allowing Blu-ray discs to proliferate and Blu-ray prices to plummet.

This virtuous cycle, at first, seems infinite for a medium that has cornered a market, but it comes to an end when a new Schelling point emerges—a new medium to which the cycle of scale attaches itself all over again.

A Schelling point, or focal point, is the intuitive choice people make without a larger communicative exchange about costs and benefits, optimal outcomes, and so on.[10] A famous analogy involves two people in New York City told to find each other with no other information provided and no way to communicate. Each person, the theory goes, would likely travel to the most iconic location associated with New York City—the top of the Empire State Building—which may or may not be the best place for them to meet given their starting locations or capabilities. Similarly, if teens circa 1970 wanted to purchase an album, they probably bought a vinyl LP even though cassette, 4-track, and 8-track alternatives likely existed. By 1982 in contrast, they would obviously purchase a cassette (a vinyl alternative might not be readily available). By 2000, they would purchase a compact disc (a cassette was likely available, but not for long). By 2020, they'd download an app.

The process reflects how a consumer market gloms on to some new medium as the metonym for music consumption,[11] without anyone having a public, ongoing deliberation about optimal outcomes for that activity. (I don't recall voting on smartphone adoption.) Applied to the manufacture of home video, the fight between Sony's Betamax standard and JVC's VHS standard was, in its early days, a fight over whether consumers would gravitate toward video *size* or video *recording time* as a Schelling point, an implicit answer to the barely formulated question in consumers' minds: What features do we want on our choice of home video cassette?[12] It turned out that consumers preferred the VHS's longer running time to the paperback-sized Betamax (as well as Betamax's purported superior video quality). The competition between LP records and cassettes can be understood the same way. Would sound quality (LP) or portability, durability, and longer runtimes (cassette) become the features toward which the consumer market gravitated, without anyone ever having a public vote about such things? The LP was always stuck at eighty minutes—forty minutes per side. The cassette figured out a way to etch ninety minutes of music onto the tape ribbon without affecting quality or price; for a few dollars more, two-hour tapes (sixty minutes on each side) were also available. (The CD's step backward in runtime—like the LP, the standard CD tapped out at eighty minutes—should have been a warning to the music industry that it had a built-in obsolescence feature.)

A debate surrounding Thomas Schelling's theory of focal points involves whether actors who lack structured communication can arrive at an optimal focal point. Imagine, again, two people told to meet in NYC: if they both started somewhere in Times Square, they might still converge on the Empire State Building even though their optimal meeting point may have been the Times Square Applebee's. For high-fidelity audio purists, the rise of the cassette was not optimal at all because they prioritized sound quality over portability. (The rise of streaming subscriptions is not optimal in my mind because I prioritize physical media.) But the market speaks, and who among us can judge its path dependencies? Is portability or music quality more "optimal"? Is physical media more "optimal" than an app on a smartphone? No one puts a gun to our collective heads; we move instinctively with the times and the vibes to a new Schelling point, a new medium, which apparently must meet unspoken needs not met by the old medium previously converged upon.

Who listens to music on LP anymore? The cassette is the thing. Who listens to music on cassette anymore? The CD is the thing. Who listens to music on

CD anymore? The MP3 player is the thing. Who listens to music on iPods anymore? The smartphone is the thing. Obviously, the jostle to become the next *thing*, the next Schelling point on a global market, fuels corporate intrigue but also industrial decisions that ignite a manufacturing base even as it mothballs another. When a market converges on a new medium, the old medium's manufacturing base begins to be dismantled, little by little.

"It always takes a little more time than you'd think," journalist Stephen Witt says about media obsolescence,[13] but eventually any technology that has ceased to be a culture's focal point will limit or cease production. A second-order effect is that the machine shops supplying the tools to make that old technology also shift production capacities to serve new markets. Imagine one hundred million Americans announce "We changed our minds and want to buy a newly manufactured version of some obsolete item or technology." Now, with demand guaranteed, imagine that no company can step up to manufacture the item because no machine shop in the world makes the tools needed to make the item. And retooling the tools from scratch is expensive and difficult enough that, even with guaranteed demand, the reboot is simply not worth the effort. That is the hypothetical endgame for an obsolete medium. Its obsolescence is, initially, triggered by simple sales numbers. At some point, however, its perpetual obsolescence is guaranteed by structural decisions made at global manufacturing sites. The next section explores how the cassette itself came awfully close to meeting that sort of guaranteed demise (and how recently popularized LPs are not immune from the neglect of a manufacturing base).

"The mixtape is American folk art," writes Matias Viegener. I think that's true, but it was a folk art reliant on a global system that allowed broke teens to purchase blank cassettes (and then blank CDs) on the cheap. Andy Warhol would have appreciated the irony. Swapping out Coke with cassette in his famous quote works well enough: *A cassette is a cassette, and no amount of money can get you a better cassette than the one the bum on the corner is listening to. All the cassettes are the same and all the cassettes are good. Liz Taylor knows it, the President knows it, the bum knows it, and you know it.*[14] (Or, in Marshall McLuhan's more delicate version: "Today, . . . the richest man is reduced to having much the same entertainment . . . as the ordinary man.")[15] There was a price hierarchy, as I said, but those chromium dioxide tapes served everyone equally well.

Certain definitions of folk art disallow mass-produced items, but preindustrial folk art always did craft with cheap, abundant, even mass-produced (for its time) material. I like to think of folk art as those aesthetic/functional things a culture creates out of its own ample detritus, what culture critic Paul Skallas would call "Lindy" materials—paints, textiles, metals, glass, and other media that have entered an equilibrium wherein the thing's increased age paradoxically *decreases* the likelihood of its obsolescence. "Lindy" refers to the Lindy effect, the observed phenomenon that the mortality rate for some nonperishable things—such as a technology, an idea, a book, or (in its original formulation) a comedian's television appearances—approaches near zero, so that, in the words of Nassim Nicholas Taleb, "every year that passes without extinction doubles the additional life expectancy."[16] These are materials and technologies that have stood the test of time, in other words, whose production and consumption are likely to continue regardless of economic or social disruptions. Americans have used paints and metals and glass to create folk art in four different centuries; they can thus be expected to do so for eight centuries more.

In contrast, the practices and folk arts that grow on the back of novel, untested media—such as a Compact Cassette—are susceptible to quick obsolescence, because the untested media themselves are susceptible to obsolescence. If mixtapes are an American folk art, they are a folk art crafted with an untested medium and thus unlikely to be described as folk art by historians in a hundred years, especially if cassette manufacturing crashes and burns at some point. Mixtapes were crafted by individuals within an identifiable cultural moment, yes, but otherwise they were a historical blip. To become Lindy, to become the stuff of folk art, a medium must survive its birth, growth, and volatile adolescence until it meets not death but stability after its dotage.

Two decades after its commercial highpoint, the compact disc is still cheaply produced. Perhaps CDs have a higher likelihood than cassettes of becoming a Lindy medium. They are, after all, a triple threat: tactile, portable, and *digital*. However, millennials and Gen Xers do not seem to have developed a nostalgic attachment to the CD like they did to the cassette, a checkmark against the CD's ability to survive its elderly stage. The cassette, in contrast, has already survived not only its volatile adolescence but its elderly and even its terminal illness stages. It was touch-and-go in the first decade of the twenty-first century. A 2009 year-end *Billboard* report on "recorded-music unit sales by configuration" includes digital tracks, digital albums, and CDs but not cassettes.[17] Even the music industry's leading publication had stopped counting cassette sales during the first decade of the new millennium. However, against all odds, the medium is miraculously alive and, by some reports, economically viable. At death's door, the cassette has refused to go gentle into that good night alongside the LaserDisc, the Mini DV tape, the 8-track player, and the VCR. How did that happen? The cassette's nostalgia factor is only part of the answer, because the global market does not care about your childhood media memories unless you're willing to pay for them.

PLANNED OBSOLESCENCE AND
UNPLANNED PERSISTENCE

The chapter opened with a question: Why can customers in the 2020s purchase newly manufactured cassettes and tape players but not other retro media? The answer starts with the industrial fact that cassette tape is the same stuff as the magnetic stripe on the back of your credit card.

In the mid-2010s, the finance industry began placing EMV chips on credit cards to store information.[18] But until very recently, consumers have been walking around with credit cards protected by 1930s technology: a magnetized tape ribbon with three tracks. Track three is usually empty; track two contains the credit card number and expiration date; track one contains the card holder name, account number, and CVC. And just as it's possible to record one cassette tape onto another cassette tape, it is indeed possible to record a credit card's stripe onto a cassette tape, and from thence onto a pirated "card." A YouTube video shows you how to do it, for those so inclined to learn. First, get a Square card reader (the cheap point-of-sale device you swipe at food trucks and other small businesses). Like credit card readers in stores, the Square reader contains a tape head, the same transducer device found in tape players to read cassettes. The card reader's head simply reads the credit card tape instead. The Square reader also comes with an external plug, to plug into a laptop, but that plug is in fact the same thing you can plug into the microphone jack of an old tape deck. So, plug the Square card reader into a tape-player mic jack, insert a blank cassette, hit *record*, then swipe a credit card through the card reader. Remove the cassette, which has now been "recorded" with the three credit card tracks. Use scissors to cut out the first couple inches of cassette tape (make it the same length as a credit card), then adhere the cut cassette tape to a library card or some other flat item. Voilà. You've just cloned a credit card.

Industrial production of magnetic tape sustained itself into the late 2010s, thanks in part to the credit card industry. However, starting in 2016, East Asian companies began shutting down large-scale tape production. In 2019, even Maxell, that corporate icon of blank cassettes, ceased global production of ferric oxide Type I tape (the only kind they still produced).[19] The transition from magnetic stripe to EMV chips on credit cards likely had something to do with this industrial pullback. Too many people had seen that YouTube video. American companies had of course ceased magnetic tape production as far back as 1984, so when the last South Korean manufacturer informed the National Audio Company (NAC) of Springfield, Missouri, that they would no longer be supplying tape, NAC president Steve Stepp began scouring the country for old tape-making equipment.

NAC was and still is one of the only dedicated cassette-manufacturing facilities in North America. There are others, of course, but their output capacity is limited; globally, cassette manufacturing seems to have become a catch-as-catch-can affair, with neither quality nor capacity guaranteed.[20] NAC had somehow found the right customers during the lean years—the first two decades of the twenty-first century (see Komurki and Bendandi's *Cassette Cultures* for a sampling of the niche bands releasing cassettes in those years)—and never abandoned the medium as nearly every other manufacturer did. Thanks to NAC, local and regional bands could release cassettes, either as a lark or an earnest gesture, well into the reign of compact disc and then streaming music.

However, NAC could not continue making cassettes without the tape.

In the early 2000s, Stepp and NAC's chief technician had already scoured the country for cassette-shell manufacturing equipment, assuming in those years the tape itself would continue to arrive from Asia. The larger media manufacturers at that point assumed cassettes would go the way of 4-tracks, 8-tracks, and any number of reel-to-reel formats. Stepp and his technician disagreed. He scooped up "wonderful, wonderful equipment, the best that the industry has ever built, at ridiculous prices," he said in an interview with *Belt Magazine*. "We were basically buying the equipment from them and if we hadn't bought it, it was going to go to landfills or to be sold for metal scrap. That unfortunately happened to way too many vinyl presses in the 1970s and we didn't want to see that happen to the tape equipment as well."[21] Stepp and other leaders at NAC bet on the long-term viability of the cassette as opposed to earlier R2R formats. More tape players than people existed in America, they reasoned. If it had been so popular in the past, the audio cassette might yet have "staying power" into the future.

The cassette has certainly not returned to 1980s popularity; however, by the 2010s, Generation X and the millennials had grown up, and the nostalgic pull of the cassette began to tug their heartstrings. (Check out the exponential rise of references to the term *mixtape* after 2000 according to the Google Ngram Viewer.) Pearl Jam, Smashing Pumpkins, and other bands began to release old or new material on cassette, and newer artists jumped onto the bandwagon. According to the Official Charts Company—which tracks such things—Lady Gaga, the Strokes, Dua Lipa, Ozzy Osbourne, and Tame Impala all had Top 20 cassette sales in 2020.[22] Today, the clothing and accessories brand Urban Outfitters features a "Cassettes + CDs" page on its website. Said page contains Taylor Swift ($29.99!), Drake ($18.99!), and even a Best of Sinead O'Connor ($17.99!), all on cassette—just click to add to your cart, alongside the Anabella sheer tutu miniskirt. At the movie theater, *Guardians of the Galaxy*, released in 2014, introduced a whole new generation to the cassette aesthetic and the coolness of the mixtape.

(A cassette plays a pivotal role in the film's emotional arc.) Sensing the vibe shift, the *Guardians* franchise likewise began releasing its seventies-soaked soundtracks on cassette, at Urban Outfitters and elsewhere. By 2022, the cassette wave had not dissipated, and New Kids on the Block went on their MixTape Tour. And if you don't have an old tape player on which to play these cassettes, Walmart still sells a Walkman clone for $19.99. For the discerning prosumer, Tascam manufactures the 202MKVII, a high-end dual cassette system for recording and playback that retails for $500. Like cassettes themselves, tape decks have rejected their own obsolescence, thanks entirely to Chinese clones—products manufactured without any official license—of earlier Japanese tape-mechanism technology.[23]

It turned out Stepp had made a good bet. The cassette was going to be around longer than the 8-track—long enough, at least, to make money off Gen X and the elder millennials during their prime earning years.

But then the tape ran out. How to source it? Stepp realized that NAC would have to do again in 2016 what it had done in the early 2000s for shell manufacturing equipment: find the machines to make tape themselves. Journalist Avery Gregurich writes, "What they found somewhere out in Nevada was a 62-foot long, 20-ton tape-coating line originally built in the 1980s that had most recently been converted into a machine for making credit card strips."[24]

The credit card saved the day. Its market for magnetic strips had kept this tape-coating machine functional, just long enough, so that it remained in usable condition in 2016, when Stepp found it. (For those interested, NAC coats their tapes with ferric oxide, cobalt, and their own proprietary ferric solution.)[25] It's not a stretch to claim, as Addison Del Mastro does, that the unlikely longevity of the credit card strip rescued the cassette-manufacturing base from oblivion, at least within North America.[26]

Stepp and his partner took the tape-coating machine apart and hauled it across the Great Plains back to Springfield. Putting it all back together and reconditioning the pieces took over a year and was accomplished with the help of retired magnetic tape engineers who graciously came out of retirement to save the cassette industry in America. Stepp says: "It was just the kindness, and there was also the fact that these guys had devoted their lives to this industry and they didn't want to see it just dry up and go away. And there was an emotional attachment, 'if I can help save this I will.' ... They had no personal gain."[27] Like Göran Bolin's Estonian and Swedish participants and all children of the seventies and eighties, the people who made the medium felt an emotional connection to the object itself, the blank cassette, regardless of whatever musical content would eventually be recorded or duplicated onto it. Without that nostalgic connection to the cassette, these "old hands" may not have provided their postretirement labor and advice. "Had we waited five more years," Stepp says in the *Belt Magazine* interview, "many of the people who were able to give us their advice would have been gone."

NAC's story offers a perfect anecdote for the simple yet complex process of planned obsolescence. The arrival of a new medium (the CD in this case) incentivizes an entire industry to retire not only the old medium (the cassette) but also its manufacturing base. The second-order effect, as I've said, is that at some point the machine shops that made the tools to make the old medium also shift their capacities. When that fabrication infrastructure disappears, so does a whole knowledge base, composed not of tooled parts but also of the people who know how the parts work and how to make the parts in the first place. As these people retire or pass away, replaced by new engineers who never learned the old equipment, a culture's ability to reproduce a rejected technology grows weaker and weaker, as the cost of rebooting an entire industry from scratch becomes prohibitively expensive, even if new demand arises. For example, in 2012, Apple announced it would manufacture certain Mac Pros in the United States. That never happened because America's tool and die industry had been so obliterated by Reagan-era offshoring that Apple found only one fabrication shop capable of supplying the little screws needed for the computers. But this Texas shop could only produce a thousand screws per day. Production ramped up, screw shortages emerged, and Apple wound up ordering the screws from China after all.[28] (Tim Cook once said, in a speech in China, that "in the U.S., you could have a meeting of tooling engineers and I'm not sure we could fill the room. In China, you could fill multiple football fields.")[29]

Japanese multimedia company Technics—whose SL-1200 turntable set high standards in the 1970s—provides another example. Recognizing in the mid-2010s that vinyl nostalgia was likely here to stay, the company decided to rerelease a new version of the SL-1200. But when executives and engineers sat down to plan the project, they discovered that the SL-1200's fabrication base was in such bad shape, it would need to be rebuilt from the ground up. "We began to study, maybe summer 2014, for the new SL-1200," explained CTO Tetsuya Itani at a 2016 British trade show where the turntable was unveiled. "We learned that it was impossible [to make the same deck], as almost all the tools for manufacturing were gone or heavily damaged—only one 'die' remained, and that was for the dust cover."[30] To Technics' credit, they did indeed remake the entire tooled edifice required to fabricate a newly designed SL-1200. Everything was reengineered from scratch, "except for the dust cover." All that upfront labor, however, led to a sticker shock for consumers. At the end of its original production run, the SL-1200 sold for under $1,000. The rereleased version sells for $4,000.

Film stock is another old medium whose manufacturers are having trouble meeting a recent uptick in demand, as taking pictures with film cameras has become a niche but growing hobby. In 2021, Fujifilm had to discontinue its popular Pro 400H negative film "because it couldn't procure a necessary ingredient to make the emulsion."[31] In 2017, Kodak began increasing prices on its film stocks but promised the profits would go to research and development to help increase supply; in 2023, Kodak film prices had doubled, but the film itself was, by all reports, even more difficult to find than in 2017.[32]

Journalist Addison Del Mastro has been following stories of phased-out, dying, and resurrected media for several years now. Although Del Mastro is interested in industrial policy, his takeaway is insightful for a book on mixtapes and the transition from physical to streaming media. "You can sum it all up this way," he writes on his personal Substack page. "Manufacturing is not like coding. So much is digital now that it feels like you can just conjure things into being. Any idea for an app or a program that you can come up with, and that current computing power can support, can be written out of nothing but lines of code."[33] Free trade, he notes, was sold in the Reagan and Bush eras on the promise that while the country lost manufacturing jobs, it would gain technological jobs in the new digital knowledge economy. America would no longer produce cassettes or computers, but it would be coding and running the interfaces of the new global village. Neoliberal and neoconservative rhetoric alike assumed that programming was just a high-tech version of manufacturing, or, put the other way, that manufacturing was just an outdated version of programming. Turns out that's not the case. "Manufacturing is an ongoing process," Del Mastro writes. "If we learn by doing, we forget by not doing.... Who knows what other everyday products are still being made on ancient factory tooling, with their popularity insufficient to support building it from scratch today? You can't store this stuff like books in a library. Use it or lose it."[34]

At some point in the late twentieth century, America (or American leaders) assumed the country had gotten as far as it could as a manufacturing powerhouse. It decided to take the old industrial knowledge for granted, assuming the knowledge could be revived if necessary. Focused on processes and technologies instead of people and institutions, American leaders assumed that if we had the industrial capacity to produce something in the past, we could always—in the abstract—produce it again in the future. The country could go all in on software development without losing the old knowledge about industrial fabrication.

Is that true? America's failure to manufacture a tiny screw for the Mac Pro suggests it's not. A similar story, followed by Del Mastro, involves pastamaker Ronzoni's discontinuation of pastina, a star-shaped macaroni, due to the company's inability to find reliable suppliers of the specialized molds required to make the intricate pasta shape.[35] Perhaps "the old manufacturer's equipment and tooling [were] worn out, and it cost too much to refresh it," speculates Del Mastro. "Or perhaps it is just difficult/expensive to design and manufacture new industrial-scale pasta dies these days."[36] The story is one more example of industrial fragility in the face of the global economy's radical whiplashes from one Schelling point to the next. Little things, which might one day become important things, get lost amid the chaos.

Vinyl LPs provide one last cautionary tale. They are, all over again, an obviously viable medium—generating over $460 million in sales in 2021—but their resurrected popularity is revealing just how hollowed out the vinyl manufacturing base had become at some point during the cassette and CD years and how hollowed out it has been allowed to remain. From the *New York Times* in 2021: "Yet there are worrying signs that the vinyl bonanza has exceeded the industrial capacity needed to sustain it. Production logjams and a reliance on bulky, decades-old pressing machines have led to what executives say are unprecedented delays. A couple of years ago, a new record could be turned around in a few months; now it can take up to a year, wreaking havoc on artists' release plans."[37] Recently, even famous artists like Adele have had to postpone release dates while waiting for LPs to be pressed. And in this case, no one can blame all the disruptions to global supply chains in the wake of the pandemic. For example, lacquer discs are needed to assemble master plates for pressing records; however, only two shops in the entire world still manufacture those lacquer discs, and in 2020, one of them—Apollo Masters Corporation in Banning, California—burned to the ground. ("We've been saying we need to fix this for years," one vinyl-pressing executive says. "Now we actually need to fix this.")[38] As more major artists get in on vinyl pressing, it puts more and more pressure on an industry sustained by decades-old infrastructure that is expensive to maintain and not easy to replace.

It's a bitter pill to swallow, the idea that Americans and even the Japanese could collectively lose the ability to make something, not because the thing is no longer viable or useful or worthwhile to the world, but because the things needed to make the thing are too expensive to refurbish, or because the institutional knowledge base—the craftspeople needed to unmothball an industry—are dead or would rather spend their retirement in hot tubs and recreational vehicles.

One reason for optimism, to be fair, can be found in the interconnected nature of industry. New media are rarely, if ever, made from scratch, ground up, with custom parts. Most of the media and technologies that surround us—nearly everything that surrounds us—is made up of parts used in other devices, other technologies, other media, all sourced from the same few tool and die shops in East Asia. I have recently discovered, for example, that the lids on medicine bottles are interchangeable. It doesn't matter the brand, the color, or the type of medicine, you can swap the lids willy-nilly. I had previously labored under the assumption that every medicine brand sourced its own separate lids. Similarly, in the nineties, the magnetic tape in my cassettes and the magnetic stripes on my parents' credit cards were likely sourced from the same fabricator, and the tape head in my cassette player was likely shipped from the same South Korean plant as the tape head in a credit card reader. The optimistic message here is that just because a medium meets its sell-by date doesn't mean the entire industrial base girding its existence will also disappear. The cassette was phased out by the compact disc and then streaming music, but bits and pieces of the cassette-manufacturing base lived on, which is why Steve Stepp was able to find a magnetic tape-coating machine in Nevada. It had been kept alive by the market for magnetic tape on credit cards.

There's a pessimistic catch. Del Mastro notes that if credit card companies had switched from magnetic stripes to EMV chips a decade or so earlier than they did, Stepp's 2016 search for tape manufacturing equipment may have turned up empty. That machine in Nevada would likely have been sold for scrap by then. The National Audio Company would have been left with just a three-year supply of tape with which to manufacture cassettes. Instead of becoming not only a preserver but one of the last manufacturers of cassettes in the 2020s, the company would have had to find a new use for its factory or go out of business altogether.

"My son and I sat down together and we said we've got to either get out of business within three years or we've got to be making tape within three years," Stepp says. "So being sort of the stubborn sort, we decided to make tape.... If we hadn't done it then it could have never been done. The equipment would have been gone and we could not have afforded to ever have it built again."[39]

There was not a Steve Stepp or a National Audio Company for the VHS tape and VCRs, the movie equivalents of audio cassette and tape player. The Japanese company Funai was the last manufacturer of VCRs and VHS tapes in the world; they marketed their wares in America as the familiar Sanyo brand. Despite selling 750,000 VCRs annually, mostly to VHS tape collectors, it ceased production of VHS tapes in July 2016, almost certainly due to South Korea's decision to stop manufacturing magnetic tape.[40] Perhaps a Japanese Steve Stepp did scour the countryside for tape-making equipment, hoping to keep the small VHS market alive, only to return empty-handed.

404: PAGE NOT FOUND

Well, so what? What if the world loses its ability to manufacture VCRs, cassettes, or any dead medium? By now, valuable content has been uploaded to the cloud, digitized, or made available on a disc of some sort. As for music, if consumers insist on an analog experience, vinyl LPs are available at hip record stores in every college town in America. (LPs, though, as I just noted, are under their own industrial strain.)

The most straightforward answer to anti-Luddite naysaying is that not everything on analog media migrated to the cloud or made it onto a digital disc. The company Legacy Box—which digitizes old photos and home VHS tapes for baby boomers—appreciates the market potential for analog media in situ. On average, VHS tapes deteriorate at a rate that will render them unusable by 2050, especially if they're sitting in a garage. But a physical medium that lasts over half a century is nonetheless more trustworthy than the cloud, which can disappear in a split second under the right conditions. Even transferring old VHS memories onto a brand-new VHS tape would provide the material with a more secure future than trusting it to the cloud.

Beyond private media, grind-house and direct-to-video horror films are often tagged as cultural artifacts that never received a digital transfer. *Mister Frost* (starring Jeff Goldblum), *Dream Demon* (starring Jemma Redgrave), and *Necronomicon* (starring Jeffrey Combs as H. P. Lovecraft) are three notable titles that exist only on VHS.[41] Even Michael Mann's infamous *The Keep* was unavailable on DVD until 2020, after much griping from its cult fanbase.

"Yes, but *The Keep* was available to stream on YouTube and Amazon!" the techno-optimist will retort, providing me a perfect opportunity to mount a stronger response to the iPhone streamer. Techno-optimists assume that content longevity on the cloud is secure and functionally eternal. I have come to believe this assumption underlies all disinterest in physical media. It is a wrongheaded assumption.

In her 2019 book *The End of Forgetting*, Kate Eichhorn writes that the psychological benefits of forgetting are just as important as the benefits of *being forgotten*. While both types of "forgetting" were intertwined in the past, she argues, "this is no longer the case" because "in the digital world, we can close our windows or even go entirely off the grid. But when we log off . . . our data shadows continue to multiply. . . . The individual's desire to forget has little bearing on being forgotten by others."[42] No doubt, the problems of "not being forgotten"—cyberbullying, unwanted virality, the conversion of our online traces into corporate and state data—continue to lack a solution, despite the best intentions of data erasure laws in America and Europe. However, without intending to minimize the pains and injustices suffered by anyone caught in a social media smear campaign or an unintended net of viral consequences, the reality is that—in the short term as much as in the long term—the internet is not forever. The 2020s are far enough along on the internet's historical timeline to conclude that the increase in the internet's data is inversely proportional to data accessibility and even data existence.

During the reign of MySpace and GeoCities, the years leading up to and following the millennial turning, parents and teachers gave us that familiar warning: *The internet is forever; be careful what you post.* Two decades later, everything I and the whole world posted on MySpace is gone, lost during a botched 2016 data migration.[43] (I do not mourn the loss, but that's not the point.) GeoCities was a popular web hosting service founded in the nineties that allowed users to create a personalized website in a "neighborhood" and browse other neighborhoods based on shared interests. GeoCities shuttered its servers in 2009. GeoCities pages fared better than MySpace thanks to the work of the Internet Archive and other digital archivists. However, archivists understandably prioritized the most noteworthy pages, so a nontrivial number of GeoCities neighborhoods never made it into an archive log. To MySpace and GeoCities, we can add AOL profiles, MSN Messenger chat and chatroom logs, Prodigy personal websites, Vine videos, Yik Yak messages, Storify timelines, and Friendster accounts to the list of early internet material no longer existing in the cloud. Anything uploaded to the internet prior to the early 2010s is not guaranteed to be accessible—a fact demonstrated by all the dead links redirecting netizens to long-since revamped home pages or 404 error messages; in fact, the Pew Research Center recently released a report claiming that 38% of web pages available in 2013 are now defunct.[44] In chapter 6, I'll highlight an article printed in a 2006 edition of *Elle Girl*, part of a hottest guy competition, a "man pageant" called "Last Guy Standing." The magazine's young audience was supposed to cast a vote for the cutest guys at the URL ellegirl.com/lastguy. Try typing that into a web browser and see where it takes you. *Elle* still exists. *Elle Girl* does not, and its web presence seems to have been scrubbed completely. Even the Wayback Machine is unhelpful.[45]

The year 2006 was a long time ago. However, recency is no guarantee against erasure. In 2023, Google updated its inactive account policy, stating that any account not accessed within a two-year period will be deleted.[46] In the same year, photo hosting site Imgur announced it would begin to delete inactive pictures, defining "inactive" along vague algorithmic lines ("a combination of total views and recent views, among other criteria").[47] And in May 2023, Elon Musk tweeted, "We're purging accounts that have had no activity at all for several years, so you will probably see follower count drop." The inactive account policy for Twitter (now known as X) was then updated with this ambiguous language: "To keep your account active, be sure to log in at least every 30 days. Accounts may be permanently removed due to prolonged inactivity."[48]

At least every thirty days? Two years? Total views and recent views? It turns out that some internet material will not survive the decade, let alone the millennium. "The internet is not forever," writes Paul Skallas, popularizer of the Lindy effect. "It feels like early social media internet (~2004–2012 or so) is entirely gone from the record."[49] Skallas argues that the unimaginable volume of data stored on server farms has grown large enough that continuing to store it is a liability, an unnecessary expenditure, for tech companies needing to tighten belts while making room for newer, ad-driven content.

Whatever the reason, both optimistic and pessimistic (in Kate Eichhorn's case) assumptions about the cloud's stability are probably wrong. Even the MySpace archive failed to make it to 2020. Just as ancient libraries were vulnerable to fire, so, too, is the internet vulnerable to corporate malfeasance or "botched data migrations." Seeing 404 error messages is so common today that the internet's archival unreliability has become a meme. One Twitter/X user posted "2003: be careful what you put online kids, the internet is forever. 2023: sorry but it looks like you went on vacation for two weeks so we scrubbed your entire online legacy from existence" (@VeryBadLlama, May 17, 2023). The economist Alex Armlovich likewise lamented in a tweet, "When I was a teenager they said be careful what you put on the internet because it will last forever. Now you try to read an econ blog from 2012 and not a single link works anymore" (@aarmlovi, September 3, 2023). We are collectively rediscovering that institutions and people, not technology and media, are responsible for transmitting information from one generation to the next. It is more likely that a nineteenth-century family Bible will survive into the next century than a Twitter post, an Instagram picture, or a TikTok video. To be sure, posting online means playing with the fire of virality—you *could* become a meme, a file, or a screen-capped picture that remains accessible on the digital map much longer than the rest of the cloud's wilderness. But this was and continues to be the exception, not the rule.

More importantly, even if the internet *were* forever, there is no guarantee its content would be easily navigable. Cultural transmission relies upon the culture's institutions, not technology or media as such. As I surveyed in my book *Excavating the Memory Palace*, and as John Gallagher argued in *Architects of Memory*, early content management systems and "data visualization" strategies historically developed within educational, religious, or civic institutions led and staffed by groups or individuals holding a stake in institutional longevity. Libraries, universities, and monasteries are the prime examples. Without an institution dedicated to content management and generational knowledge transmission, there is no guarantee that content will be accessible or, if accessible, easily navigable after its creation.

No single institution, however, has a stake in the internet's longevity. It is too decentralized. And institutions that own a stake in a specific corner of the internet—like MySpace or Imgur—have proven unreliable and fickle. The Google search bar is the closest thing we have to a full internet management system, but even there, content management is offshored to algorithms informed by how content is *used*, not by a desire to make access useful and robust. Math, not a librarian, guides users to the requested content, and the math seems to have gotten worse and worse at interpreting what a user is really looking for. (Imagine a library that organizes its shelves according to what people check out most frequently, and you have an idea of the Google approach. Better yet, imagine a librarian who guides a patron not to a requested title but to popular titles containing the same words as the requested one.) "Google search is dying," claims Isaiah McCall in a Medium post. "Search engines have stopped behaving like databases and are giving suggestions instead of results because an algorithm believes it knows your intentions and objectives better than you."[50] Anyone who has relied on Google in recent years for anything more complex than finding a restaurant's menu will be sympatico with McCall's complaint. Even if the desired information is *there*, somewhere in the digital wilderness, the terabytes of information stored on the cloud are worthless without good heuristics to guide users through it; otherwise, they are left looking for a needle in a stack of needles. While the Internet Archive and its Wayback Machine remain good models of archiving, Google and other search engines seem to have lost their heuristic edge in guiding netizens through the thickets.

I'll return in the final chapter to these problems and what they mean for the future of American music and musical cultures. Between here and there, the next chapters wade through the transition years between a physical and a streaming media infrastructure—a confusing decade when MP3 files rearranged our relationship to music, the mixtape lost its status as a living and breathing custom, and "mixtape" caught on as a metaphor at the same time music freed itself from tapes, discs, and every other durable medium.

NOSTALGIC CYCLE 2.0

In *Mediated Nostalgia*, Ryan Lizardi describes the DVD box set—of TV shows and film trilogies—as an object producing "a focused nostalgic gaze defined strictly by media."[51] In other words, the box set produces nostalgia for itself and for the moment of its consumption, not for its content, and not for whatever nostalgic echoes the content contains.

The box set of the television show *Freaks and Geeks* provides Lizardi's primary example. Released in 1999, the show was an early portrayal of the 1980s as crafted by sentimental Gen X filmmakers. The show was canceled after one season. Nixed so quickly, *Freaks and Geeks* should have become as memorable as any other network show that lasted a single season: *Cupid, Greg the Bunny, Goodtime Girls, Jennifer Slept Here*. However, like the single-season shows *Firefly* and *My So-Called Life*, *Freaks and Geeks* received a second chance on home video and DVD, where it gained far more viewers than it had found during its original broadcast. These shows' afterlives can be explained in part by critical acclaim but mostly by the rising popularity of their stars after the fact—Claire Danes in *My So-Called Life* and Seth Rogen and James Franco in *Freaks and Geeks*. (The goodwill Joss Whedon had accrued with *Buffy the Vampire Slayer* helped give *Firefly* a second shot at post-TV life.)

The *Freaks and Geeks* DVD box set was released in 2004. Lizardi describes the box set and its bonus-feature commentary tracks as doubly backward-looking objects. The show was created to capture America's nascent nostalgia for the 1980s,[52] but the commentary tracks—recorded by the show's actors and producers—along with the wistful presentation of the box set itself, wound up producing nostalgia for the late 1990s, the years of the show's production and doomed television broadcast. Almost none of the banter in the commentary tracks references the 1980s or the filmmakers' memories of growing up in that decade. Despite commenting on a show steeped in eighties references and eighties aesthetics, the actors and filmmakers spend most of their time focused on what had occurred during production in 1998-1999. "We miss each other," Judd Apatow says at one point.[53]

Lizardi notes with interest how rarely the show's source and origin—the 1980s—becomes a discursive touchstone on the box set's commentary tracks. Indeed, it's like a commentary track on a World War II film that never mentions the war. Then again, the whole point of a commentary track is to reminisce about the show's production. I imagine it's easy to find a war film on DVD whose commentary track never references the war—it would be a version of a media effect we're all familiar with. When a friend and I recall a memory existing nowhere but our heads, we speak of past time. When a friend and I look at a picture of a memory, we say, "I remember when we took this picture."

In use, media always force a double mnemonic imprinting—the moment recorded and the recording of the moment. We become accustomed to the fact. Our minds want to create not just memories but the mediation of memories via a screen. Judd Apatow's and Paul Feig's reminiscences about making a TV show in 1998 made to reminisce about the 1980s is not unexpected; it's not much different from my friend and I reminiscing about taking a picture.

In extreme cases (and for those old enough), the reflexive habit we've developed to imprint memories twice and at once—the smartphone's automatic duplication of memory—can lead to a subtle form of the Mandela effect for content consumed in the pre-smartphone past.[54] Like *Freaks and Geeks*, certain shows and films released in the 1990s and early 2000s became popular on secondary media after their initial release, via reruns or home video. This secondary popularity occurred not *too* long after the initial releases—a matter of four or five years—meaning that both the initial releases and their afterlife popularity emerged along with the internet and social media. In the 2020s, I have observed that some older viewers have developed a tendency to believe they experienced the *original* distribution of this sort of content—even though they almost certainly did not. If so many people had watched *Freaks and Geeks*, *My So-Called Life*, or *Firefly* when they were first released, the shows would not have been canceled after the first season. To television we could add, most famously, the film *The Shawshank Redemption*, which performed poorly at the box office but became an audience favorite on VHS, DVD, and cable television.

I know, objectively, that I never watched any of these examples during their first releases, but my mind, in the 2020s, now accustomed to the simultaneous imprinting of fact and artifact whenever cameras and screens are involved, wants to make up the memories anyway. It's like my mind cannot comprehend such a great distance between the imprinting on film of *The Shawshank Redemption* or episodes of *Freaks and Geeks* and my earliest memories of watching them. *Surely, I watched that episode on television? Yes, that one time, I know I watched it on . . . No, that was on DVD too.* To be sure, this media Mandela effect could be an artifact of old age, but if so, I'd argue it is old age influenced by the media ecology of the past quarter century.

Hypermediated life messes with personal memory, at the very least. Mediated memories—constantly engaged—mess with personal memory too. Are you *sure* you saw *The Shawshank Redemption* at a movie theater and not on cable TV? What 1990s content can you be sure you watched in the 1990s? You might be misremembering! This is the retroactive consequence of the smartphone's demand: *pics or it didn't happen.*

If you aren't persuaded by the media Mandela effect, simply swap it out for the less controversial fact that our personal memories—in our imaginations, as we recall them—are not coordinated or evoked at all like the scroll of an iPhone camera roll or a Facebook history. Personal memory relies on idiosyncratic cues, personal associations, and serendipity, not on chronology, thematic curation, two-dimensional space, or algorithmic sorting. In his chapter on mnemonics in *Institutio Oratoria* (*Institutes of Oratory*), the

Roman orator Quintilian describes memory well. Memory, he says, can present to our minds "so many old facts, revived after so long," both when we are seeking after those facts and, more surprisingly, when we are not seeking them at all—even when we're trying to sleep! Memory sometimes "forget[s] recent events" yet recalls distant ones. We cannot recall what happened yesterday and yet retain a vivid impression of "events from our boyhood." Memories "refuse to present themselves" when we try to recall them, but then they "occur to us by chance," returning to us long after we'd forgotten they were lost.[55] This is Quintilian's pre-Proustian description of involuntary memory, our natural, scattered memoryscape that operates via heuristics—sensory, emotional, random, idiosyncratic—different from the tight logics that underlie the digital organization of silicon memories.

In the 2020s, consumers rely on digitally curated mnemonics more often than they engage in natural reminiscence. Maybe this explains why a glitch has surfaced in our traditional cycles of memory and collective nostalgia. We immerse ourselves for hours at a time in content—often, content produced from our own lives—that is organized on a flat screen via chronology, algorithm, and two-dimensional space, logics completely foreign to natural memory. The digital logic nevertheless computes within the natural memoryscape. Time, as much as sense perception, reorients itself in our minds. Creating a new memory in 2004 on a DVD commentary track about a show developed as a nostalgic portrayal of the 1980s, the actors and producers of *Freaks and Geeks* had developed a nostalgic appetite for 1999. The lesson to be learned from this confusing sentence is that capturing external memories on a screen invites nostalgic retrospective, both in the present and in the future, but not always about the past that incited the initial memory-making. No, that's a confusing sentence too. Maybe the lesson is simply this: as we continue to externalize our memories onto our phones, every hour of every day, it's no wonder that nostalgic cycles have begun to short-circuit. Memory itself has been zapped. All the grandmotherly warnings were correct: Taking a picture of yourself takes a piece of your soul.

5: A RHETORIC AND POETICS OF THE MIXTAPE

Nick Hornby published *High Fidelity* in 1995. Stephen Frears released the popular film adaptation in 2000. The book and especially the film represent number-one-with-a-bullet highpoints for pop-culture depictions of the mixtape. (The film *Get Rich or Die Tryin'*, starring 50 Cent, is a highpoint for depictions of rap mixtape culture.) Sliding into second place is *The Perks of Being a Wallflower*—novel by Stephen Chbosky published in 1999; film released belatedly in 2012—a coming-of-age tale whose protagonist and supporting characters are always making compilation tapes for one another. Rounding out this Top 3 list of Most Popular Mixtape Books/Films is probably Rob Sheffield's *Love Is a Mix Tape*, a bestselling memoir from 2007 about the *Rolling Stone* editor's life and his loss of a spouse to a sudden heart attack.

The *Perks* film was released late enough on the media timeline that it had as much to do with popularizing cassettes among younger millennials and Gen Z as *Guardians of the Galaxy* did two years later. Remember, however, how deep the timeline is: Philips released the Compact Cassette in 1964. Margie B. Olsen made that mixtape for her anniversary in 1973. Jehnie Burns writes that *High Fidelity*, *The Perks of Being a Wallflower*, and *Love Is a Mix Tape* "exhibit the first generation of mixtape novelization," and that's a good word for it.[1] America's audio archives reveal that people have crafted custom playlists—for paramours, family, and friends—since the 1940s, before Nick Hornby and Stephen Chbosky were born. A mixtape *culture* didn't exist back then, and the word "mixtape" would not be coined until the eighties or nineties. But the *Perks* novel (1999), the *High Fidelity* film (2000), and certainly the *Perks* film (2012) all postdate the analog era and its years of mixtape swapping as an active youth ritual. Only Hornby's novel can be read as a primary source, and even then, a later one. Both novels, certainly both films, and Sheffield's memoir are best categorized as end-of-the-line reflections on a twentieth-century media culture coming to a close. By 1999 and 2000, teens and young adults had switched to making mix CDs and discovered digital files called MP3s. The first iPod dropped in 2001, just one year after the release of the John Cusack film. When *High Fidelity* hit theaters, the mixtape was already becoming, not a thing people made anymore, but a nostalgic touchstone for a generation about to face a Gutenberg-scale media revolution.

In the 2020s, the mixtape has become, not just a touchstone, but a rhetorical life jacket for those who experienced the analog-to-digital revolution and feel drowned by its lifeless abundance. The New Kids on the Block went on their MixTape Tour in 2022. Popular NPR show *Radiolab* released an excellent, wide-ranging series called "Mixtape" in 2021. In 2020, the documentary *Analog Love* interviewed Henry Rollins and others about the continuing impact of mixtape culture, three decades after its death. Google's Ngram tool reveals an exponential growth of references to the term *mixtape* in the digital millennium. Gen X and elder millennials, now old and starting to notice gray hairs, if any hair remains, seem to have settled on the mixtape as an analog talisman to conjure youthful sparks and musical memories rendered obsolete not just by time but by digital media.

Having turned into a rhetorical trope, mixtapes demand at least one critical reflection in a book about them, especially before I place the cassette on a pedestal in the final chapters. The previous chapter set the cassette against an industrial backdrop, draining a few ounces from the mixtape's nostalgic power. Before leaving the analog era, I want to bleed out the rest of the nostalgia, framing mixtapes as the sociological purview of what TV critic John Carman once called "self-indulgent white brats."[2] The fact of the matter is, the mixtape has attained cultural staying power and become a metaphorical commonplace thanks in part to its middle-class milieu and the young males who made, popularized, and enjoy reminiscing about private mixtapes. No figure better epitomizes that milieu than the protagonist of *High Fidelity*, Rob Fleming (a.k.a. Rob Gordon, as winningly portrayed by John Cusack).

SELF-INDULGENT WHITE KIDS: A CLOSE READING OF *HIGH FIDELITY*

About one of his sister's boyfriends, Charlie, the protagonist in *The Perks of Being a Wallflower*, says, "He is always making mix tapes for my sister with very specific themes. One was called 'Autumn Leaves.' He included many songs by the Smiths. He even hand-colored the cover." In the book, the sister gives Charlie the "Autumn Leaves" mixtape without bothering to listen to it herself. "I took the tape, but I felt weird about it because he had made it for her," Charlie confesses.[3] Later, he tells his sister about a good song on the tape, and she thanks him, because now she can mention it to the boyfriend when he asks.

The girl doesn't listen to the tape! Worse, she lies about listening to the tape! To be fair, she decides to listen to it a few pages later, but it's still a funny moment because it confronts the egotism that fueled so much mixtape-making in the hands of adolescents, mostly (but not only) adolescent males. Says indie musician Dean Wareham, of Galaxie 500, "The message of the tape might be: I love you. . . . Listen to how I feel about you. Or, maybe: I love me. I am a tasteful person who listens to tasty things. This tape tells you all about me."[4] Thurston Moore says, "Mix tapes are like matchmaker forms. But why must your match have to be so like yourself—do you just pretty much love yourself? Is there a desire to convert your lover into you?"[5]

Many mixtapes—not all, but a lot—were made to reflect the maker, not the darling or the boyfriend they were given to. (Fair play, of course, for mixtapes made as a personal item for the car or the Walkman.) Despite the deep interpersonal gesture of making someone a mixtape, its fabrication was often managed by Narcissus rather than Cupid. But the true Don Juan, even at 16, knew the best mixtape went the other way around, containing songs from bands or artists the other person had turned *you* onto, songs that hit the other person's dopamine receptors. It's the epiphany Rob Fleming has at the end of *High Fidelity*, the idea to make a mixtape of things Laura would want to hear: "When Laura hears the opening bars she spins round and grins and makes several thumbs-up signs, and I start to compile in my head a compilation tape for her, something that's full of stuff she's heard of, and full of stuff she'd play. Tonight, for the first time ever, I can sort of see how it's done."[6] To be fair, one can frame the self-indulgent playlist (here's stuff *I've* been listening to; here's stuff *I* really like) as an earnest deed of sharing (here's stuff that moves me; I hope it moves you too) or romantic revealing (here's stuff that makes me think about you). But that generous reading easily dovetails back toward egotism (here's stuff that makes me think about you . . . and aren't you deeply interested in what makes me think about you—wouldn't you like to know what it's like to be me thinking about you?).

From a distant enough perspective, the protagonists of *High Fidelity* and *The Perks of Being a Wallflower* are the same person at different life stages. White, male, middle class, prone to fits of emotional immaturity (not a big deal for teenaged Charlie; a bigger deal for thirty-five-year-old Rob Fleming). Such fits are universal to humanity, but Rob and Charlie wallow in them longer and more frequently than is allowed in other racial or socioeconomic contexts. Rob's emotional immaturity is a symptom of stunted self-awareness. He is still, at thirty-five, an adolescent. Laura, the mature voice, explicitly confronts Rob about his juvenile character: "You've lived half your life, but for all you've got to show for it you might as well be nineteen, and I'm not talking about money or property or furniture."[7] However, that line doesn't arrive until late in the book, so for most of the story, the sympathetic reader can remain as oblivious about Rob's immaturity as Rob does.

Hornby's novel is less guilty than Frears's film of romanticizing Rob's emotional stunting. But Rob Fleming remains likable, and his unwillingness to become less self-centered seems curiously tied to his identity as a music lover and mixtape creator. "What really matters is what you like, not what you *are* like," he says.[8] The whole story comes across as a wink-wink, nod-nod affair. The reader is not put into a critical or even an ironic frame of mind, for example, by the waggish opening passage where Rob fames his entire story as a ranked list of girls.

> My desert-island, all-time, top five most memorable split-ups, in chronological order:
>
> 1. Alison Ashworth
> 2. Penny Hardwick
> 3. Jackie Allen
> 4. Charlie Nicholson
> 5. Sarah Kendrew[9]

But what kind of man thinks about women from the past in terms of a ranked list? Rob, record store owner and rabid music consumer, is of course riffing on the Top 5 hits trope, which grants him immunity. Still, ranking girls is a thing teenage boys do. Abstracting individuals as numerals—hardly even objects—is a pastime of the adolescent or the spiritual adolescent. Teenage boys at least have the cowardly decency not to initiate contact with the people they rank; Rob does not have that decency.

In a Top 3 countdown of Rob's most self-centered, emotionally unaware moments, let's consider the opening passage number 3. Number 2 is when Laura tries to have sex with Rob in the back of a car after her father's funeral. Laura gives Rob the call about the sudden death—*"My dad's died,"* *she sobs, "my dad, my dad"*—and two pages later Rob has already turned attention inward: "I have thought about the stuff I want played at my funeral," he confesses.[10] He goes on to observe that "people who have dead parents, or dead friends, or dead partners [are] the most interesting people in the world" and that, at least, is turned outward. Offhand but sincere, the opposite of self-centered. However, when Rob finds himself in the car with Laura, his self-preservation instinct kicks back in. Laura explains her reason for leaving the wake. She has been thinking and talking about her father all day, and now people want her to think and talk about him some more. She's tired. "Listen, Rob," Laura says, "I want to feel something else apart from misery and guilt. It's either that or I go home and put my hand in the fire." She drives them to a lonely spot her father once took her for walks. "Do you want to get in the back?" she asks. Rob, skeptical at first, clears some space amid the "empty cassette cases." The kissing commences, then the undressing, and then Rob interrupts:

> "You know with Ray . . ."
> "Oh, Rob, we're not going to go through that again."
> "No, no. It's not . . . are you still on the pill?"
> "Yes, of course. There's nothing to worry about."
> "I didn't mean that. I mean . . . was that all you used?"
> She doesn't say anything, and then she starts to cry.[11]

To be fair to Rob and Hornby, the book was written in the 1990s, during the AIDS epidemic. They had been trained by a dozen PSAs to think about such things. But then Laura reminds Rob, in tears, that she is *Laura*, the woman Rob was sharing his life with just a few weeks ago. Given the unhappy circumstances, *I'm concerned you have an STD* should land not just on our Top 3 list here but on a list of Worst Possible Things Said by a Male Protagonist during a Romance Scene. It betrays Rob's complete lack of self-awareness, yes, but also trust in a woman whose influence is, at last, pushing him to love not "girls" but a specific person. Apparently, that influence registers on Rob's radar as just another random fling with whom he needs to worry about venereal disease.

Self-centered moment number 1 in this deconstruction of mixtape dignitary Rob Fleming occurs after the funeral, when Rob and Laura's relationship has "resumed its normal course" but before Rob's last-page epiphany about making mixtapes Laura would actually want to listen to. Postcoital, he asks Laura about sex with Ray (played by Tim Robbins in the film), the man she has had a short fling with during their weeks apart. Over a dozen or so lines of dialogue, Rob becomes increasingly desperate to hear details, despite Laura never having asked to hear about Rob's "extracurricular activities" with another woman during the same time.

> "I don't care. I just want to know."
> "Want to know what?"
> "What it was like."
> She huffs. "It was like sex. What else could it be like?"

... And so it goes. I want to know (except, of course, I don't want to know) about multiple orgasms and ten times a night and blow jobs and positions that I've never even heard of, but I haven't the courage to ask, and she would never tell me. I know they've done it, and that's bad enough; all I can hope for now is damage limitation.[12]

Laura has just lost her father, she and Rob have reconciled after being apart, and all Rob wants to talk about is the other guy's penis size—while he and Laura are in bed together!

The scene, reimagined in the film as slapstick humor instead of selfish and unmanly behavior, is innocuous as far as encounters with male sexual insecurity go. Rob, for his part, wisely shuts up, and Laura rewards him with a graceful endnote. However, Rob's pestering—"I don't care, I just want to know"—reveals a deeply flawed character. Rob, at thirty-five, wants to know the details because he wants to know where he ranks in Laura's mind. Is he better or worse than Ray? Is he number one with a bullet or at the bottom of the charts? Believing that Laura thinks about sexual experiences in these terms—as Rob himself does—is another sign of emotional immaturity. Rob can't imagine, even as Laura tells him explicitly, that it's not like that for her. More than just self-indulgent, the moment shows an unsteady mix of egotism and insecurity in a protagonist whose cinematic double was, for a while at least, the pop-culture reference point for mixtapes.

Rob's attempt to goad Laura into revealing details about Ray isn't entirely unlike the egotistical style of mixtape-making. Such was the style of Rob's first tape for Laura, which buries the one song he knows she likes "in the middle of side two," surrounded instead by songs *he* thinks she'll like, songs *he* hopes will make her think of *him*—"oh, there are loads of rules" about making a mixtape.[13] In the throes of gathering and dubbing, the egotistical mixtape maker is driven less by rules, however, and more by his own barely understood motivation: *Here are songs that make me think about her, and I know she must be interested in me thinking about her, because I'm deeply interested in her thinking about me.* Rob when he's pestering Laura in bed and the egotistical mixtape maker are both pursuing the same impossible thing: direct knowledge—direct experience, even—of how you exist in someone else's head. Adorno says, "What the gramophone listener actually wants to hear is himself, and the artist merely offers him a substitute for the sounding image of his own person, which he would like to safeguard as a possession. The only reason that he accords the record such value is he himself could also be just as well preserved. Most of the time records are virtual photographs of their owners, flattering photographs—ideologies."[14] Although the mixtape has become a metaphor for nineties nostalgia, among other things, it could just as well be a metaphor for middle-class selfishness or self-indulgence. Framed ideologically, the mixtape with its customized playlist can be seen as nothing more than a physical icon or idol representing the maker. It is *me* in plastic and magnetic form, and what more precious object could there be?

I realize I'm performing a garage psychoanalysis on Rob Fleming here, and I've tactically avoided his moments of self-awareness ("with the emphasis on *guy*, self-centered, blind, and stupid"; "I can't think of the adult expression"[15])—but I'm trying to expose a whiff of emotive decadence that, although universal, is fairly associated with the mixtape. Rob Fleming—especially Rob as played by John Cusack—is the most popular incarnation of private mixtape culture. But what kind of culture throws out as its exemplar a thirtysomething whose self-worth rests on knowing whether his latest girlfriend thinks he was a better lay than Tim Robbins? Probably a culture whose most enthusiastic participants, in one way or another, for better or worse, identify with Rob Fleming. In the next section, I'll discuss how the mixtape has turned into a metonym for the nineties and a metaphor for love and nostalgia; however, I think it would be perfectly possible to use the mixtape as a metaphor for selfishness.

THE MIXTAPE AS A RHETORICAL FIGURE

Jehnie I. Burns's *Mixtape Nostalgia*, which I've cited at length, contains a comprehensive overview of the mixtape's cultural and rhetorical diffusion in the first two decades of the twenty-first century. She charts the number of songs whose lyrics reference mixtapes (over forty since 2010),[16] the proliferation of books mentioning mixtapes, the rise of podcasts about cassette culture, a mixtape card game, and corporate and crowdfunded attempts to re-create the analog music experience for digital listeners (most of which are banal; Apple Music's "mixtape" service is simply a digital playlist with a custom JPEG attached to it). Burns's excellent compilation is a valuable resource for anyone interested in the widespread adoption of the mixtape trope over the last two decades. "No longer a point of everyday life," she writes, "mixtapes became a point of nostalgia."[17] She follows the cassette's and the mixtape's evolutions from tangible objects to "idealized concepts" sustained by a heavy dose of "techno-nostalgia" from the now middle-aged children of the seventies and eighties.

The mixtape has survived the digital revolution as a metaphor but also as a metonym and what I'll call a figure of arrangement. The word *mixtape* no longer denotes a physical item people make and share but an ever-more-popular figure of speech. Even in *High Fidelity*—steeped in music culture and the love of physical media—the *mixtape* (although Hornby never uses the exact word) is more than just a reference to a customized cassette. By the end of the narrative, the mixtape becomes a metaphor for Rob's slow but steady emotional maturation.

"Love is a mix tape" is the last line as well as the title of Rob Sheffield's book, and for him, the mixtape is unambiguously a metaphor: "The rhythm of the mix tape is the rhythm of romance, the analog hum of a physical connection between two sloppy, human bodies. The cassette is full of tape hiss and room tone; it's full of wasted space, unnecessary noise. Compared to the go-go-go rhythm of an MP3, mix tapes are hopelessly inefficient."[18] Sheffield is defining the messy reality of love in this passage. Love is sloppy. Love is human. Love is full of noise and wasted moments. Love is disorganized—until, of course, you intentionally shape it as you shape a mixtape. Like all memoirs, *Love Is a Mix Tape* narrativizes a life that does not come equipped with a narrative arc or a readymade lesson to impart. Life, death, love (not just the romantic kind), and most things worth writing about do not, in fact, lend themselves to easy description. That's when we reach for metaphor, simile, and other rhetorical figures.

However, the simplest—and to be honest, the most ubiquitous—use of the mixtape trope is to treat it not as a metaphor but as a figure of arrangement. By that I simply mean ordering the contents or chapters of one's book as though they were songs on a mixtape compilation. Used this way, the mixtape is a stand-in for a table of contents, and its metaphoric potential is not coaxed out otherwise. C. R. Asher's self-published book *Some Shit Off an Old Mixtape: A Selection of Freeform Verse* is the bluntest application of this organizational tactic in the Google Books archive; its chapters are titled "Tracks." Stefanie Honeder's *Heartbeat: A Yoga Symphony Mixtape*, Absolutely Anwar's *The Written Mixtape: Volume One*, Zachary Burlingame's *Damp: A Poetry Mixtape*, and Brad Abraham's comic book series *Mix Tape* are just a selection of titles that use the mixtape as a figure of arrangement, likening its curation of songs to the book's careful compilation of chapters, poems, essays, stories, or autobiographical anecdotes. This method tries to deliver the same emotional impact as more sophisticated uses of the mixtape trope (metaphoric or metonymic), but most of the time, the content in these titles has little or nothing to do with mixtapes, cassettes, or music, so the attempt falls flat.

A more complex rhetorical use of the mixtape is to turn it into an "emotional through line"[19] that recalls the mixtape not just as chronological *arrangement* (i.e., a table of contents) but as an arrangement *of music* that contains emotional highs, lows, and crescendos as well as diminuendos. Sheffield's *Love Is a Mix Tape* famously begins each chapter with a picture of a mixtape he created in the past. However, one after another, the transitory playlists come to represent not just the chronology of Sheffield's life but the whiplash of emotional content that accompanies his life trajectory, from the rush of meeting his wife to the ache of becoming a widower. When we get to the final line—"love is a mix tape"—the reader is thinking, not about chronology at all but about the mixtape's inimitable clash of loudness and softness, of major and minor chords, of congruity and incongruity, of tape hiss between tracks, all of which creates a beautiful unity by the end of it. The likeness between a personalized compilation of songs and our own cobbled-together lives is explicit at this point and is what gives the comparison its whole value. More than figures of arrangement, Sheffield's mixtapes are, at first, emotionally associative objects, and then, on the final page, a magnificently earned metaphor.

C. S. Lewis reminds us that the best similes and metaphors provide either an "emotional echo or an emotional contrast to the business at hand," allowing a writer to turn a single note into a "symphony" by bringing to bare on the reader whatever themes or images the author wants, for whatever purposes.[20] The mixtape's "echo" of course can't help being nostalgic, and the best authors—like Sheffield—lean into the fact. However, beyond the mixtape's ability to make a passage reverberate into the reader's imagination with more yearning than it might otherwise possess, another reason the mixtape has become a popular metaphor is that, as a single note, it easily allows authors to grasp at the entire symphony of their life and all those ineffable feelings that come along with reflections on love, life, death, and, in Sheffield's case, the anticlimax following death. When the business at hand is as delicate as all that, the mixtape—itself a physical collection of songs expressing something ineffable—ends up being a valuable metaphor to lean on (so valuable, in fact, it's at risk of becoming a cliché). When Sheffield tries to sum up all he has learned about life and love, he has no choice but to offer a metaphor.

The cliché is an intermediate state between a living and a truly good and dead metaphor: *I've come a long way* (life as a journey) or *My life is in ruins* (life as a building). The problem with a cliché is that it has lost its power to convey the depth of what someone really wants to convey. It has also, relatedly, lost its power to provide *meaning*, as in *purpose* or *value*, which is another important effect of metaphor. "A person's life, when viewed from one objective angle," writes psychologist Mark Landau, "amounts to a heap of ephemeral moments devoid of purpose. But that's not how most people want to see it."[21] Landau notes that having a sense of purpose in life correlates with positive life outcomes and feelings of life satisfaction. So how do people develop a sense of purpose? Identifying with a larger entity, such as a nation or an ideal or a baseball team, is one strategy. Belief in an afterlife is the most common strategy of all. Landau suggests that metaphoric thinking is yet another equally pervasive strategy for finding purpose in life. "Although people may not fully comprehend what their life is for, they are intimately familiar with the uses of myriad objects, events, and activities. They know, for example, that using a compass is for reaching a desired destination; violent confrontations are for defeating enemies; and athletic events are organized so that one of several competing parties can be determined a winner. Hence, representing life metaphorically in terms of such concepts may project onto life a clear and convincing purpose."[22] We don't need to look any further than holy texts to find obvious examples of metaphor used not only to make an abstraction clearer ("meaning" in one sense) but also to provide people with a sense of purpose and value ("meaning" in the other sense).

Similarly, "love is a mix tape" ends up being a good metaphor because it gives us "meaning" in both senses. It turns a purely intangible emotion into a physical item (the first sense, making an abstraction clearer), but it also provides a sense of purpose. It achieves the latter because the mixtape is exactly the sort of thing a marriage or other long-term romantic commitment actually looks and feels like. It's a DIY artifact that takes time and effort. It never turns out *exactly* how you'd imagined it, which is not a bad thing. Knowing it can never be an ideal mix, you must still put intention into the sort of thing you want it to become if it's to become something worthwhile. It is a bespoke compilation of distinct songs, not a narrative in any sense, but it's *your* compilation (yours and the other person's), so it develops a kind of narrative only the two of you can read or recognize. It is something made but also given, and in the giving, you receive all the satisfaction you could ask for. With time, however, the mixtape begins to represent the past as much as the present, as we realize that songs on a mixtape are not the same now as they were back then. Listening to a mixtape at fifteen is different from listening to it at forty. The songs no longer overwhelm us with a rush of emotional urgency, but with any luck, our hearing has nonetheless grown deeper and more appreciative than ever ("I don't love you like I used to," as Russell Dickerson's country song says). The mixtape thus evokes evolving identities that are yet inscribed—here is the important part—on a durable medium, which is, in my reading, one of the most hopeful images of love in the Western pantheon of images for love. "Love is a mix tape" offers not only a suggestive but a purposeful image. Imagistically and emotionally charged with both senses of "meaning," it's no wonder that the mixtape has become a popular metaphor, long after the youth ritual itself has disappeared.

Another good metaphoric use—although, as we'll see, it's also a metonymic use—can be found in Chelsey Johnson's *Stray City*. Toward the end of the novel, Johnson sends the protagonist, Andrea, into the attic to drag out old pictures and VHS tapes of her daughter's father, whom the daughter has never met.

And here were the cassettes: a few mixtapes from Ryan, a microcassette from an answering machine she no longer owned. They had lived such analog lives then. Letters, photocopied zines, videocassettes, mixtapes in a Walkman. It used to take her hours to make a mixtape. That was the art of it—you had to measure your time so carefully, rationing those forty-five minutes per side, and sequence with precise intent since the order of the songs was fixed forever. Time then was more like space—you traveled it like land, minute by minute, mile by mile. You were always stopping by a Kinko's to copy or print something, or the post office to collect mail. . . . You had to *go* to things, to people. What went on here, in this town, in your orbit, constituted ninety-nine percent of everything that happened.[23]

Johnson starts with the observation that a tape ribbon's material length corresponded to its runtime. The fact suggests the simile, "time then was more like space"—referring to the "analog lives" of the 1990s, best measured not by the clock but by the physical space one had to traverse to get anything done in those pre-internet years (almost but not quite as substantial as the time-space one had to traverse in the years before train or automobile). Just as a cassette's time was bounded by its length, Andrea's life was once bounded by the spatial orbit of her daily surroundings. So far, so good. However, the time-as-space metaphor is heightened in the ensuing sentences, when Johnson contrasts the old, spatially reckoned mode of living with the destruction of distance brought about by digital technology and social media: "Now it seemed only fifty percent or sixty percent of life happened here—your sense of what was going on flooded in from everywhere, all the time, at the same time."[24] Drowning in real-time updates about far off things, from people whom she has not interacted with in the flesh for years, Johnson's protagonist reaches for the cassette mixtape—always advertised in minutes *and* feet—as a metaphor for a simpler, predigital, epistemically quieter life. At this point, however, Johnson's mixtape is becoming a metonym as much as a metaphor.

A figure not unrelated to metaphor, metonymy names something by invoking a specific attribute or object associated with it.[25] Referring to journalists as "the press," to language as "a tongue," and to the tech industry as "Silicon Valley" are all examples of metonymy. When Marc Antony asks the crowd to lend him their "ears," he means their collective attention. I'd suggest that certain mixtape metaphors are really mixtape metonyms, in which the mixtape invokes the whole media infrastructure of America in the eighties and nineties. The phrase "cassette era" is clearly a metonym for those decades. The *Stray City* passage is one of the more poignant examples of a mixtape metonym, which is why I quoted it at length (and it takes the whole passage to fully unspool), but many other authors draw upon the mixtape trope not metaphorically but as a metonym, an associative stand-in for the analog vibe of the late twentieth century, the last moments before digital ubiquity swallowed America whole.

In the last section, I suggested the idea that mixtapes could be used as a metaphor for middle-class indulgence. The closest thing I've found on that score is a remark in Yvonne Prinz's *Vinyl Princess* (a book which the author described as "*High Fidelity* for kids"[26]). Gifted a CD by a boy, Allie, the protagonist, says: "Could it be a mix CD, the mating call of the romantically challenged?"[27] As mixtape metaphors go, this is one of my favorites. It plays on all the self-centeredness I tried to call out in Rob Fleming, but despite its teen-girl snark it also contains a euphemism and thus manages to be forgiving rather than biting. It's not Rob's or any other boy's *fault*. They're just *challenged*. Courtney Smith, in her essay anthology *Record Collecting for Girls*, takes an even more forgiving stance toward the mixtape as self-indulgence; for Smith, it's not at all a bad thing that mixtapes tend to represent the giver rather than the receiver. "When guys make us mix tapes and play us songs," she writes, "they aren't just showing off. They're trying to tell us some truths about themselves through the sounds and words of an intermediary."[28] Through Smith's generous lens, the mixtape represents a certain style of male communication, one she has come to appreciate. In fact, directly comparing a mixtape to the personality of its maker is a similar, not uncommon metaphor to be found in the archival wild. For example, a character in Joe Meno's *Hairstyles of the Damned* says, "To me, the tapes were what made me like her, then love her so much: the fact that in between the Misfits and the Specials, she would have a song from the Mamas and the Papas."[29]

Last, consider Jane Sanderson's romance novel *Mix Tape*. On the back cover blurb, the mixtape provides an image for the excitement of a newly rekindled relationship: "Daniel was the first boy to make Alison a mix tape. But that was years ago. And Ali hasn't thought about him in a very long time. Until Dan's name pops up on her phone, with a song from their past. Ali can't help but respond in kind. And so begins a new mix tape."[30] Combining backward-looking nostalgia with forward-looking expectation is of course the secret mix that gave Nicholas Sparks's book *The Notebook* its bestselling success. However, I call attention to Sanderson's derivative novel because its front cover provides a rhetorical novelty: the visual mixtape metaphor. An unspooled mess of magnetic tape from two cassettes connects around the cover's perimeter, representing what I imagine are all the worthwhile difficulties of romantic connection. We did, after all, find it worthwhile to respool all that tape with our pencils when it came undone.

A SARGASSO SEA OF DEAD MEDIA

Before pivoting away from the mixtape metaphor, it's worth asking why mixtapes have become a trope in the twenty-first century. The Google Ngram Viewer proves the fact, but why the cassette? Obviously, when handled expertly, it offers a good metaphor for love and other indefinable things. It also provides an evocative metonym for the last noninternet decades this world will ever know. But still—why not the Polaroid camera? The floppy disk? Pagers? Cordless phones? Try plugging those and other retro words in the Google Ngram Viewer and comparing the results with "mixtape." Something about the mixtape must set it apart from any number of defunct media from the end of the last millennium.

The last chapter described mixtapes as American folk art or DIY artifacts. One important reason for mixtape longevity is the simple fact that a mixtape took more time and effort to create than a Polaroid snapshot, an answered page, or a returned call on a cordless phone. Floppy disks contained cool stuff, but teens did not put the cool stuff onto the disks themselves, they just booted it up from a command prompt. In contrast, and unlike the Polaroid or the pager, the mixtape did not in any way foreshadow the immediacy and efficiency of the digital infrastructure to come. The mixtape took time—gathering songs, dubbing songs, handwriting playlists, doodling J-card art, speaking messages between songs into a cheap microphone, finding time to deliver the tape. Across America, these moments collectively added up to a cultural *thing* we now refer to as mixtape culture. We loved our Polaroid photos, but they were far too instantaneous to create a cultural moment.

In 1928, Paul Valéry already recognized the logical endpoint of industrially reproduced art, with its immediacy of delivery and impact. In a short essay entitled "The Conquest of Ubiquity," he says the following (and it is worth quoting more fully this time):

> Works of art will acquire a kind of ubiquity. We shall only have to summon them and there they will be, either in their living actuality or restored from the past. They will not merely exist in themselves but will exist wherever someone with a certain apparatus happens to be.... Just as water, gas, and electricity are brought into our houses from far off to satisfy our needs in response to a minimal effort, so we shall be supplied with visual or auditory images, which will appear and disappear at a simple movement of the hand, hardly more than a sign.... [W]e shall find it perfectly natural to receive the ultrarapid variations or oscillations that our sense organs gather in and integrate to form all we know. I do not know whether a philosopher has ever dreamed of a company engaged in the home delivery of Sensory Reality.[31]

Impressive foresight for 1928. Marshall McLuhan wouldn't do better. Interestingly, Valéry also recognized that music—the most acute, immediate, and emotionally impactful of the arts—would be the first art, and, thanks to the phonograph, already was the first art to be made instantly available "at will, anywhere on the globe and at any time."[32] However, while Valéry's sage observations apply (not in equal measure) to the radio, the LP, the cassette, the compact disc, the MP3 player, and the streaming playlist, they do not apply to the mixtape. For its creator, the mixtape was not at all instantaneous. The cassette mixtape did the one thing that few media rituals did in the automation age: it forced teens and young adults to *slow down*, to gather, to craft, and, under the least narcissistic conditions, to consider the emotional effects of the compilation ("I start to compile in my head a compilation tape for her, something that's full of stuff she's heard of, and full of stuff she'd play"[33]). Apropos Valéry's prediction, even the listener received the mixtape as a unique object, something different from the mass-produced album. The fact that a mixtape had been customized for us informed the way we listened to it. The effort of its creation transmitted itself onto the magnetic tape. We sat on the ground next to the tape player, or maybe lounged back in a bed or on a window seat, and really listened to the thing. Nothing on the tape was "content," especially when a song on it resonated. *Stop, rewind, play* would be our response. *Stop, rewind, play*, as we attempted to relive serendipity again and again. The opening credits to the Jason Reitman film *Young Adult* make excellent use of the effect, capturing Charlize Theron's sweet anticipation as she waits for the tape to reverse across the tape head, so she can relisten to a song over, and over, and over—those seconds of anticipation being something like the moment before an orchestral performance when the oboe hits A and all the other instruments tune in.

The cassette mixtape, in other words, squared a circle: it found a way to offer the immediacy of mechanically reproduced sound without sacrificing the entire experience of live music as a spatial, tactile, time-consuming, three-dimensional *event*. All music sets molecules vibrating, but, with all due respect to Valéry's foresight, the resonance of music on headphones is distinct from the flesh-space resonance of music in a crowded venue. The way sound wavelengths bounce and resound against the walls and ceilings—not to mention the physical closeness of the spectators in the middle of it all—makes live music and mediated music two distinct experiences. Sound, writes Byron Hawk, is both a "material vibration and experiential relation,... a quasi-object—part energy, part material force, and part relational exchange—that is entangled via resonance."[34] I'd argue that the cassette mixtape came as close as any other physical medium to reproducing at least an echo of the tactile, sonic qualities of live music. The tactility

I've already explained, in this chapter and the last. In addition, the mixtape was a shared item, a "relational exchange," meaning the music on a mixtape was not yours alone. Material and relational, it sparked something like the joy of driving to a concert with friends, and in this case, the concert was a festival because it included more than one band. The uniqueness of the mixtape also provided an echo of live music's distinctiveness. Just as every version of a song at a concert was unique to that concert (it had never been played that way before and would never be played just that way again, which is why concert bootlegs remained popular in the 1990s and early 2000s), so, too, did the mixtape exist as a bespoke performance; no one had ever heard these songs in just this way before.

All this, I think, is why physical media in general and mixtapes in particular remain culturally relevant so deep into the digital revolution. We continue to realize that music should be something to touch, to take up space, to materially exchange—not just something to hear. And, lacking a concert ticket, nothing turned music into a tactile, embodied, relational experience quite as much as making or receiving a mixtape.

All those moments of exchange explain why mixtape nostalgia had already deepened as early as the release of *High Fidelity* in 2000, one year after Napster had gone live and five years after hackers had released CD-ripping software into the wilds of the early internet. John Cusack dubbed records onto tapes in the theaters, but outside, the MP3 had introduced the world to the most radical aural novelty since the wax cylinder: sound mediated without a durable surface. The year 2000 also saw the release of Lawrence Lessig's book *Code*, an early warning shot signaling the internet's vulnerability to hyperregulation not by the state but by corporations whose digital arsenal could undermine legal doctrines of fair use, first sale, and traditional conceptions of ownership. *High Fidelity* and all mixtape nostalgia appeared, in other words, as an immune response against an abrupt injection of digital ubiquity into American life. On either side of 9/11, there was a sense among twenty- and thirty-somethings that the analog-to-digital transition—despite availing ourselves of its bounty—was doing something to music that we could not yet describe but felt powerless to stop.

6: MUSIC WITHOUT A MEDIUM

Every generation, at a certain middle-aged point, begins to long for its youth. Not every generation finds its youth inaccessible after a media revolution. Imagine being a scribe in Gutenberg's Holy Roman Empire or an aged cowboy in Henry Ford's America. When these revolutions occur, it's understandable that an aging generation clings not to the content but to the objects of its former life. The content lives on; the media do not. The scribe's manuscript still circulates, just not in his handwriting. The cowboy can travel fast, faster than ever, just not on a horse. The dominance of the Western in 1920s and 1930s movie houses can be explained by the memories of old men as much as by the enthusiasm of young boys.

The compact disc was released in the United States in 1983. Codeveloped by Philips and Sony in a rare case of cross-cultural collaboration, its sales overtook LPs in 1987[1] and surpassed cassettes in 1991,[2] maintaining market dominance until the end of the nineties. *High Fidelity* and *The Perks of Being a Wallflower* were encomiums to a dying medium. They didn't seem so at the time, as I recall, because we still had our old cassettes, and "mix CDs" still required effort—not as much effort as a tape, but enough that teens failed to notice a change when they started burning files onto CDs instead of dubbing songs onto tapes.

In hindsight, the blank CD-R was the first step toward the transubstantiation of music into content, a conversion that accelerated with the iPod's "1,000 songs in your pocket" and terminated in the streaming playlist. At their cheapest, after they had outsold LPs and become the consumer focal point for music consumption, blank cassettes still cost anywhere from $0.84 to $4.00 per cassette, depending on quality and runtime. Cheap, but not nearly as cheap as blank compact discs would one day become. An economy of scale is as much a metaphor as an accurate description of market effects. The more an item gets produced, the cheaper it becomes, in both the economic and the social sense. Making a mix CD took the same amount of time as making a mixtape—an hour or two—but it was much,

much *cheaper* on CD. Ten dollars for a five-pack of cassettes wasn't chump change to a teenager in the eighties and nineties. But twenty dollars for a stack of fifty blank compact discs in 2000? The math worked out to chump change per unit.

Stephen Witt's *How Music Got Free* is probably the best social history of the CD era and the CD's slow murder by MP3. Jonathan Sterne's *MP3: The Meaning of a Format* provides the most thorough overview of the era's technical details and industrial intrigue. Riding the Media Bits, the personal website of Leonardo Chiariglione, chairman of the Moving Picture Experts Group (MPEG), established in 1988 to standardize digital encoding formats, hosts a valuable first-hand retrospective on the digital revolution.[3] And Charles C. Mann's longform essay, "The Heavenly Jukebox," published in *The Atlantic* in September 2000, provides valuable early reporting on the music industry's response to the (accidental) release of MP3 encoders to the public. The short version is that the compact disc was the first medium in sound history to store music as a series of zeros and ones. The digital substrate of the disc made music easier and cheaper to manufacture, ship, and store, but it also made it possible to rip music away from the disc. Once consumers figured out how to get music off the discs and onto hard drives, the music industry, musical culture, and music consumption would be confronted with a media revolution whose effects still resonate nearly three decades later.

"WE'RE MAKING A HUGE MISTAKE"

Early advertisements for the CD promised "Pure, Perfect Sound Forever." The compact disc could offer "Perfect Sound Forever" because it was imprinted with enormous amounts of audio data made possible by digital technology. The CD offered the highest fidelity rendering of music the world had ever heard, captured by cutting-edge studio equipment and copied perfectly onto each CD unit. From the beginning, record executives were uncomfortable with the whole idea. "We're making a huge mistake," the head of Polygram is reported to have said. "We're putting studio-quality masters into the hands of people."[4] It remained a physical object—a relevant qualification—but it was still a revolutionary item, because before music could free itself from physical media, it first needed to get digital. Recalling the CD era in a 2015 interview with the *Guardian*, former Virgin Records executive Jon Webster puts it bluntly: "Once you made a CD with ones and zeroes, it was only a matter of time before that was converted into something that was easily transferable."[5] Although a CD doesn't contain "files" as such—it contains a continuous stream of linear pulse code modulated audio—its grooves can be accessed via computer operating systems as though it contains discrete CDA files (compact disc audio files). For a few years, like a bunch of dopes, music publishers and less technically inclined consumers believed a CD player was required to access the files; sound engineers and savvy hackers, however, would cure us of that illusion.

The illusion worked great for the music industry at first. Like any new medium, the CD had a slow start following its release, but within a decade, the compact disc had become such a high-fi success that global music sales topped $1 billion in 1992 and $2 billion in 1996. Even though the CD was cheaper to manufacture, store, and transport than cassettes or LPs, music publishers did not drop album prices but in fact raised them, allowing profit margins to swell. Consumers failed to see the discrepancy. A blank cassette with case and J-card, at peak abundance, cost a buck or two. A cassette album priced at ten to fifteen dollars seemed fair dinkum. It never occurred to us that twenty dollars for a CD album and twenty dollars for a fifty-pack of blank CDs might indicate a sharp practice on the part of the music industry. In 1995, a CD cost ten to fifteen cents to manufacture. The jewel case cost thirty cents. Yet the average price of a prerecorded CD album rose to $16.98.[6] "It was simple profiteering," claims Stephen Witt in an interview accompanying the release of his book. "[Labels] would cut backroom deals with retailers not to let the price drop."[7] Webster, the former Virgin Records executive, deems the claim unfair. Virgin and other labels put more money than ever before into finding and promoting new talent, and it's not as though raising prices on a new medium—even though it was cheaper to manufacture than the old medium—was a rare practice in technological history. Webster admits, however, that "in the 90s we were awash with profitability and became fat, to be honest."[8] The CD promised perfect sound forever. And music labels spent money as though the CD would be around forever too. The Virgin Megastore and the celebrity wealth of Richard Branson are good symbols for the excess profits of music publishers during the compact disc's short reign.

Unsurprisingly, the media industry—companies like Philips, who had developed the cassette, and Sony, who had partnered with Philips to develop the compact disc—knew that digital music would not stay chained to the CD for long. As early as 1990, while music publishers got fat on album sales, Philips was already preparing for the CD's obsolescence, developing a universal format standard for compressed digital audio. "Digital audio" of course covered a lot of nonmusical ground in the early days of the internet, DVD, and digital broadcasts. However, well before the rise of the internet, sound engineers had already understood the radical potential of digital technology for music delivery and consumption. Converting a master recording into a digital file, stored on a hard drive, could completely change how the world listened to music. The arrival of digital music would not entail another upgrade to a new medium—as from cylinder to disc or disc to tape or tape to tape cartridge—but would mean a quick stab of punctuated equilibrium into the evolution of audio technology, closing the book on music devices altogether.

But what about "Perfect Sound Forever"!? How could the CD ever be topped? I recall, from my perspective as a young and broke consumer in the late nineties, that the CD seemed like an end-of-history medium at the time. Not that fifteen-year-old me would have put it that way. It just felt like I'd be listening to music on these discs the rest of my life, such was their quality compared to LP or tape. To be sure, we all recognized the shortcomings. The CD sounded better than anything that came before it, but durability and portability were the twin costs paid by its high-fidelity digital data. The CD jewel case was larger than the cassette in its case, so you couldn't keep as many of them in your glove compartment or center console. More importantly, however, the CD was far less resilient than the cassette. The CD returned us all to the "don't scratch it!" fussiness that had typified the LP decades. It was also more susceptible to skips and pauses when played on a portable device, such as a car stereo or a Discman. Anyone who grew up listening to cassettes on a Walkman before transitioning to a Discman will recollect the frustrations. The Walkman happily jostled in your pocket. You could turn it upside down, left or right without interrupting the tape head's mechanical certitude. But the Discman needed to lay prone and undisturbed to operate without interruption. You couldn't go for a jog with the earliest versions of the Discman.[9]

Despite all that—despite the fussiness—I and millions of other Americans believed, in the moment, that the CD's Perfect Sound quality would outweigh the medium's downsides. Sony never figured out how to stabilize the Discman, but car stereos got better at steadying the disc against pothole-induced skips and pauses. Maybe they'd come out with a scratch-resistant disc someday. The possibilities for development seemed endless. Like the flush music publishers, I assumed that, here, at the end of the millennium, after a parade of wax cylinders, LPs, 8-tracks, and cassettes, music had finally achieved its ideal form.

However, neither I nor the music industry were in tune with history. As perfect as music sounded on a CD, the cassette and the VHS had already taught the media companies that portability, durability, and longer play-times were what Americans wanted on their music (and video) media. A digital format that could maximize all three ends at once would in short order become the new Schelling point, even if the format sacrificed a degree of audio quality in the process. The cassette's magnetic tape, after all, wasn't as warm as a lacquer disc. The consumer-vibe shift moved in its direction anyway. Ripping music from a CD onto a hard drive would likewise lower the music's quality; however, media companies like Sony were confident that a truly digital music format (Perfect Portability Forever) could be made *good enough* that consumers would not care about a slight reduction in sound quality.

Decades of psychoacoustic research supported their confidence. Philips's MP2 and its rival, the MP3, were both developed on the back of psychoacoustic research into the human ear's capacity to apprehend sound. The gist of the research is that the human ear is an imperfect medium for capturing sound. The auditory world it allows the brain to perceive is something of a fiction. The ear evolved to identify human speech and predator sounds but is otherwise lousy at catching the fine nuances of pitch and timbre that audiophiles claim to hear. (The philosopher Thomas Nagel once made a similar claim about the whole human sensorium, comparing our five senses with the bat's apprehension of things via sonar sense.) Promising "Perfect Sound Forever," the compact disc was impressed with herculean amounts of audio data—much of which, researchers realized, was as inaudible to the human ear as a high-pitched dog whistle. The point of the MP2 and MP3 was to deliver compression formats that reduced the size of digital audio files "to between 1/10th and 1/12th of its original size without a recognizable loss of sound quality, which is accomplished by simply removing the frequencies that ordinary people cannot hear anyway."[10] And in the early nineties, the point of this compression was to make digital audio more suitable for transference across the globe's nascent digital media infrastructure, including but not limited to the internet. The music industry was completely unprepared to control, much less profit from, compressed audio formats at the time, such was their confidence in CD supremacy.

Because no human ear could hear, much less appreciate, the high-fidelity precision encoded on the compact disc, German pioneers of digital music predicted early on that the CD's delicacy was pointless and ultimately detrimental to its survival. Upon the CD's initial US release in 1983, electronics engineer Dieter Seitzer called it a form of technological "overkill," a "maximalist repository of irrelevant information, most of which was ignored by the human ear" because the ear had not evolved to perceive all those minuscule modulations of duration, pitch, intensity, timbre, and so on.[11] All the psychoacoustic research backing Seitzer's point is not easy reading. It involves, for example, the upper limits upon which neurons can phase-lock their action potential, neuronal signals containing delayed copies of themselves, and so on and so forth. The whole business reminds me of questions regarding child language acquisition or the comparison of bird song and human language. The interface between scientific research and philosophical or theological speculation grows thin at the margins.

More practically, psychoacoustic research was an extension of telephony research from the early twentieth century that attempted to answer such basic questions as, "What was the minimum amount of signal that could be sent down the line and still be intelligible as speech? What parts of the audible spectrum were important to hear for intelligibility and which were not? How did the listener's ear react to different sonic conditions?"[12] According to German scientists like Seitzer and his student Karlheinz Brandenburg, a key takeaway from telephony and psychoacoustic research, as it related to digital music and audio, was that compressing the CD's voluminous data into a more compact form would not only retain digital music's crispness for the human ear but also perfect the CD's portability to a degree unimaginable prior to the analog-to-digital revolution. Audio compression would allow a song or a whole opera to be made instantly available with nothing more than a "simple movement of the hand," as Paul Valéry had predicted in 1928.

Seitzer himself applied for a "digital jukebox" patent in 1982: the idea being to distribute music from a centralized server to keyboard-enabled requests, delivered through the new digital phonelines that Germany had begun to install in the early eighties. "Rather than pressing millions of discs into jewel cases," Stephen Witt explains, "everything would be saved in a single electronic database and accessed as needed. A subscription-based service of this kind could skip the manifold inefficiencies of physical distribution by hooking the stereo directly to the phone."[13] Good idea! However, Seitzer was a couple decades too early. His patent never went anywhere, circa 1982, because few consumers owned digital phone lines at the time (dial-up internet connectivity, in other words). And even if they did, sending music through a phone line required a degree of audio compression that was theoretically possible but not technically feasible due to the limitations of consumer devices.

In those years prior to the development and popular uptake of America's digital infrastructure, the music industry apparently had no interest in audio compression formats, much less in a digital jukebox (i.e., a streaming subscription model). Throughout the 1990s, publishers and artists believed the cutting edge of music consumption would continue to be the compact disc, that "maximalist repository" of audio quality. And they seemed to be right. CD sales overtook cassette sales just as the cassette had overtaken LPs—a slow but steady vibe shift not unlike the phase transition that turns water into steam after a never-ending process of adding heat. Slowly, then all at once, tape players disappeared from car dashboards,[14] and cassettes disappeared from retail shelves, replaced by jewel cases and shiny digital discs.

Meanwhile, in the background, as consumers began to worry about something called the Y2K bug, nonmusical digital audio settled into its own future. During the compact disc's short reign as the premier music medium, without consumers noticing or caring, a digitally compressed audio format—the MP2—was indeed being standardized onto CD-ROMs, DVDs, and other digital sound sources.

In 1988, Jonathan Sterne explains, the International Organization for Standardization (IOS) had formed the Moving Picture Experts Group (MPEG) and charged it with standardizing a format for digital video and audio. As its name suggests, the group was initially composed of video-encoding experts. In the autumn of '88, however, MPEG established an audio subgroup, which issued a call for proposals for an audio compression algorithm. In response, the subgroup received fourteen compression algorithms, from major players such as Phillips, AT&T, and Fujitsu, as well as from Fraunhofer-Gesellschaft, a German research group.[15] Over the next three years, these encoding/decoding algorithms were compared, demonstrated, and further developed by the rival companies. In 1991, MPEG settled on three audio compression formats as the new "standards," which they called *layers*: MPEG-1 Audio Layer I (MP1), MPEG-1 Audio Layer II (MP2), and MPEG-1 Audio Layer III (MP3). MP1 and MP2 had been developed by Philips, in consultation with French and Austrian research groups, with the MP1 being a simplified version of the MP2. Both formats were simple, however, insofar as they required less time and power to compute than the competitors' encoding/decoding algorithms. The MP3 was developed at Fraunhofer-Gesellschaft. More computationally complex than Philips's MP1 or MP2, it had the saving benefit of sounding better.

Fraunhofer-Gesellschaft was (at the time) a comparatively small consortium dedicated to applied science research and development. The head of the division charged with developing a digital audio compression format was Karlheinz Brandenburg, student of Dieter Seitzer, the "digital jukebox" inventor who had declared the CD an "overkill" medium. Brandenburg and Seitzer were engineers, first and foremost. They were nerds, in other words, working for an organization defined by the same Germanic drive for engineered perfection that gave the world Mercedes-Benz and BMW. In a head-to-head format war—even one overseen by a standards group like MPEG—Fraunhofer-Gesellschaft was never going to win against a legacy media powerhouse like Philips, a conglomerate that understood politics, marketing, and the power of relationships (with MPEG, for example) in addition to engineering. That MPEG allowed Fraunhofer-Gesellschaft and Brandenburg's MP3 to slide into the standards at all is a minor miracle.

However, when it came time for media companies to pick a standard and ship a product, Philips's MP2 format emerged as the de facto standard, with MP1 offering a simplified backup format (it was used, for example, on the short-lived Digital Compact Cassette). After MPEG's standards announcement in

1991, Philips's MP2 made its debut on CD-ROM video games; throughout the decade, it found its way onto LaserDiscs and DVDs, HDTV programming, early audioconferencing software, and many other devices and media. The German engineers who had pioneered the superior MP3 format, including Karlheinz Brandenburg, watched their own digital compression format sit unused. The MP3 may have offered superior audio quality, but it also took more computer processing power, which not all devices or consumers had access to at the time. Eventually, Fraunhofer-Gesellschaft pulled funding from Brandenburg's audio division, and Brandenburg found himself going cap in hand to various trade shows, hoping to find customers to license his superior, if slightly more complex, compression format.

The story of how the MP3 went from unemployed underdog to music-freeing revolutionary is told to excellent effect in Witt's book. (Brandenburg's first breakthrough customer would be the NHL. The league appreciated that the MP3 format captured the sounds of the sport more crisply than the MP2—puck hits, ice scrapes, crowd noise, and so on—for their new digital broadcasts.) As format wars go, this one was never as public as the Betamax versus VHS battle or the comparatively bland scrap between Blu-ray and HD DVD, but its consequences would eventually net the Fraunhofer company hundreds of millions of dollars in licensing royalties.

The story's unexpected twist came in 1993, when an anonymous hacker—a Star Wars fan who went by the pirate name SoloH—got ahold of Brandenburg's compression algorithm. To demonstrate the adaptability of MP3 as a musical medium as well as a generalist audio format, Brandenburg and his division had developed an MP3 encoder, or, more colloquially, a program for ripping and burning CDs. It wasn't the most advanced MP3 encoder, just a demonstration program that could be shown to potential customers, such as the still-uninterested music publishing houses. The program sat on an unprotected computer at the University of Erlangen. SoloH hacked into the computer's file system and stole Brandenburg's MP3 encoder. Recognizing that the compression algorithm could be improved, SoloH released an updated version of the encoder onto his personal website, hosted in the Netherlands. Over the next several years, his "project," as he called it, saw the release of seven versions, each encoder improving the audio quality of the last. In Witt's words, SoloH was "patient zero" in the MP3 revolution. Every encoder downloaded from his website meant one more person who could rip digital audio from a compact disc onto a hard drive as an MP3 file—and from there onto a blank disc or, more commonly, onto the internet, where it could be shared with anyone in the world.

Fraunhofer threatened to sue SoloH. The hacker eventually pulled his MP3 encoder from his personal site, but the damage had been done. Other hackers picked up the slack. An Australian hacker released an early encoder named 13enc,[16] Tord Larson improved encoding speed with bladeEnc, Winamp received over three million downloads in 1997, and, as Hendrik Storstein Spilker and Svein Hoier recap the history, many other engineers and hackers contributed their own codecs "with further refinements, working on the features they found most important," either sound quality or user interface design.[17] Fraunhofer released its own proprietary program in 1995, WinPlay3, but you couldn't beat freeware when it came to price. And even WinPlay3 found itself "redistributed among Internet users in modified or hacked versions."[18] Released into the wild, the MP3 format's rise took hardly any time at all, compared to the decade-long emergence of cassette and then compact disc. By the late nineties, millions of young consumers had bought a proprietary burning/ripping program (I have no idea if the one I bought was officially licensed to use Fraunhofer's technology) or downloaded a freeware encoder, making *MP3* an acronym for digital music.

The social success of that file extension is a remarkable feat. Everyone knew what an MP3 was even if no one knew what it stood for or where it came from. Awash in digital acronyms—MPEG, DIVX, WAV, WMA, M4A, A2B, AAC—the only format that kids ever put an article in front of was *the* MP3. In September 1998, news outlets humorously reported that *MP3* had surpassed *sex* as the most searched term on the internet.[19] The MP3— hacked out of a computer lab in Germany and gifted to the world—became so dominant that even Apple was forced to provide MP3 capabilities for iTunes and iPod, despite AAC being its preferred format. As the new millennium got on its way, any device or program with pretenses as a music medium needed to stamp itself with "MP3."

MIX CD: THE MIXTAPE'S LAST STAND

Although prerecorded music had shed its skin, tactile media still played a role in American music cultures in the late nineties and the aughts. On either side of 9/11, waning but not dead, the CD encouraged consumers to keep sharing music via tactile media. After all, circa 2000, the MP3's Perfect Portability Forever remained a theoretical construct. For college kids sharing MP3s on Napster or Kazaa, the format was a medium in the strictest sense: an intermediary, a means of *transference*, not a final form. It allowed consumers, via their computer hard drives, to transmit a song from disc to blank disc or, after 2001, from disc to MP3 player. Deep into the first decade of the twenty-first century, as I recall, both CD albums and CD-Rs with handwriting on them were common sights at parties, in glove boxes, and on bedroom shelves, even though an MP3 player had made its way into at least every third person's pocket by 2007—the year iPod sales peaked at $50 million annually.[20] So, despite the radical new technology of compressed digital audio, young adults continued to fashion mixes on blank CDs with songs ripped from other CDs, downloaded from peer-to-peer (P2P) networks, or grudgingly purchased from iTunes. Without a doubt, people listened to MP3s on desktop computers and laptops as well—via headphones in the library or at work; sans headphones when we had our rooms to ourselves. But we made MP3s "real" by transferring them onto a durable medium. We had no choice. iPods were always expensive, and hard drives remained clunky things, no more portable than an old turntable. Music awaited the invention of a pocket-sized computer to detach itself well and truly from all dedicated music media.

The iPod, other MP3 players, and integrated music/video/camera contraptions like Kodak's MC3 were all protosmartphones. And the iPod's thousand-song playlist, playable for ten-hour stretches, offered a trial run for the streaming music app. In earlier chapters, I emphasized the MP3 player as a physical, dedicated music medium, and it was that. But the mixtape's last stand relied on the compact disc, not the iPod. I described in chapter 3 the DIY similarities between creating a mixtape and creating a mix CD. As a medium that kept mixtape-making alive into the early 2000s, the CD had another important feature: unlike the MP3 player, it was the last dedicated audio medium manufactured separately from its playback device.

From the time of Edison until the development of compressed digital audio—over a century of audio improvements—prerecorded audio had relied on an inscribed surface and a device to play back the inscription. Wax cylinder and phonograph, lacquer disc and turntable, magnetic tape and tape head, compact disc and CD player. The existence of an item imprinted with the coveted audio, distinct from its playback device, was the baseline reality of mechanical sound reproduction for the entire twentieth century. It set the precondition for the invention of the "album."

As with wax cylinder, LP disc, tape reel, and tape cartridge, the CD took up space separate from its player. It was an object added to life's surroundings, granted a right of prominent display, or tossed straight into a car's center console. The CD's music was materially stored, could be physically shared, and had been literally *cut*. Millennials and Generation X will recall their ability to spot a blank CD by squinting for those minuscular grooves that appeared on a disc's reflective surface when it had been etched with audio. Even though the CD's digital inscription contained the means of its own obsolescence, music on a CD remained a material engraving on a durable medium, played back on a separate device. The CD preserved the traditional media architecture. No one felt a radical shift, as I have said, when they started burning songs onto digital discs instead of dubbing them onto magnetic tapes. The sound quality improved, and that was a good thing. The runtime exceeded that of the cheaper cassettes, and that was a good thing too. However, the limitless ubiquity of digital media was not anticipated by the compact disc. Like the LP and the cassette, the CD had a runtime limit, beyond which sound quality would be compromised to an unacceptable degree. In the seventies, artists wanting to record lengthy concept albums had to release double records; in the nineties, artists wanting to do the same had to release double discs. *Mellon Collie and the Infinite Sadness* (the Smashing Pumpkins), *Tusk* (Fleetwood Mac), *He's the DJ, I'm the Rapper* (DJ Jazzy Jeff & the Fresh Prince), and *All Eyez on Me* (Tupac Shakur) are good examples of albums that neither the LP nor the CD could handle on a single unit. The compact disc still obeyed the rules and limitations of flesh-space.

And this is why I must stab the MP3 player in the back. I've described it as a "dedicated music medium," but it made a sharp pivot away from physical media and toward the disembodiment of streaming music. It was the first consumer music device to break free from the rules and limitations of material space and tactile media. Late nineties MP3 players—such as the Rio PMP300—held just thirty minutes of music, but Apple mastered the digital magic in short order, releasing the first-generation iPod in 2001: "1,000 songs in your pocket."

In the history of audio technology, the MP3 player can be described, like many inventions from the millennial turning, as a placeholder device: a pocket-sized computer before pocket-sized computers.[21] There was never any such thing as a mix MP3 player because MP3 players represented nothing less than a lifelong music collection, and no one could meaningfully share such unfiltered abundance. Cost played a part. Even the cheapest MP3 players at the time bottomed out at $200 or more. First-generation iPods cost $399. I suppose some rich consumers gifted an iPod with favorite artists preloaded onto it, but such an extravagance could never catch on as a general trend. Also released in 2001, Apple iTunes allowed users to create playlists ("create" being a generous verb, since it entailed nothing more than dragging file icons into the iTunes window). But Apple never made it easy, in the early days, to share or "sync" iPods together—they synced to specific *devices* logged into an iTunes account. In 2001, playlist sharing was still easier to do via blank CD. Plus, the cost issue again: not many teens or young adults owned a portable MP3 player in the first years of the twenty-first century. They were much more expensive than a Discman and not much cheaper than a nice car stereo system. Personally, I did not own an MP3 player until 2008. I continued to rely on mix CDs to customize my life soundtrack, as did many consumers during the first years of the twenty-first century. Apple sold only eight million iPods in 2004.[22] In 2008, it sold over fifty million iPods, a sales peak likely aided by the release of the cheaper iPod Shuffle. This peak, however, overlapped with the rise of the smartphone market.[23] Ultimately, MP3 players were rendered obsolete before they had a chance to become a universal Schelling point for music consumption.[24] It never made much sense to spend a few hundred dollars on a music-only device instead of $499 (the cost of the first-generation iPhone) on a pocket computer that could play music in addition to doing a thousand other things.

A materially inscribed object, the compact disc sustained mixtape culture not just beyond the cassette era but beyond the release of the MP3, the Y2K millennial turn, and even Apple's release of iPod and iTunes. As I mentioned a few paragraphs ago, I don't recall CDs, CD players, or the Discman disappearing entirely from the American landscape until 2010 or thereabouts. Of those mix CDs and fully burned CD albums still in my possession, I made or was given most of them after college: 2008 or 2009. Thanks to the CD—and thanks to the recurring fact that any new audio medium takes about a decade to become America's latest musical Schelling point—mixtape-making lasted almost a full decade into the digital millennium. Consider again the CD album sales data, this time paired with smartphone and iPhone sales data.[25] The Recording Industry Association of America (RIAA) reports that nearly a billion CD albums shipped in 2000. In 2005, that figure had dropped to 700 million shipments. By 2010, however, the CD had lost its status as a consumer Schelling point, and a meager 250 million CD albums shipped that year. In 2009, global smartphone sales remained under 200 million units sold annually. That figure rose to nearly 300 million units in 2010, then to nearly 500 million units in 2011, and to nearly 700 million units in 2012.[26] The iPhone likewise began its ascent in earnest in 2010: $5.5 million in sales in the first quarter of that year spiked to $23 million in the first quarter of 2012.[27]

That millennial overlap—between digital music's climb and the compact disc's slow but steady fall, roughly from the late nineties until 2010—saw mix CDs live long enough to be etched with a prototype of social media music: songs downloaded from Napster, Kazaa, LimeWire, Gnutella, and other P2P networks. Despite the compact disc's lingering relevance in the first decade of the 2000s, the socially shared MP3 did indeed give young listeners their first taste of the "everything everywhere all at once" effect that would, by 2010, begin to short-circuit America's entire cultural complex.

THE LAST DAYS OF PIRACY

About seven years before the release of Apple's pocket-sized computer, MP3 file sharing networks had already fulfilled Paul Valéry's prophecy of digital ubiquity—all music made available with a "simple movement of the hand." At the turn of the millennium, a Borgesian library of musical content, from

Abba to Zeppelin, had suddenly materialized on young adults' desktops and laptops. I vividly recall making my first mix CD with music downloaded from Napster. Most of the CD contained songs ripped from my personal disc collection, but I wanted Eric Clapton on it too, because its recipient and I had recently attended a Clapton concert. I owned Clapton albums on cassette, but I was not savvy enough to know how to transfer songs from magnetic tape onto the hard drive. So, I typed "napaster.com" into the desktop browser, downloaded the peer-to-peer program, and searched for "Wonderful Tonight," "Tears in Heaven," and of course "Layla." There they were—MP3 files sitting on someone else's hard drive. I double-clicked each one in rapid succession.

For those too young to remember or too old to have never tried it, Napster and other peer-to-peer networks, such as LimeWire or Kazaa, did not provide access to songs stored on their own servers. What they did was provide a Schelling point for individual users who wanted to exchange MP3 files among themselves, from one user's hard drive to the next. Peer-to-peer networks were nothing new; the protointernet is fairly described as an extended P2P network. However, Napster was the first P2P network (1) devoted to music sharing, and (2) developed with a graphical user interface (GUI) that made it easy to search for music available across the network. A user searched for a song by title or artist, and the results provided an indexed list of other users on the network from whom the song could be downloaded. The Napster GUI served as an easily navigated portal between users' music collections. The GUI also offered information about users' internet connections and "ping" measurements, a test of the roundtrip communication time between hard drives. This information made it easier to know which MP3 file would transfer more quickly than the others. *Quickly* is of course a relative term. In the halcyon days of dial-up internet, a five-minute song took anywhere from five to sixty minutes to download. The day I downloaded the Clapton songs, it took well over an hour. I busied myself with chatroom gossip while they downloaded, not realizing that messing around online slowed the download speed (*kilo*bytes per second!) even more, but I needed the songs, so the wait was worth it. ("Tears from Heaven" did not make it onto the CD; I realized just in time that it was not an appropriate song for a girlfriend's mix CD.)

Napster went live in June 1999. Swift as an arrow, the RIAA, with A&M Records as the lead plaintiff, sued Napster in December 1999. P2P networks had gone live not long after SoloH released the hacked Fraunhofer encoder in 1993. However, early P2P networks did not promote themselves, did not offer user-friendly GUIs, and in general did not attract attention. Once networks started doing all three of those things, the RIAA took notice. The RIAA had also taken notice of MP3 players. In 1998, it sued Diamond

Multimedia, maker of the early MP3 player mentioned in the previous section, the Rio PMP300. In a decision that safeguarded all digital music to come, the judge in that case ruled that the noncommercial copying of music from hard drive to digital audio player constituted fair use, under the novel legal doctrine of space-shifting, or the ability to access legally purchased content via multiple devices.[28]

Knowing that the Diamond Multimedia lawsuit would be a longshot—the Audio Home Recording Act of 1992 had already made copying for private, noncommercial use perfectly legal—the RIAA's first collective legal action against P2P networks occurred in 1997: Fresh Kutz and Parsoft were the P2P networks targeted and taken down in that early legal action.[29] In 1999, Napster likewise made its web presence known, and for whatever network-effect reasons, its popularity soared compared to all previous music sharing networks. By March 2000, it had clocked over twenty-five million unique global users and fifteen million American users—nearly all of them high school and college students. Napster became so popular on college campuses in 2000 that its users overloaded university networks, forcing administrators to block access to the service. "A recent survey of 50 universities found that a third had banned their students from using [Napster]," reported a *BBC* article at the time.[30] Luckily, I still lived with my parents, so I had free rein to keep the computer on all night, downloading thirty songs at a time (which did indeed take all night—sorry, Mom and Dad).

It was a hell of a time to be a young music fan, the late nineties and early aughts: downloading songs, ripping songs, burning songs, making compilation CDs for the car or for lovers or for friends, and not paying for anything but the blank CDs, which were cheap. While media companies and software developers profited, the music industry had no idea what to do with the new reality. (Ditto the film studios and other content industries.) The early aughts correspond to a preciously short period when established content producers had no idea how to make money on the internet. Music freed itself from physical media, but both artists and the RIAA had failed to prepare for the moment. Charles C. Mann, in his article "The Heavenly Jukebox," sums up their fears circa 2000: "Technophiles claim that the major labels, profitable concerns today, will rapidly cease to exist, because the Internet makes copying and distributing recorded music so fast, cheap, and easy that charging for it will effectively become impossible. Adding to the labels' fears, a horde of dot-coms, rising from the bogs of San Francisco like so many stinging insects, is trying to hasten their demise."[31] Caught unaware, and not sure how to make online payments "effective," the music industry and established musicians lashed out. Alongside the RIAA, the band Metallica famously sued Napster. At one point, drummer Lars Ulrich showed up to Napster headquarters (a tiny office located above a bank in

San Mateo, California) with boxes of printouts showing users who had, in a single weekend, downloaded or uploaded Metallica songs on the network. A group of former Metallica fans showed up too, taking a sledgehammer to their Metallica CDs while shouting, "Fuck you, Lars, it's our music too!"

Napster lost both lawsuits. It filed for bankruptcy in 2002. However, other P2P networks—such as LimeWire and Kazaa—waited in the wings. If anything, pirated music became more common after Napster's downfall. I pointed out in chapter 3 that kids dubbing mixtapes in the eighties never thought of themselves as music pirates, but this time around, with the Napster case so public and fraught, teens and young adults were very aware of what it meant to download MP3s online. It was a common activity, to be sure; all over again, we did what the technology allowed us to do. But we knew—our parents and newspapers reminded us—that it was technically "illegal."

Still, we downloaded. After all, if individuals were guilty of copyright violations, so, too, were software companies that sold CD-ripping programs at Best Buy, MP3 player manufacturers like Apple, and of course media companies like Philips, Sony, and Fraunhofer who had developed digital compression formats in the first place. Despite my parents' warnings about downloading music, I recall a sense of general impunity in the air. "Litigation is almost always more expensive than the actual award," media historian Josh Sheppard says. "The threat is central to the process."[32] I don't think many teens were aware enough to put it so clearly, but the sense of impunity did flow from the feeling that, if it was just personal use—if we weren't downloading gigabytes of songs, burning them onto CDs, and selling them on streetcorners—the threat (which we knew was real) would never hit us personally. Corporations gave us the equipment, after all, so why should we be liable for using it? At first, it seemed like the RIAA agreed with us. Napster fell in 2001. The P2P networks Aimster and Grokster fell in 2002 and 2003, respectively. The Grokster case—brought by movie studios, not music labels—made it all the way to the Supreme Court in 2004. The question was whether technology producers could be held liable for intent to induce copyright infringement. Lower courts had ruled in Grokster's favor. The Supreme Court disagreed, finding in favor of the movie studios in a unanimous decision penned by Justice David Souter. The court held that companies who distributed and promoted software enabling copyright infringement could indeed be held responsible for "secondary liability." Grokster was used so widely to infringe copyrights that it seemed to have been the sole purpose for its development and distribution. Also, the court held it would be immensely difficult for copyright holders (namely, the studios) to deal with each individual infringer. The "only practical alternative," the court concluded, was to sue the software provider.[33] I vaguely recall the news reports about the ruling—mere background noise to a twenty-one-year-old—but insofar as it registered, my personal takeaway was that, contrary to my parents' warnings, if anyone was going down over MP3 sharing, it would continue to be the software companies, not individual users. LimeWire's lawsuits began in 2006, as did Gnutella's. The Pirate Bay headquarters were also famously raided in 2006.

My parents, however, turned out to be correct. In the same year as the Gnutella lawsuit, the LimeWire lawsuit, and the Pirate Bay raid—2006—the RIAA did the unthinkable: it sued an individual. A short time later, in 2007, Apple would release the first iPhone. In retrospect, the timing of the events seems curious—as though the music and media industries had simultaneously, and in concert, announced the closing of the digital frontier. The law had caught up. Content now needed to be accessed in the approved way, via smartphone and subscription.

One of the individuals sued for sharing music in that strange year was Jammie Thomas, a young mother of four from Minnesota. Although she had used Kazaa to download over a thousand songs (who among us had not done the same?), Capitol Records, leading the suit, held her liable sharing only for twenty-four, presumably the songs with the greatest monetary damages attached to them, including Aerosmith's "Cryin," Gloria Estefan's "Rhythm Is Gonna Get You," Guns N' Roses' "November Rain," No Doubt's "Hella Good," Reba McEntire's "One Honest Heart," and, with a bit of cosmic irony, Destiny's Child's "Bills, Bills, Bills."[34] The statutory relief sought by the record companies ranged from $5,000 in a pretrial settlement offer to $1.9 million in a June 2009 trial (which the record companies won). Thomas's response to the whole ordeal typified the response by most individuals caught in RIAA lawsuits in the middle and late aughts: a complete refusal to cooperate or settle with the RIAA, followed by bankruptcy proceedings. Thomas, by then Thomas-Rasset, declared bankruptcy in 2013, refusing the RIAA's final offer of a lower settlement in exchange for her making a video about the evils of copyright infringement.[35]

The next domino to fall was the case of *Sony BMG v. Tenenbaum*. In 2003, when he was twenty, Joel Tenenbaum had already been given a cease-and-desist letter, along with an offer of paying $3,500 to avoid a lawsuit. Tenenbaum never paid up, and the lawsuit finally arrived in 2007. (Again, it's curious that the RIAA timed all its lawsuits so closely to the release of the Apple iPhone.) This lawsuit focused on thirty-one songs, including Limp Bizkit's "Leech," Red Hot Chili Peppers' "Californication," and the Smashing Pumpkins' "Bullet with Butterfly Wings" (Tenenbaum was more of an alt-rock fan than Thomas).[36] Like Thomas's case, the Tenenbaum lawsuit devolved into what one judge called "retrial hell." Settlements were offered, Tenenbaum refused, court resumed, eventually another settlement was offered, but higher this time, due to ensuing legal fees incurred by the RIAA. Tenenbaum went through various pro bono lawyers but never retained them.

In a June 2008 hearing, a judge involved in the case, Nancy Gertner, admonished the RIAA for creating such a legal mess. She didn't have kind words for Tenenbaum either (he had ignored cease-and-desist letters, after all), but by 2008, Tenenbaum was just one of many, many young consumers targeted by the content industries. A trend had emerged. "They bring cases against individuals," Gertner said, "individuals who don't have lawyers and don't have access to lawyers and who don't understand their legal rights." Some individuals recognize the threat and go to great lengths to cough up the initial settlement price. Too many individuals, however, are blindsided and not savvy enough to understand the dangers of going to court—the RIAA's legal fees rise, so do the statutory damages, and so do the settlement offers. If these individuals balked at $3,500, they would of course balk at $35,000, thereby launching the cycle of never-ending statutory judgments, never-ending appeals, and never-ending retrials. Gertner summed it all up: "Counsel representing the record companies have an ethical obligation to fully understand that they are fighting people without lawyers, to fully understand . . . that the formalities of this are basically bankrupting people, and it's terribly critical that you stop it."[37] Too late for Joel Tenenbaum, though. He was ultimately ordered to pay $675,000 for copyright infringements. He declared bankruptcy in 2015.

The Electronic Frontier Foundation estimates that, in 2006, the RIAA began litigation against twenty thousand music fans who had shared files on Kazaa, Gnutella, and other P2P networks.[38]

Lashing out, however, was simply the content industry's first step toward regaining control. In hindsight, it's all so obvious that the anarchic, techno-optimistic ethos of the "free internet," popularized by glossy cyberpunk magazine *Mondo 2000* and epitomized by P2P sharing networks, would never be allowed to last. Did we really think the record companies and movie studios and publishing houses would let us have fun like that forever? Did we really think established artists like Metallica would stand by and watch their album profits drop, forcing them to return to the bad old days of radio and LP, when bands had to constantly *go on tour* to get rich? Way back in 1987, the RIAA had already announced its preferred tactic against this whole digital-file business, intimidating Sony with lawsuits if it released the world's first digital audio format, the Digital Audio Tape.

The Wild West of the late nineteenth century was a blip on the historical timeline—just a decade or two between the outlaws, the fur traders, the homesteaders, and gamblers and the arrival of jails, lawyers, railroads, and telegraphs. The early aughts of the twenty-first century were likewise a brief

Wild West of content piracy, a time when software companies sold CD-ripping programs on retail shelves just a few aisles away from the officially released albums whose liner notes contained FBI-stamped injunctions against burning and ripping. While software producers and of course media manufacturers profited from the widespread adoption of the MP3, music labels and established artists understood that the digital file's escape from CD confinement threatened to turn the entire music industry into—what? No one knew. Postmillennial youth may not believe it, but in this historical blip—the early and middle aughts, essentially—music labels and all established content producers saw the internet as a threat to neutralize rather than as a new medium to exploit. A mix CD of songs downloaded from Napster or Kazaa might end up as evidence in the discovery process at trial.

The content industries needed some sort of integration with the media and software industries. The uneasy alliance between media manufacturers and content producers goes back to the earliest days of mechanically reproduced sound. Arthur Sullivan hated sheet music printers. Most composers hated piano-roll makers and restaurant jukebox vendors, who didn't pay royalties. In the 1980s, Polygram and Elektra refused to share ad space with Maxell and other manufacturers of blank cassettes: "The Record Industry Goes to War on Home Taping," as the headline read.[39] In the 1990s, the RIAA attempted to legally block the release of digital music formats in America until Congress stepped in to provide financial cover with the Audio Home Recording Act of 1992. The RIAA's attempt to block Diamond Multimedia's early MP3 players was not an intuitive reaction so much as a standard operating procedure.

When would it all end? Could the new millennium and digital ubiquity finally provide the grounds for a lasting truce, aligning the incentives of media and content once and for all? In 2006—that year again—Hilary Rosen, former CEO of the RIAA, made one of the earliest official comments about this need for incentive alignment between media and content in her response to criticism about the RIAA's slew of individual lawsuits: "For the record, I do share a concern that the lawsuits have outlived most of their usefulness and that the record companies need to work harder to implement a strategy that legitimizes more p2p sites and expands the download and subscription pool by working harder with the tech community to get devices and music services to work better together. That is how their business will expand most quickly."[40] The historical division of labor between content producers (artists and publishers) and media manufacturers (Sony, Philips, Apple) created opposing corporate strategies that at different times harmed the former, which ultimately threatened the latter. Media companies had dabbled in forming their own content production divisions—Sony and Philips both controlled their own labels, just as Apple would one day own a movie studio—but such ventures tended to escalate rather than ease the traditional tensions between the content creators and the media manufacturers, especially in the uncertain years following the MP3's accidental release.

The timeline of that corporate interplay goes beyond the scope of this book, but if Napster is a metonym for the musical Wild West of the year 2000, the metonym for today's tightly controlled mediascape would be an Apple Music account or a Samsung TV preloaded with streaming content. The integration of music and all entertainment into a single-screen access point—the smartphone—turned out to be the winning strategy for both media and content industries. Dieter Seitzer had been right all along. Consumers valued portability and convenient access over quality and tactility. His 1982 "digital jukebox" idea—songs sent to a device from a central server via keyed requests—was about to become a reality.

THE LAST LIVING MIXTAPE

As established music labels combined forces with legacy media companies to regain control of and make money from the internet, the first order of business, as we saw, was to destroy the peer-to-peer networks. The next order of business was to make examples of tens of thousands of individual users, creating a global chilling effect. The third order of business, as Hilary Rosen laid out, was to align those old divisions between media manufacturers and content creators and publishers. Such conglomeration was not entirely new—as I glossed above, Philips, inventor of the Compact Cassette, had released classical music recordings since 1950 under the label Philips Phonographische Industrie, and Sony had incorporated its own music label in 1968. But these ventures were typically perceived as a media company flex rather than a move toward content integration in general. To make money off the internet, everyone needed to give up that old multipolar media landscape and, if not join forces, at least agree to new conventions of engagement.

For music, it didn't take long for the strategy to reveal itself and pay dividends in the form of the streaming subscription model, enabled entirely by the rise of the smartphone. Because I've veered far enough away from mixtapes at this point, annual sales since the iPhone's release in 2007 will need to stand in for any sort of smartphone history. It experienced a relatively quick takeoff compared to the decades-long emergence of the cassette and compact disc. From 2007 to 2008, it went from one million to ten million units shipped and grew quickly from there.[41] I leave it as a rhetorical exercise for the reader to compare the "units shipped" chart with statistics on music media sales since 2007.[42] I can sum up the data as follows:

In 2004, digital song or album downloads accounted for only 14.3% of total music unit sales; the CD, 80.4% of total unit sales; and the cassette, 0.5% of total sales (unsurprisingly, 2004 was the last year cassettes made it into the accounting at all). The 2006 lawsuits worked their magic, however, and by 2007, people were paying for digital music. The stats reversed: CD sales in that year accounted for only 27% of total unit sales, while digital units had jumped to 71.2% of sales volume. Now, to be clear, in 2007, these digital "sales" were paid downloads for songs or albums. That 71.2% of total sales volume equaled over 1.3 billion individual song or album downloads. Over the next few years, those numbers—total units and percent of total units—would continue to grow in favor of digital downloads, which, in the next chapter, I will graciously count as a sort of lingering, digital version of "owned" music media. The CD's market share—in both total units and percent of total units—continued its decline, dipping below 10% of total unit sales in 2014 (138.7 million units sold).

But starting in 2010–2012, a curious thing began to happen. As smartphone sales swelled, the percentages of tactile media versus digital downloads remained the same; however, the *total number* of units began to shrink dramatically as streaming music (paid subscription or ad-driven) began to rise. In 2022, digital downloads still comprised about 70% of total market share, and CDs had even inched a bit higher to 11.8% of total sales. However, by 2022, percent of market share had become a completely worthless statistic: that 70% for digital downloads translated to 200 million individual song or album downloads—contrasted, above, with 1.3 *billion* song or album downloads in 2007. The same can be said for the CD. It's 11% share in 2022 translated to a mere 33.4 million units sold, contrasted with 2014's 138.7 million units. In 2022, in fact, counting every and any music-only format, only 282.4 million units sold (including, to reiterate, digital downloads). In 1973—when the RIAA began tracking format distinctions—over 600 million individual units were sold, in any format.

TL;DR: Even if we generously count digital downloads as "tactile media," fewer tactile media—in raw totals—were sold in 2022 than at any other point since the RIAA began keeping detailed records. Almost three times as many tactile media units were sold to the American public in 1973 than in 2022. Streaming music had ascended.

Standing somewhere within that time span is 2006–2007: the year of the smartphone; the year of the Kazaa lawsuit; the bellwether year for corporate control of digital music; the death knell for tactile media. It is thus fitting and, by now, unexpected, that when I went looking for the last trace of mixtape influence—the last beat of its material heart—I discovered a spiritless listicle in *Elle Girl* from 2006. As far as I can tell, it is the last nonnostalgic, nonmetaphorical, nonironic, completely literal reference to a "mixtape" in the Google Books corpus. It occurred in what *Elle Girl* called "Last Guy Standing":

> Check out our latest scheme to track down the coolest guy in the U.S. Hey, it's a man pageant.
>
> ... Welcome to the fifth episode of Elle Girl's yearlong dude contest. Each issue, our contestants perform a revealing task, and you vote for your favorite at ellegirl.com/lastguy. This month, we asked the boys to create a hypothetical mixtape for the girl of their dreams (plus throw in one song they're embarrassed to like).... Now, see who shares your musical tastes. Then vote!⁴³

This mixtape "challenge" is completely unassuming, proposed without a hint of techno-nostalgia, media irony, or metaphorical baggage. The boys each offer a list of four or five songs, including a short description of why each song would make it onto their romantic mixtape:

> **Dylan Reider, 17, Westminster CA**: Syd Barrett "Two of a Kind": "This song is about two people who are meant to be together." Devo "Beautiful World": "I don't like all my mixtapes to a girl to be super-sappy." ...
>
> **Josh Romero, 23, Tucson, AZ**: OK Go "You're So Damn Hot": "This song is a great way to start the mix, and the compliment doesn't hurt."⁴⁴

And so on. This *Elle Girl* challenge is the exact opposite of titles like *Love Is a Mix Tape*. It is a literal request for a custom song compilation. Note that everyone was making compilations on CDs by 2006, but *mixtape* is still the go-to term for the staff writers.

I know, it's not an actual tape, just half a dozen imaginary mixes, each designed to portray the personality of its maker (which the egotistical mixtape had always done). But when it comes to mass media and shared culture, *Elle Girl*'s "Last Guy Standing" challenge seems to be the last living example of mixtape culture in the wild. Born sometime in the 1940s on lacquer disc; developed on reel-to-reel tape in the 1950s and 1960s by home-audio enthusiasts, pirates, and DJs; consummated on cassette as a pop-culture phenomenon in the 1980s; given a name sometime in the 1990s; and miraculously sustained on compact discs through the first decade of digital music, the ritual of mechanically dubbing songs from multiple albums onto a blank medium—to create a custom playlist for a friend, a family member, or a crush at recess—finally limped onto the pages of *Elle Girl* in July 2006 as a hypothetical object made by half a dozen cute boys in a man pageant.

Scattered mix CDs would continue to be made and even shared for a few years yet—charming vestiges by 2010—but as far as American youth culture is concerned, this 2006 *Elle Girl* issue bore witness to the death rattle of the mixtape.

RIP, old friend.

NOSTALGIC CYCLE 3.0

"*The Wedding Singer* takes place in 1985 and came out in 1998. Imagine a blockbuster nostalgia movie released now set in 2010" (@dante_eats, Twitter/X, November 2, 2023). I come across a social media post like this at least once a day. The point can be made more extreme by pushing it back an additional decade. The early 2000s were twenty years ago, after all, so it should theoretically be possible in the 2020s to make a "period" film set in 2003—like *Almost Famous*, *The Last Days of Disco*, *Dazed and Confused*, and other 1990s films set in the 1970s. The vast cultural gap between Led Zeppelin and Nirvana, the Sugarhill Gang and Tupac, and bellbottom jeans and ripped saggy jeans is as quantifiably large as the gap between 2003 and 2023, but culturally—musically, cinematically, fashionably—the gap seems tiny in comparison.

A similar meme template is "X event is closer in time to Y event than to today"; for example, "Bob Seger's 'Old Time Rock and Roll' was released closer to the invasion of Poland than to the modern day." (Fact check? True.) Sure, these viral moments could just be middle-aged millennials—the first generation to come of age with social media—comparing psychological notes on the aging process. But let's use a pivotal event in millennial psychology—9/11—as a test case for this posited idea that the quantitative time gap and the qualitative cultural gap have somehow diverged. As I write this in September 2023, twenty-two years have passed since 9/11. Here is a list of events and media releases that occurred twenty-two years *before* 9/11, in 1979:

The Iranian Revolution—the shah was deposed, and student militants took hostages at the US Embassy.
Rhodesia became Zimbabwe.
The nuclear power plant at Three Mile Island, Pennsylvania, underwent a partial meltdown.
McDonald's introduced the Happy Meal (no toy yet).
Disco Demolition Night at Comiskey Park in Chicago—fans rushed the field, blew up a crate of disco records, then rioted. The rioting and explosion ruined the field, forcing the White Sox to forfeit the game to the Tigers.

On television, *This Old House* premiered in its first season on PBS, the Daytona 500 became the first full NASCAR race to be broadcasted, and the final episode of *All in the Family* was viewed by forty million people. On the sound waves, the Sugarhill Gang's "Rapper's Delight" became the first rap single to reach the Billboard Top 40, Barry Manilow won a Grammy for Best Male Pop Vocal Performance (for "Copacabana"), and the Year-End Hot 100 Singles included Rod Stewart's "Da Ya Think I'm Sexy?," the Village People's "Y.M.C.A.," and the Knack's "My Sharona."

It'll require different efforts of imaginative vision, depending on your birthday, but the question to ask is whether the cultural-historical gap between 1979 and 2001 feels the same as the gap between 2001 and 2023. To help kickstart the imagination, we can note that the alt-rock band the Smashing Pumpkins sang nostalgically about 1979 in their song "1979"—released in 1996. To my knowledge, no nostalgic odes to 2006 were released in 2023. For those too old or too young or too skeptical to participate in the experiment, however, it's easy to bring up news footage on YouTube of that day in September 2001. Watching those news clips, the world looks radically different than it did in 1979. Does the world of 9/11 look radically different from the world of 2023? Or have mass culture's cycles of cultural overturn slowed since then? I also recommend repeating this experiment with 2007, the year Apple released the first iPhone: a gap of sixteen years that takes us forward to now and backward to 1991—the year of Nirvana's *Nevermind*, Extreme's "More Than Words," Operation Desert Storm, and Clarence Thomas's confirmation on the Supreme Court. Equal in years, are the two timelines equal in cultural distance? Or is the distance between 1991 and 2007 somehow more *real* than the difference between 2007 and 2023?

7: THE INFINITE PLAYLIST

THE SMARTPHONE AND ITS CONSEQUENCES: A DISASTER FOR THE HUMAN RACE?

The smartphone's absorption of physical media, I wrote somewhere in the last chapter, is an example of punctuated equilibrium, the evolutionary idea that speciation occurs in short, radical bursts between long periods of stasis. The smartphone is a radical burst, a novel device whose similarity to immediate predecessors—the pager, the portable digital assistant (PDA), the MP3 player, the laptop, Kodak's music/video/camera device the MC3, even the BlackBerry with its QWERTY keyboard—simply throws its newness into stark relief. I've used the metaphors of "phase transitions" and "Schelling points" to illustrate how a medium slowly then all at once corners a market without consumer debate, just as heated water slowly then all at once turns into steam. The phase transition metaphor can also apply to the adoption of the smartphone. In this case, all those digital predecessors are the heat, and the smartphone is the boil. They came into being and went obsolete so that an always-with-you, pocket-sized, internet-connected computer could burst into existence. Cloud access via eyewear and gaze pattern will be the next "revolution," but compared to the shift from laptop to smartphone, its impact will be narrow: the speed of cloud access has reached its sensory limit with the smartphone. (Direct neural access to the cloud will be the next revolution, without quotes.)

Sci-fi speculation aside, the smartphone did at least stop music media's tactile evolution from cylinder to disc, disc to magnetic tape, tape to cartridge, cartridge to cassette, and cassette to compact disc. That evolutionary lineage—physical inscriptions requiring a playback device—is now extinct. The same can be said about the growth of film stock toward VHS tape, DVD, Blu-ray, and 4K. The smartphone ends the twentieth century's well-trod cycles of industrial development and obsolescence; it is a knife through the heart of physical media's ouroboros. What comes next, nobody can guess.

I am not enough of a Valéry scholar to know if his prophecy—all content made available anywhere in the world with a flick of the hand—represents techno-optimism or ironic skepticism, or if, like Marshall McLuhan, he was simply commenting on the tendency of things.

In this final chapter, I adopt McLuhan's position on media history, both its long periods of stasis as well as the radical punctuations of its equilibrium. The position is best summarized in Ecclesiastes, chapter 1, verses 9–10:

> The thing that hath been, it is that which shall be; and that which is done is that which shall be done: and there is no new thing under the sun.
>
> Is there any thing whereof it may be said, See, this is new? it hath been already of old time, which was before us.

Marshall McLuhan's insistence on the all-encompassing effects of media should not be taken to mean that media introduce anything new into the course of human history. Each new medium simply rolls into itself the content of the old medium: the content of cinema is photography, for example, and the content of print is the handwritten book of the Middle Ages. The new media environment "processes the old one as radically as TV is reprocessing the film. For the 'content' of TV is the movie."[1] McLuhan does note that the speed of electric technology's development is perhaps a novel historical change that has made humans more aware of the totalizing effects of new media: "Today technologies and their consequent environments succeed each other so rapidly that one environment makes us aware of the next. Technologies begin to perform the function of art in making us aware of the psychic and social consequences of technology."[2] However, McLuhan's main point in *Understanding Media* is that even revolutionary technologies like the printing press or the smartphone never introduce new *content* into human experience; rather, they escalate the scale of the old medium's impacts and usher in new mediated ecologies that reshape the grounds of human experience. The twentieth century's rapid technological upgrades, its ever-quickening cycles of obsolescence, have made humans hyperaware of that escalation and reshaping.

All technologies extend the human body and therefore expand human action. The horse extended human legs and feet: in succession, so did the spoke-wheeled chariot, the carriage, the locomotive, the car, the airplane, and the spaceship, each extending the social and psychic (and environmental) consequences of the transportation media that preceded it. Whether or not the automobile's impacts existed, in embryo, in horse and chariot is a provocative thought experiment more than a historical question. Steppe warriors on chariots did bring about a regional cataclysm comparable to the global one threatened by the combustion engine, but we needn't be technological determinists to admit that media's path dependencies are locked in from an early age. Robert R. Johnson's rhetorical frame on technological determinism is helpful. Our lives are entangled with technology—from the combustion engine to the air conditioner—so it's no wonder, Johnson writes, "that interpretations of technology as agent are likely to result. Put another way, when technologies accompany cultural changes it often is not clear who or what is controlling or influencing the change, and the appearance that humans have lost control is a commonly rendered conclusion."[3] Technology seems to exert agency over our lives, in other words, and the *seeming* is as powerful as the *being*. Arguments about the technical necessity of media succession miss the rhetorical effect, which influences both the average user and the engineer. Moore's law—the idea that the number of transistors in an integrated circuit doubles every two years—has produced smaller and smaller computer devices whose processing powers grow stronger and stronger. "Smaller is better" is the path dependency underlying Moore's law. However, no law of physics required increased computing power to correspond with circuit *size*. In an alternate universe, computing power could perfectly well increase on clunky desktop towers. However, when Gordon Moore posited the idea in 1965, it primed the entire network of consumers, corporations, and engineers to accept the premise. The size-power correspondence locked into place, the stage was set for consumer devices to become more portable, to burst out of the office, to splice themselves ever more deeply into daily existence. "As we begin," McLuhan says, "so shall we go."[4]

Nowhere is the point more clearly illustrated than in the evolution of music media. Once sound could be mechanically reproduced, all Lars Ulrich's anxieties were immediately put into play. As we saw in chapter 2, nineteenth-century composers had already lamented that manufacturers of player piano rolls robbed them of revenue, and Arthur Sullivan had tried to sue Americans who performed his revues, royalty free, with bootlegged sheet music. Mechanical inscriptions on cylinder (recall Lionel Mapleson at the Met), lacquer disc, and magnetic tape, each in succession, exacerbated or heightened the tension surrounding the copying problem. "Home tape is killing music," the industry cried, even as Amstrad advertised its dual cassette decks with the slogan: "It tapes tapes!" From printed sheet music and player piano rolls to magnetic tape and of course the digital CD, music inscriptions made it easier and easier for music to be copied and shared, copied and shared, copied and shared. That was the trajectory or, less mechanistically, the *tendency* built in from day one. The release of the digitally compressed MP3 file onto the world's computers and, a few years later, the world's smartphones consummated that trajectory. With the MP3—to riff on a bit from *This Is Spinal Tap*—music could get none more copiable. Likewise, from turntable to portable R2R recorders to the Walkman to the MP3 player to the invisible MP3 files on a phone, music also became more portable as it became more easily copied.

Greater reproducibility and greater portability weren't music media's only built-in trajectories. In a 1950 commercial catalog, reel-to-reel tape manufacturer Ampex provided a list of Ampex Applications, with "Continuous Music Services" listed as a professional use for their R2R tapes and players: "In providing up to eight hours of continuous music without attention from an operator, the Ampex Model 450 sets new standards of economy and convenience for Muzak franchises and other users of background music."[5] The advertisement demonstrates that, even in 1950, professional-grade R2R equipment—like the expensive model 450—had already taken a great leap forward in another one of music media's path-dependent developments: the march toward an infinite playlist. "Up to eight hours of continuous music"! Not many people had access to that kind of device in 1950, but the path dependency was there, the tendency to push music media toward a never-ending playlist: an engineering goal set without engineers ever meeting in synod to set it. Today, of course, consumers take it for granted that the infinite digital playlist is the Platonic ideal toward which all musical inscriptions have strived since Edison's two-minute runtime cylinders. All roads lead to Spotify.

The smartphone is the endpoint of music media's path dependencies. Runtime: infinite. Portability: everywhere. Copies: innumerable. Even from a McLuhanist perspective, the smartphone is something of a novelty because it reprocessed not just music media but all consumer media that preceded it.[6] Music, camera, video, and book all had their unique development trajectories, but the smartphone absorbed all trajectories into itself and is currently reprocessing them. The content of the smartphone is the CD, digital film, digital camera, and the print book all at once, among dozens of other things—map, clock, calculator, mail, and (as we often forget) telephone. It absorbs the path dependencies of all those technologies too, and in a sense fulfills them because they have now been replaced with whatever built-in tendencies the smartphone possesses (too early to tell). The smartphone—in conjunction with the COVID-19 pandemic—is even reprocessing our understanding of live music with the rise of the "virtual concert": an event held at a particular time and place within a metaverse gaming environment, where a musician's avatar performs before the avatars of gathered fans. In March 2020, rapper Travis Scott held a series of virtual concerts within Fortnite's gamescape; the first one was "attended" by 12.3 million Fortnite players, the largest concurrent gathering of users ever recorded in the game space.[7] Not just music media but music itself is being reprocessed by a whole new set of engineered rules and interface designs.

Ditto film. Ditto the camera, which, on a smartphone, turns everyone into a professional photographer. Ditto the map, which now navigates for you instead of helping you navigate. The era of dedicated physical media is over; their evolutions are finished. The smartphone is their endpoint.

Like the computer, the smartphone is a medium of media or, more accurately, a "medium to end all media," as Geoffrey Winthrop-Young describes Friedrich Kittler's view of the computer.[8] Of course, the computer needed to attain pocket-sized portability to end all media. We still used atlases and car stereos, after all, long after the personal computer had made its way into our homes and offices. Now, however, consumers no longer require dedicated devices for different sorts of content consumption or different sorts of mental or communicative work. Unlike the computer, the smartphone makes its processing power instantly and effortlessly accessible. That always-with-you portability turns out to have exerted a greater psychic and social effect than the development of a medium of media per se (i.e., computer or laptop). Like the Walkman, the smartphone is a private music device that disengages its users from their environment while hyperengaging their aural sense. Like the television, the smartphone locks its user into a hot, high-resolution experience. Like the Polaroid camera or the tape recorder, the smartphone encourages its user to engage with reality by commodifying it into remediated, shareable "content." Using McLuhan's famous distinction, we can say that the smartphone is both a hot and cool medium, even within the same moment, as when we compose a text while streaming a music app. Other times, it whiplashes users back and forth between hot and cool engagement, as when we pause a movie to answer a phone call, then "hang up" and go back to the movie. I'll come back to McLuhan's hot and cool media at the end of the chapter, where the distinction will help to explain why the mixtape's death was guaranteed the moment Apple released the first iPhone. The distinction will also assist my final appeal—a McLuhanist rendering of arguments made in chapter 3—to the importance of physical music media.

THE SMARTPHONE AND ITS CONSEQUENCES: STUCK CULTURE

Even if the smartphone has not been a disaster for the human race, it has arguably fried America's collective mnemonic circuitry. The contrast between pre- and post-smartphone cycles of nostalgia and media turnover suggest that culture has both sped up and stopped, simultaneously and paradoxically. Due to our always-on social media and twenty-four-hour news cycles, culture changes, or *seems* to change, rapidly with apps, updates, and viral trends. Nothing solidifies into a mass cultural phenomenon in which a critical mass of people participates long enough to make it a *cultural thing* reflected on in later years. The result is what social critic Paul Skallas calls "stuck culture." (It's possible to blame personal computers, the internet, and social media, but to reiterate, my running hypothesis is that if the internet had never burst out of our home offices, its social and psychic effects may not have been as noticeable as they are today.)

"There just doesn't seem to be that much difference between 2002 and now," tweets journalist Holly A. Bell (@HollyBell8, February 1, 2022). "I wonder if our cycle of nostalgia has slowed," tweets Dr. James Joyner, a security studies professor at the Marine Corps University Command and Staff College. "Nostalgia for the late '50s was huge by the early '70s. There's little wistfulness for the aughts now" (@DrJJoyner, February 1, 2022). To repeat the comparison from the introduction, social media and smartphones have exacerbated a trend that began with cable television. Presented with a hundred channels rather than five, we channel surfed until we ironically settled on five channels all over again, but with this distinction: now we were all watching five *different* channels. Cable TV struck a minor blow to the shared media environment enjoyed throughout the twentieth century. Social media and the smartphone have done the same thing to all content, with a more wholesale destruction of shared media.

Stuck culture is the result, and its impact not only on music but cinema and other arts is increasingly noticeable. In 2016, Skallas wrote, "Half of the top 50 movies released were a remake or a sequel, representing a 312 percent increase since 2000."[9] In his 2022 article in *The Atlantic*, Ted Gioia points out a similar trend for music: "Old songs now represent 70 percent of the U.S. music market, according to the latest numbers from MRC Data, a music-analytics firm. . . . But the news gets worse: The new-music market is actually shrinking. All the growth in the market is coming from old songs."[10] Even as culture proliferates in a thousand niche spaces online, the vestiges of the last century's mass media infrastructure still dominate with old content. The music industry no longer puts money into shaping and promoting new talent—as it did in the highly profitable CD decade, which gave us boy bands and rock-rap and Brit pop—but instead it invests in back catalog music, securing future licensing rights to songs and artists from twenty, thirty, or in the case of the Beatles, sixty years ago.[11]

Two things seem to be happening to explain the 2007–2023 media consumption cycle. First, where shared, legacy media do exist—most prominently on the cinematic screen but also on radio waves and at venues like the Super Bowl. The same pre-2007 content is continuously recycled. Snoop Dogg, Eminem, and Dr. Dre performed at the 2022 Super Bowl halftime show; movie studios devote more screen time to sequels and reboots than ever before; alt-rock radio is stuck playing Red Hot Chili Peppers on repeat. Second, where media have fragmented into the customizable spaces of streaming content—from YouTube to Spotify to TikTok to Twitch—consumers have become so overwhelmed by the rush of new content that, aided by their own self-reinforced algorithms, they end up consuming and reconsuming only the safest and most familiar music and videos, most of which, again, is old content. Decision fatigue exists.

When "new music" meant a dozen songs released on a local radio station any given month, there could be such a thing as new music. When new music means tens of thousands of channels and streaming options, we retreat into old music. Or, at best, we retreat into old music more often than we strike out into the stream's overwhelming rush of content. In the same article mentioned above, Gioia cites a report from music analytics firm MRC Data showing that in 2018 the two hundred most popular new songs accounted for only 10% of total streams. As bad as that sounds, the report goes on to note that by 2021, the two hundred most popular new tracks accounted for less than 5% percent of total streams.[12] It's worth repeating the statistic from the other direction: in 2021, 95% of total streams came from music that was *not* in that year's new Top 200. That 95% includes legacy content that music companies are investing heavily in—the Beatles, Fleetwood Mac, Taylor Swift, and so on—as well as the long tail of niche artists who, altogether, number in the tens of thousands but whose streaming totals are individually paltry.

Although our niche, algorithmically tailored music apps seem to offer an impossible myriad of songs (which we rarely dive into), American music culture at large never shifts into a *new* shared cultural phase. "Culture is no longer made," writes Skallas. "It is simply curated from existing culture, refined, and regurgitated back at us. The algorithms cut off the possibility of new discovery."[13] And where new discovery is possible, he continues, the sheer volume of "new" music overwhelms us. We "retreat" back into the easily navigated media monoculture of the twentieth century or, at best, into those two or three niche musical corners with which we are comfortable. Streaming service Tubi's 2023 ad campaign—"Find rabbit holes you didn't know you were looking for"—emphasizes the contradiction of media abundance and algorithmic restraint.[14]

The noticeable, regular cycles of change produced in the last century's mass media ecology helped to conjure the sharp distinctions between decades and cultural phases. The distinctions never overlap with decades perfectly, but when it comes to shared media from the twentieth century, nearly anyone can tell if a song, a film, a technology, or a fashion trend emerged in the 1920s, 1950s, 1980s, or 1990s. These cyclic waves of development and obsolescence were themselves a new development, made possible by electricity and its mass media infrastructure, as well as tight corporate control over its content: what Skallas calls the "media monoculture." Within the monoculture, for example, a single radio station in Los Angeles—KROQ, along with its hitmaker DJ Rodney Bingenheimer—could singlehandedly make a music artist popular. Whatever new bands KROQ decided to play would soon play across the country.[15] Likewise, a handful of Hollywood studios controlled the movie theaters, a few networks and megacorps regulated radio and television, a limited number of fashion houses decided what was cool to wear, and a countable number of publishing houses decided what people should read. Twentieth-century media were *mass* because they reached everybody; however, cultural production was a top-down affair, its levers controlled by a select few. That's why culture changed at a regular rhythm. The gods of media and content could respond to and shape tastes, allowing market signals to turn into path dependencies. It's the logic of culture under capitalism.[16]

The smartphone changed all that. It gave consumers far more choice of content than had ever been available before, and it gave them immediate access no matter where consumers found themselves. Consumers no longer *had* to go to the theater, *had* to watch network television, *had* to listen to radio stations, *had* to read what the publishers printed, or *had* to follow the fashion houses. We *had* to do all those things in the twentieth century because no alternatives existed (except, of course, DIY media produced under the radar, such as mixtapes and zines).

But the smartphone screen peddles a thousand alternatives, in part because *we* became our favorite content. Videogame and lifestyle streamers on Twitch claim a bigger audience than both cable and network television.[17] Bloggers and Instagram influencers set the tone for fashion and home decor.[18] Self-published authors gather tens of thousands of readers on Amazon and social media (but never tens of millions—such celebrity relied on a media monoculture). Bandcamp and YouTube host the sounds of new musical acts that will never sign a record contract. Whole new genres of music—such as chillwave or new retro wave—emerge and spread in the fractured social media ecosystem without ever making themselves known to anyone not cued into those niche spaces. The legacy media infrastructure still exists, but its lever controllers are aware that they no longer monopolize content production or even content distribution—which explains why, understandably, they no longer take risks, specifically the risk of being tastemakers and culture shapers. Again, in the last century, consumers had no choice but to go along with the monoculture's tastemakers. Today, the randomness of virality and network effects guide consumer taste. For legacy media, that means a box office bomb or a poorly performing streaming network can risk stock tumbles, as the Walt Disney Company has rudely discovered, or swift bankruptcy, as the ill-fated Quibi network learned.[19] On the smartphone, there is always, somewhere, more appealing content.

The vestigial spaces of mass or shared media—movie theaters, network and cable television channels, streaming channels branded with legacy names, radio stations, clothing stores, Barnes and Nobles bookshelves, the Super Bowl halftime stage—have thus been locked into stasis. Stuck culture. The media companies and the content producers play it safe: recycled content continues to make money, after all, so why mess with it? Their attempt to milk last century's analog content into the digital future is what keeps superhero movies and sequels in the theaters (in contrast to the last century's regular clip of genre turnover) and what will keep KROQ locked in to playing 1990s and early 2000s alt-rock until Jesus returns. It's why everyone dressed in 2023 the same as in 2007. It's why a thirty-year-old Fleetwood Mac song helps sell electric cars.[20] Mass culture refuses to shift into the next gear.

Online culture, of course, changes every minute. Niche content, musical and otherwise, fills every corner of social media. However, algorithmic sorting counteracts the liberation of content online, producing the same feeling that culture is stuck. It's a pure media effect, engineered into the user interface and its backend design. On streaming devices, every song listened to, every show binged, and every podcast bookmarked determines what pops up in the interface tomorrow. From one perspective, I suppose, this situation is preferable to the old monoculture, where corporate suits and market reports determined what played on the radio, went out on television, hit the theater, or made it to the bookstores. However, from another perspective, the algorithm is more, not less, deterministic and domineering than the corporate suits. It's no longer possible to wax eloquent about the internet's "liberation of content," as Lev Manovich and others could do in the late 1990s and early 2000s, those halcyon days of P2P sharing and a Google without search engine optimization.[21]

The dominance of old music catalogs on streaming music apps is a case in point. Playing by algorithmic rules, old music's past dominance is a guarantee of its continued and future dominance. New music exists in abundance, but the algorithm is not going to guide listeners to it. In "The Eternal Revenue Stream of Led Zeppelin" for *Rolling Stone*, Amy X. Wang writes, "Monetizing a fusty back catalog is no longer a matter of releasing box sets to existing fans so much as it is curating an artist strategy—or in some cases, a track-by-track strategy—to hook in devotees and new listeners alike. Spotify and Apple Music have made that infinitely easier. While many modern artists complain of music-streaming services' low royalty rates, record companies like to think of streaming as a source of long-tail, and possibly eternal, profit: A slow and steady trickle of money that builds up to a massive pile over time." Wang concludes, "That philosophy works particularly well," both for legacy acts as well as for older one-hit wonders or noniconic acts who are yet "deemed full of new potential to reach young consumers, despite not having released music for years."[22] Every new crop of thirteen-year-old boys was always going to find Led Zeppelin, but there's something about the algorithmic certainty of it now that makes young listeners passive recipients of music rather than active discoverers of it. And I personally find it odd that the few songs most of my undergraduates know tend to be very old; nearly all of them will have heard A-ha's "Take on Me," but not many can agree on the current one-hit wonder.

Finding new bands or artists online requires active wayfinding, even willful defiance of "suggested" links. Most listeners are not primed for that sort of engagement, however, which is why sixteen-year-old girls in the mid-2020s, like sixteen-year-old girls in 2007, are big fans of Taylor Swift and why it was probably an easy production decision to put "Take on Me" in the 2023 (reboot!) *Super Mario Bros. Movie*. Algorithmic tailoring is a self-reinforcing delivery mechanism. It guarantees similarity of content. Your taste is a list of tags. Serendipity is off limits. So, too, is the subtle fact that similarity of musical content is something best apprehended, not by an algorithm, but by you, the individual listener, informed by your idiosyncratic sensitivities, your uniquely attuned preferences, and your whole historical development as a music listener. For example, I have yet to find the algorithm that can reliably place Bach's Prelude and Fugue in B Minor and deadmau5's "Strobe" into the same playlist, even though both hit my dopamine receptors for similar reasons (neither contain lyrics, for one, but even that binary fact seems to allude the algorithm). And yet we have come to implicitly trust or at least accept algorithmic sorting effects. The ethos of digital abundance makes consumers believe their options are limitless. However, because every tap on the play button predetermines what music may or may not be consumed in the next minute, hour, or day, the algorithm keeps content more limited than any corporate suit ever did in the media monoculture.

And yet—here's a bitter pill to swallow—the algorithm knows us well. It knows we shut down when faced with the vastness of the cloud's musical universe, just as 3.5 million Google search results mean we don't click beyond the third link. Even when the algorithm strikes out into the cloud's terabytes of abundance—when, for example, a music app asks if you like this new song—consumers have already been primed to tap *no* and to retreat to the safe familiarity of their tailored music experience. New music that would lift your soul is being recorded and released in vast quantities. Consumers are free to seek it out. They may even discover it. But with every stream, the algorithm encourages them to fall back into the regular beat of music they already *know*. Discovery is cut off because there is simply too much to discover. The simpler, analog monoculture was tightly controlled, but at least it provided us with a dozen new songs every month.

Instead, to return to the main point, the smartphone has made culture stuck. I've overstated my case here, of course. New music circulates in multiple spaces online and even in local concert venues: from lo-fi to underground rap to "core-core" on TikTok, which, Josh Sheppard notes, follows a trend of "adding -core to things" to describe various regional musical cultures.[23] But these cultures are no longer coordinated or promoted by a top-down media monoculture. New musical cultures are not *shared media* in the twentieth-century sense of that term, because the vestiges of shared media in the 2020s are much more interested in legacy content than new acts. The new stuff is locked forever on the phone: on Bandcamp pages and YouTube playlists. There will be no more superstars; no more Sammy Davis Jrs., Madonnas, or even Pitbulls because the smartphone killed the media infrastructure that made superstardom possible.

The ease of recording and distributing music online plays a role too. There were always a lot of garage bands, but now they all have a SoundCloud to promote. In 1971, William Jovanovich imagined a future in which new technologies would allow everyone who wanted to, to be a "published" writer. "Everything will be published," he wrote, "and it will belong to everybody—power to the people. . . . Every man will become at once a writer, a publisher, librarian, and critic—the literary professions will disappear."[24] Musicianship and sound recording, by default, provide greater barriers to entry than writing, but the internet's universalization of distribution obviously has a lot to do with the deluge of new musical content. Hardly any of it, however, is allowed onto the few remaining stages of shared media. New artists may have a million fans, but they will never have a hundred million fans. The ambient media environment no longer manufactures superstar acts, so new artists can no longer take part in a well-defined cultural moment. Shared media and last century's media monoculture were one and the same, after all. The former relied on the latter.

There is a hidden virtue in the default "niche" status of new music and new musical cultures, such as the new retro wave or lo-fi rap scenes. New artists will never be famous or rich, but that's merely a return to the reality faced by musicians throughout history. (As Charles Portis portrayed in his expose on the "new Nashville sound," quoted in chapter 2, it wasn't too long ago that country artists had to tour to make money because profits from record or album sales didn't trickle down to the artists in any great quantity.)[25] The hidden virtue, today, is that new artists no longer need to rely on the distribution network of the media monoculture; they needn't even rely on the old production network, given the accessibility and quality of consumer recording technology. New artists can and do cultivate a fanbase without labels, publishers, producers, or professional sound engineers. They can produce the music they want, hustle it online, monetize it for whatever profits might come, and tour when they cross a popularity threshold. New artists and their fanbases emerge from the bottom up again, rather than from the top down. This new reality provides musicians with artistic and financial freedom, and it also means that cultures and fandoms that develop around a musical style are generally free from the corporate commodification that often bastardized, diluted, or exploited cultures made famous within the last century's media monoculture (the story of N.W.A and gangster rap is the best example of that dynamic, but plenty of country music fans hated to see what happened to the sound in the 1960s, when a handful of producers in Nashville—led by Chet Atkins—decided to make honkytonk popular by fusing it with pop). As new artists and listeners settle into happy contentment with the new media architecture—producing and consuming music in their corners of the internet, meeting in small venues here and there, a comparatively minor but dedicated scene—new music will likely have many bright decades ahead of it. Thousands of bards will arise to wander the digital landscape, most of them good, some of them better than the Beatles and Taylor Swift.

It's too bad you'll never hear most of them.

THE SMARTPHONE AND ITS CONSEQUENCES: CONTENT FOR LEASE

Music by the wandering bards is not free from the smartphone's new rules. The content of the smartphone is the CD, but the smartphone reprocesses the CD, which means the CD must operate according to the new medium's logic. The smartphone was released just after the music industry unleashed mass lawsuits against individuals downloading free music on their personal computers and laptops. It was the device that tamed the Wild West of the late nineties and early aughts, subduing outlaws like Napster and Kazaa. With the outlaws publicly hanged (bankrupted) and their posses scattered (sued), the Apple iPhone rode onto the scene. Here was an entirely novel content-access device. From 2007 onward, consumers slowly acquiesced to its demands and began to listen to music in the approved manner. The digital frontier had been closed. The MP3 freed music from media inscriptions, but the marriage of the media and content industries—exemplified by the smartphone—helped to lock music up on server farms in the Nevadan desert.

The most significant consequence of the new digital architecture is that I don't own any of its content. I own a content-access device. When it comes to music, I own a high-tech radio or jukebox, which, unlike old radios, must be replaced every few years. Also, unlike radios, there is no way I can record from it onto a cassette. Also unlike radios, some stations I pay to listen to—every month. I personally did not consent to these new rules, but collectively, we purchased the devices—drawn like moths to the new Schelling point—which establishes consent as far as the economy is concerned. No one voted on VHS or Betamax, Blu-ray or HD DVD, but we did make purchases. If we don't like the new rules of content access—always leased, never owned—maybe we should have continued buying cassettes, CDs, VHS tapes, and DVDs instead of iPhones. Ceding content to the cloud, it turns out, has meant ceding content ownership to the owners of the cloud. In September 2023, for example, I opened the Spectrum TV app on my smart television, surfed to ESPN, pressed OK on the remote, and—"WALT DISNEY COMPANY, THE OWNER OF THIS CHANNEL, HAS REMOVED THEIR PROGRAMMING FROM SPECTRUM."[26] I was suddenly reminded that layers upon layers of digital chokepoints stand between me and the content I want to access.

The fair-minded Luddite will concede that corporate battles over ownership, licensing, and distribution rights are nothing new. Taylor Swift recently rerecorded her earlier hits because she did not own the songs' master rights. Big Machine Records did, which then sold the rights to megamanager Scooter Braun in 2019.[27] Swift's royalties on "Love Story" paled in comparison to the publisher's ongoing profits. In the last century, such matters did not concern the consumer. Purchasing music in the old days entailed a singular acquisition of a physical item, which consumers could listen to, sell, or give away as they saw fit (the first-sale doctrine). Corporate rights transfers or industry intrigue did not revoke that purchased LP, cassette, or compact disc. A lawyer would not barge through the door at dawn to repossess an old album, explaining that Warner Music no longer owned this artist's catalog, so you'd need to purchase the remastered CD issued by Sony Music Entertainment.

In the streaming era, however, licensing battles can indeed affect the consumer's ability to access content. My inability to access ESPN for two weeks is a good example. Similarly, in early 2023, Warner Bros. Discovery sued Paramount for not providing new *South Park* episodes to the former's streaming platform, HBO Max (now called Max). Four years earlier, in 2019, Warner/HBO had paid a remarkable $500 million for streaming rights to the *South Park* catalog, which, according to the lawsuit, included new episodes planned for development. Paramount, however, was not handing over the new episodes to HBO Max, steering customers via targeted advertisement to its own streaming service, Paramount+, as the access point for new *South Park* episodes. For at least a year, HBO Max subscribers—who assumed their subscription included access to all *South Park* episodes—were not able to view the new episodes.[28] This sort of content variability is nothing new on streaming services. Today, consumers take it for granted that content comes and goes on Amazon, Netflix, Spotify, and Apple Music. We pay the subscription fee anyway because inertia is a strong force.

In the last century, the physical media infrastructure made it possible to purchase or record content once and for all on a durable, owned object—cassette, CD, VHS, DVD, and so on. The content's longevity or accessibility did not depend on the digitally updated whims of its playback device. Of course, the jukebox is an old technology that asked customers to pay a small fee for a single listen; when Dieter Seitzer patented his idea for a digital jukebox in 1982, did he imagine a future in which jukeboxes were the most popular way to consume music? In the 2020s, cloud-based streaming apps have turned all music consumers into jukebox or radio listeners. It's all ad-driven music or pay per view now, a flat fee for content access, and as with the jukebox, the content is stubbornly stuck to the devices we use to access it.

Some streaming services—like Amazon—make it easy to download specific songs and movies and TV episodes directly to a hard drive, a discrete file accessible to the user even without internet access. Some services—like Spotify—provide download capacity but make it difficult, requiring consumers to use a specific app or device to access discrete audio files. Ad-based services—like YouTube—do not offer downloadable files at all. Third-party programs will download YouTube music for you, but malware is a risk with such services.

The reality is that today few consumers go out of their way to download streamed content onto a dedicated hard drive, which is the only way to duplicate the old media infrastructure's certainty of ownership. According to the RIAA, paid music downloads represent less than 3% of the music market.[29] The majority of music consumers share the techno-optimist's assumption that, as long as they keep paying the fee, the content will remain accessible in the cloud. However, anyone who has lost access to an old iTunes account, found themselves unable to stream a *South Park* episode, wondered what happened to *Friends* on Netflix or *Top Gear* on Motor-Trend, or realized that an original version of a song is no longer available on Pandora will understand the practical downsides of cloud-based content access, even without raising larger ethical concerns. Today, when distribution or ownership rights change, or when new editions are released, media companies and content owners don't need to send lawyers to our doors; they simply make content unavailable. It is as easy as Yahoo deleting

GeoCities, MySpace conveniently "losing" twelve years of data, and Elon Musk terminating Twitter/X accounts that haven't logged on in a month. The internet is not forever, I argued in chapter 4, and neither is the content we take for granted.

Paul Skallas suggests that the internet is not forever because data storage has grown onerous enough that it is now a strain on bottom lines, a cluttered obstacle to new growth.[30] Or it could be that media companies no longer want to be associated with older, socially problematic content (such as *Elle Girl* and the "Last Man Standing" pageant). Or maybe media companies are crap at maintaining their own archives. Whatever the reason, "404 not found" error messages have become a set feature of the internet, just as content disappearing from apps has become an accepted feature of the streaming experience.

My defense of physical media, here and everywhere else, is nostalgic but also economic and, for lack of a better word, utilitarian. I simply do not *like* my relationship with music in the smartphone age. I know I'm not alone: physical music sales, primarily LPs, are creeping up. The easy disappearance of song versions is part of the problem; the inaccessibility of certain artists and catalogs is another part. However, one of the most revealing issues with streaming music is that when serendipity strikes (and it strikes rarely), and I hear a good new song, if I'm not quick to bookmark or write down the titular information, I often have a difficult time tracking it down again. Song catching was a problem in the analog era as well, but the current digital infrastructure has deformed it from a joyful pursuit into a search-optimized annoyance. Searching for a specific song becomes an object lesson: when it comes to new music (and music in general), there are no specific songs. Songs on a screen devolve into a stream of cheap and disposable by-products of instant accessibility and infinite runtime.

To be fair, popular music has always circulated as a disposable item. It repeats clichés, employs familiar chord structures, and delivers its total emotional impact in thirty seconds. As a genre, pop music is an effective illustration of planned obsolescence. "These songs are meant as throwaways," writes Joshua Harmon, "to be replaceable by other, similar songs on next week's Top 40."[31] However, streaming apps make all music disposable—from Bach to Bananarama—because that's the point of the streaming media architecture: everything everywhere all at once. Music is no longer a well-organized library of songs and sounds and artists; it is a stream, emitting from a device with which we consume all sorts of barely differentiated streams. The smartphone converts all human art, expression, and knowledge into an economy of scale: abundant, easily transferred, and impossibly cheap. It converts art into "content," in other words: a flat sameness of form delivered via a 2D screen.

I invoked Andy Warhol in chapter 3 as an early adopter of a technology (the portable tape recorder) that rearranged his sensory relationship with his immediate environment. As explained by biographers and Warhol himself, he recorded even the most mundane conversations, converting his interpersonal relationships into a commodity that could be duplicated infinitely. Long before the arrival of personal computers, smartphones, or social media, Warhol had conceptualized identity as mass-produced sameness of form. For Warhol, however, a world in which identities were as regularized as chain grocery stores would be a good one: a world without anxiety or strife. When everyone is alike, everyone can be liked.

Hal Foster compares Warhol's ideal identity with French literary critic Roger Caillois's description of the "psychasthenic subject," whose identity is "not similar to something, but just similar."[32] Coke bottles and Campbell's soup cans are the exemplars here: you could say that each one *looks like the other ones*, but it's more accurate to say they are all *alike*. Coke bottles and Campbell's cans are *the same*, and for Warhol, that flattened, mechanically reproduced sameness is their virtue. "If Warhol's notion of identity does entail similarity, to something, perhaps it's the similarity of the widget, the generic, mass-produced item," writes Charles Reeve. Warhol's quip about Coke cans—"All the Cokes are good and all the Cokes are the same"—is an evaluative judgment, according to Reeve. Warhol means that "all the Cokes are good *because* they're the same. . . . Sameness means predictability, which means easiness. No variable means no choice, which means no thought, which means no effort."[33] The self—identifiable from other selves—does not survive Warhol's commodified conception of identity. Commenting on "the great Warhol figures," Fredric Jameson likewise noted the outcome of Warhol's "sameness is good" philosophy: it means "not merely a liberation from anxiety but a liberation from every other kind of feeling as well, since there is no longer a self present to do the feeling."[34]

Blake Stimson updates Warhol's philosophy for the digital era. Connecting it with Warhol's Eastern Orthodox upbringing, Stimson claims that, for Warhol, "self and society are synchronized by locating all the action at the boundary or screen that divides them."[35] For Warhol, the TV screen was an Orthodox icon of sorts—transmuting complexity into a kissable, knowable simplicity. Although Warhol did not live to appreciate it, the smartphone is indeed an icon, filling the same role of condensing the world into a two-dimensional rectangle. Unlike the religious icon, whose purpose is to inspire transcendental reflection on spiritual realities, the smartphone literally flattens life—and, unlike the television, it exerts influence every waking hour. It should not be controversial to claim today that the smartphone's promise of self-invention, endless optionality, and infinite media experiences is a false promise. The user interfaces are sleek; they extend a customizable veneer. However, for all its tailored temptations, the smartphone screen is not a pivot away from the twentieth century's mass commodification but a distillation of it. The Detroit assembly line starts to look like an artisan craft shop compared to the flat *alike*-ness of life and art accessed via the smartphone. The comparison is expected: each new media environment, McLuhan argues, "turns its predecessor into an artform." The age of mechanization allowed the old agrarian mode of life to take on an artistic ethos, and so, too, will the digital age allow us to "see the entire process of mechanization as an art process."[36]

More completely than the factory assembly line, the smartphone and social media achieve Warhol's ideological vision. They make all art and expression seem "the same"; they mass produce individual expression to a degree not possible in the last century, which manufactured endless copies but offered no mechanism for mass delivery or circulation to the individual. On a smartphone, however, Warhol's "sameness" meets its greatest potential. A feed of shared photos—babies, graduations, birthdays, life updates!—turn into glazed eyes and unthinking reaction clicks. Likewise, songs emanating from a screen end up feeling far too much *alike*, just one bit of content circulating into and out of consciousness without much distinction. To some extent, this conversion of life and art into a flattened "sameness" can be equated with "content," in Kate Eichhorn's sense of the word: a thing that exists for no other communicative or aesthetic purpose than to copy or share itself widely. Eichhorn points to the Instagram egg as an example of content that has no meaning to communicate. Literally a photo of an egg, the Instagram egg was posted by @world_record_egg as a joke to see if it could become the most liked image on the site. It succeeded, accruing more than fifty million likes. The Instagram egg is content in its purest form: a thing that "circulates solely for the purpose of circulating."[37] After a while, it begins to feel as though every photo and every song flowing through the smartphone screen exists merely to circulate.

I suppose all this is a new rendering of McLuhan's observation that specialist technologies (such as print) detribalize humans into distinct identities, while nonspecialist technologies (such as the smartphone or TV) retribalize humans into a collective form of engagement—McLuhan's "global village." At first glance, the viral spread of the Instagram egg seems like an example of collective engagement, "restor[ing] a tribal pattern of intense involvement" that, in his optimistic moments, McLuhan believed may yet produce a global village wherein everyone is intimately involved in the same, low-resolution forms of media engagement. However, clicking "like" on an Instagram picture is hardly engagement in the sense McLuhan understood it or in the sense anyone means it today, despite what we call it.

McLuhan's distinction between detribalizing and retribalizing technologies reiterates his distinction between hot and cool media, which reiterates his distinction between high-resolution and low-resolution media. McLuhan conceptualized low-resolution media as cool because they require the user to provide some sort of literal or mental engagement to feel "complete," such as with a telephone conversation or a newspaper comic or an aphorism. In contrast, high-resolution media are hot because they hyperengage one or two senses totally and intensely, requiring no engagement whatsoever on the part of the users, lulling them into flesh-space passivity.[38] The woman chatting on a low-resolution cell phone in 1999 ("Can you hear me now?") is engaged with a cool medium and is thus truly engaged. The man glued to his seat in a movie theater or blissed out with a Walkman is engaged with a hot medium and thus fully disengaged from his immediate surroundings. We have five senses, and the more a technology hyperengages one or two of them, the more likely we are to shut off the other senses as compensation.

McLuhan imagined the new, "electric" media ecology—the internet, in essence—as one in which the user would engage the entire central nervous system, at low resolution, to participate. The electric media would produce a new, collective engagement on the part of its global users, an engagement quite different from the hot media environment of film, print, and other technologies that disconnected users from their immediate environments and detached them from home and village (print, after all, helped to create national identities, the original "global village" effect). Although McLuhan knew that life in a village could be unpleasant because everyone is always in everyone else's business, in his more sanguine moments, he imagined that the coming media environment might "extend our senses and nerves in a global embrace.... Electricity points the way to an extension of the process of consciousness itself, on a world scale, and without any verbalization whatever.... Today computers hold out the promise of a means of instant translation of any code or language into any other code or language. The computer, in short, promises by technology a Pentecostal condition of universal understanding and unity."[39] The hundreds of millions of teens and young adults in tune to the same viral patterns on social media—from clicking on the Instagram egg to joining a virtual concert in Fortnite—do seem to live in something like a "global embrace." However, what McLuhan failed to realize was that the oncoming digital media architecture would heat up, not cool down, the senses (primarily the visual and auditory senses), thereby *disengaging* users from their environments as much as any film or book had done.

Today, the sort of "engagement" enabled by the smartphone hasn't produced a global village so much as a million disconnected islands. And on any given island, the collective engagement looks nothing like the old rituals of tribal life so much as a collective daze, of the sort that drew Plato's condemnation against the rhapsodes and sophists. Whatever corner of Twitter/X or Instagram we lurk in, whatever the algorithmic path of our TikTok videos, the content we consume does not exist as a center of global life but merely as a thing to be consumed and circulated. Indeed, "engagement" on social media doesn't mean engagement at all; it simply means heightened circulation and recirculation. Hence the terms *engagement bait* or *click bait*. In the concept of *virality*, engagement and circulation are one and the same. The result is that the ostensibly distinct content scrolled through in flatland ends up feeling "the same," like an aisle of Coke bottles or Campbell's soup cans. "When data move instantly," McLuhan wrote in a more analytical and less sanguine moment, "classification is fragmentary. Data classification yields to pattern recognition."[40] Digital content is not able to be classified, in other words, because it is not content at all, in the old sense—it is information, data.

It is difficult, for example, to conceive of an album in the new digital ecology. Contrasted with Rob Fleming's well-organized cathedral of LPs on shelves, songs on a smartphone are interchangeable. The smartphone makes it impossible to experience music as anything but an endless data stream. "An album is simply a data dump now," says Jon Caramanica, pop music critic for the *New York Times*. "The minute albums hit streaming services, they are sliced and diced and the songs are relegated to playlist slots, and everything after that is a crap shoot. The truth is that albums worked as a medium only because everyone was a captive.... I wouldn't be surprised if the next generation of pop stars finds ways to never release an 'album' again—they'll just drip music out, one automated-brain-chip-download at a time."[41] For the same reason, it's impossible to conceive of a digital mixtape. The whole point of a mixtape was its uniqueness. The digital playlist—songs algorithmically sorted or tapped/dragged into a window—is the pale simulacrum, the best the screen can offer to mimic mixtape-making. But it's too high resolution: one sense overly engaged, leading to a general disengagement from the flesh-space environment. Compared to dubbing songs from cassette to cassette (all the while doodling on a J-card), a digital playlist's engagement factor is near zero. The playlist itself, like a file folder on a Windows desktop, is an ad hoc expediency; the files can easily be dragged elsewhere or deleted altogether.

If songs on a smartphone cannot be meaningfully grouped into albums, neither can music be easily differentiated from everything else we tap, drag, do, and consume in flatland. As Twitter clones demonstrate, even the interface designers have stopped trying to differentiate one app from the next.

Digital content's sameness emerges in part because the economic and engagement incentives are by now built into the flatland experience. Every post written, every movie enjoyed, every song wept over begins to feel transactional. Commercial music always had a blatant economic incentive, but purchasing a physical album or record used to be a once-and-done affair; the transaction didn't follow me home and announce itself every time I dropped the needle or pressed play (more on that in the next paragraph). On a screen, every song, every time I listen to it, generates an economically motivated interface effect. The song's real backend purpose can't be ignored: data collection. Just one more input for algorithmic tailoring, one more engagement point tracked by the media conglomerates who license the content (and who, since the days of Northern Songs Ltd., rarely give the artists or sound engineers anything like a fair cut). For music accessed on nonsubscription services, every song feels like an interface effect generated by targeted third-party ad delivery; the song could just as well be a Pornhub video as far as the ad services are concerned. At its worst, purchasing music online from niche, lesser-known acts via Bandcamp or Apple Music starts to feel like charity—a quarter dropped into the hat of the digital gig economy, "a mass deskilling of labor that was once valued," as Eichhorn describes that economy.[42]

The anti-Luddite chimes in: How does describing digital music as "content" or as a mere interface for "targeted ad delivery" not apply to all mass-produced musical inscriptions from the last century, on CD, cassette, 8-track, and LP? In fact, how does it not apply to every cultural artifact from the last century? McLuhan in 1964 could already write: "We have reached a point of data gathering when each stick of chewing gum we reach for is acutely noted by some computer that translates our least gesture into a new probability curve or some parameter of social science."[43] Chapter 3 is a preemptive defense of my position here. The simple answer is that by providing consumers with a dedicated inscription (*the* CD, *the* cassette, *the* LP, to which we can add *the* stereo or *the* Walkman), a musical medium could be integrated into a unique life trajectory, like any other mass-produced object that yet accrues special attachments and meanings over the course of its lifetime in our possession: a child's stuffed animal, a first car, a worn t-shirt, or pair of jeans. Contra Warhol's philosophy, the fact that an item was mass-produced never precluded the possibility that nostalgia and unique, idiosyncratic associations might imprint on the object. Uniquely cut diamonds emerge from the same mine. In the mixtape's case, the consumers did the cutting.

Mixtape makers co-opted mass commodification; they didn't consummate it. Mixtape makers may have been working with mass-produced items, but their effort and motivations were unique to them and their lived experiences. Eichhorn similarly contrasts the twentieth century's "content industries" (equivalent to Skallas's "monoculture") with online content, stating that "even if trite or trivial, or worse yet, dangerously merging the boundary between culture and pure amusement," all the images and sounds produced by and circulated within last century's media monoculture "were still doing and communicating something. Can the same be said of the Instagram egg?"[44] I'd argue that one reason last century's content felt differentiated—mass-produced yet somehow unique in the experience—is the simple fact that it still produced not just "something" but *things*.

A tactile, dedicated object for musical enjoyment—that was the small pleasure of the media monoculture, a pleasure the smartphone takes away. Recall Göran Bolin's Swedish and Estonian subjects, nostalgic for records and cassettes and radios that were obviously items of mass production and consumption. For all its faults, the last century's media monoculture allowed music to be touched, loved, collected, shared, and owned. Maxell may have fabricated ten million cassettes each year, but *I* made that New Wave mixtape shared with the punk rock girl, and *she* made the punk rock mixtape shared with me. Virgin Records may have sold six million copies of *Siamese Dream*, but *I* owned the copy that [redacted] put into the CD player before giving me my first kiss. In the media monoculture, once a mass-produced item entered your hands, it was, despite all its mass-produced-ness, yours to keep and make memories with. Money had been swapped, but the economic incentive underlying music production did not announce itself with every spin.

No one makes memories with a smartphone. If anything, we *commodify* memories with it, converting life into content for engagement points or, in extreme cases, monetization. Also, the phone is a catchall tool. Dedicated to life and work in general and not to any one sensory, emotional, or aesthetic experience, the smartphone's potential for emotive attachment is neutered. It may be our musical medium, but it is also the thing we use to pay bills, check email, order food, find dates, watch porn, and place sports bets. We're as likely to develop emotional attachment to a smartphone as to a desktop tower.

I would like to believe that the future of music is not stuck to this medium of media. The smartphone, in my view, reprocesses music with generally negative effects. The joy of collecting music is gone because it provides no objects to collect; the anticipation of sharing music is gone because it offers nothing to share; pride of ownership is deflated because music is forever leased. Consuming music via a medium of media rather than a dedicated medium also means that social media and other distractions too often interrupt the flow of musical pleasures. Unlike the turntable or the Walkman, the smartphone does not invite long, leisurely sessions with a favorite artist or composer. No one has conducted a survey for me to cite, but based on conversations with students, my feeling is that, following the smartphone's playlist-ification of music, the tradition of young friends gathering in a room together to listen to a full album has nearly disappeared. I'm tempted to explain why I think its disappearance would be tragic, but at that point, my utilitarian defense of physical media would turn into a nostalgic one. I'll simply note that, as a music lover, I feel toward the smartphone the way UCLA librarian Lawrence Clark Powell felt toward information scientists: "To them books in large numbers are merely a nuisance, and they spend their time trying to think up substitutes for them, jargonizing about automation, mass media, retrieval of information, and the dissemination of knowledge."[45] From Powell to Nicholas Carr, many authors have defended the book as a superior textual delivery medium compared to the computer (just as many once defended the codex against the book). I am simply providing the same defense for physical music media. A shelf stacked with hundreds of LPs, CDs, and cassettes is, for more reasons than I'm attempting to enumerate here, superior to a decillion of songs on a pocket-sized computer.

"God has given us music," wrote Friedrich Nietzsche, "so that above all it can lead us upwards. Music unites all qualities: it can exalt us, divert us, cheer us up, or break the hardest of hearts with the softest of its melancholy tones. But its principal task is to lead our thoughts to higher things, to elevate, even to make us tremble."[46] Or Boswell, if you'd prefer: "I told [Johnson], that [music] affected me to such a degree, as often to agitate my nerves painfully, producing in my mind alternate sensations of pathetic dejection, so that I was ready to shed tears; and of daring resolution, so that I was inclined to rush into the thickest part of the battle." (To which Samuel Johnson famously replied: "Sir, I should never hear it, if it made me such a fool.")[47] Given music's centrality to the human experience—some people can go without movies, most people can go without books, but few people live without music—the smartphone's reprocessing of music is worth pushing back against if we don't like what it's doing to our relationship with and experience of this most vital of human arts.

If we don't want to lose the joys of collecting, sharing, and owning music, the straightforward reality is that we need to buy physical media. Physical music sales are creeping up, but as chapter 3 described, the cassette's manufacturing base is coming off life support, and the LP's manufacturing base needs a capital injection. It seems unlikely that media manufacturers will develop new tactile media formats for music. Aligned more closely with media publishing companies than in the last century, they, too, are all in on the streaming subscription model. And why wouldn't they be? It's a successful model—*leasing* music instead of encouraging single purchases. To paraphrase Orwell, if you want a picture of the future, imagine a boot withdrawing fifteen dollars from your bank account every month, forever.

Compact discs, the National Audio Company's cassettes, and the LP revival—last century's media, in other words—are the holdouts. (Too late for VHS.) To reiterate a statistic, the RIAA's 2022 sales report shows that 84% of all music sales were generated by streaming-service revenue.[48] And digital downloads—despite being available to every consumer on the market—accounted for only 3% of sales. Physical media (CDs and LPs and a tiny but growing number of cassettes) represented 11% of sales, an upward trend from 9% in 2019, but physical media are still a distant second to the supremacy of streaming playlists. Until consumers give media manufacturers an incentive to develop new physical media, we Luddites must rely on old formats to keep the physical manufacturing base alive, and to keep content accessible on something other than a smartphone. As the industrial demise of VCRs and the pastina macaroni demonstrate, some physical media may pass a point of no return. Even with a potential market, they are no longer viable and thus no longer produced because the costs to unmothball an industrial base are too great. Consumers must give the boot its fifteen dollars in perpetuity. Viewed in that light, the National Audio Company's stubborn commitment to magnetic tape manufacturing seems like an act of radical defiance.

COOL MIXTAPES

To a degree not endorsed by McLuhan, media theorist Friedrich Kittler underscores technology's internal logic of development—isolated from economic or consumer influence—as the steering force of media evolution. For Kittler, the mechanical advances involved in a medium's development set the stage and create the desire for subsequent developments that supersede the ones preceding it: "Humans are merely along for the ride," summarizes Geoffrey Winthrop-Young.[49] "The unique medium sets other media free," in Kittler's words.[50] A medium dictates how humans may, may not, or must develop it in its next iterative phase. In *Kittler and the Media*, Winthrop-Young pushes back against Kittler's "anti-sociological, anti-economist, and anti-humanist bias against grounding technological innovations in social context, economic imperatives, or the desires of individual or collective subjects."[51] To an extent, I'm inclined to agree with Kittler. The compact disc converted music into binary characters, setting the stage for digital compression algorithms like MP3 or AAC. Digital compression algorithms made it possible for Apple to put a thousand songs in our pockets. It was then a small leap from the MP3 player to pocket-sized computers that convinced America and the globe to discard physical media altogether. That's why I've emphasized the media's path dependencies as well as the Schelling point metaphor, a reminder that no one votes on these technical developments. "As we begin, so shall we go."[52] We vote with wallets, and we vote only on what the engineers provide, and the engineers *themselves* rarely if ever meet in synod to debate how things should go. I don't recall ever asking for a thousand songs in my pocket before the Apple iPod advertised a device for keeping a thousand songs in my pocket. The scratch precedes the itch.

Is this technological determinism? In *User-Centered Technology: A Rhetorical Theory for Computers and Other Mundane Artifacts*, Robert R. Johnson provides a helpful summary of arguments about technological determinism. Given how enmeshed our lives have become with technology—from the combustion engine to the motherboard to the AC unit—and given that our way of living has arisen from centuries of diffuse processes always producing newer and more efficient machines, Johnson writes, "It should not surprise us that interpretations of technology as agent are likely to result. Put another way, when technologies accompany cultural changes, it often is not clear who or what is controlling or influencing the change, and the appearance that humans have lost control is a commonly rendered conclusion."[53] I like this summary because it is not mired in arguments about the veracity or varieties of technological determinism but instead points to technology's rhetorical effect on the average consumer. Technology *seems* to exert agency and power over our lives, and the seeming is more potent than debates about the reality. No one will recall a referendum, a ballot initiative, or a national vote on adopting the smartphone or the automobile. Yet here we are, society and environment utterly changed by both—and a thousand other things.

If all media history is an attempt to understand whether, and when, human agency or technical logics guide the direction of media development, the mixtape is a good anecdote in that history because it complicates both a technological as well as a purely sociological explanation of media turnover. The mixtape both utilized and subverted the medium's internal logics. Mixtape culture could not have existed without the cheapness and abundance of magnetic tape; however, mixtapes had little to do with the cassette's path toward greater portability and greater runtime. The cassette may have created the desire and conditions for infinite and infinitely portable digital music, but the desires motivating mixtape creation were in direct opposition to those tendencies. Mixtape culture required the cassette's widespread adoption, but it can't be described as any sort of by-product of the technical logic that led from magnetic tape cartridges—the last analog music medium—to music qua digital information. If anything, the mixtape represented a medium digging in its heels against the next (and final) stage in its trajectory toward digital freedom.

Forty years after its peak existence, and twenty years after its unnoticed death in the pages of the defunct *Elle Girl* magazine, the mixtape remains a media oddity. It was a media-enabled practice, to be sure, but more than one music medium enabled it: 78 rpm disc, R2R tape, tape cartridge, and compact disc. The cassette tape and its playback devices happened to hit a sweet spot of affordability and portability, turning mixtape dubbing into a culturally recognized artform for two decades. However, as I hope chapter 1 proved, the idea to compile and share bespoke song mixes goes back to the 1950s, 1940s, and probably earlier. Sound archivist Patrick Feaster sets Christmas 1940 as the moment when media companies began to advertise the idea of home disc-recording. Machines like the Wilcox-Gay Recordio made it affordable(ish) for middle-class families to record radio broadcasts onto blank discs. Even earlier, however, in the 1920s, phonograph "albums" were literal album books: collections of empty sleeves for whatever discs the consumer wanted to curate into them. Even in the earliest days of wax cylinders, at the advent of the twentieth century, Edison sold portable boxes for storing and transporting multiple cylinders.

The urge to co-opt mechanically reproduced sound technologies for personal ends stretches back to the earliest moments of mechanical sound inscription. The compulsion has nothing to do with the path dependencies of the sound media themselves. From Edison's cylinders onward, music media have progressed toward improved portability, greater runtimes, and (in fits and starts) better sound quality. Cassette mixtape culture relied on these path dependencies but was not defined by them. If the mixtape relied uniquely on the ratio of portability and quality found on the Compact Cassette, there would be no mix-discs or mix R2R tapes. Chapter 1's "Cornhusker Special" wouldn't exist: a mix 78 with a paltry fifteen minutes per side, on a medium with middling sound quality that couldn't be played in a car. Regarding runtime, as I recall, the mixtape had no use for a neverending playlist. Most cassette mixtapes I made or received contained dead tape hiss after the last song. The whole point of the mixtape was special curation, after all, not "more and more" songs.

If *infinity* and *immediacy* sum up the last century of music media development (an infinite number of songs, played with minimal tactile involvement), nothing was less infinite or immediate than a mixtape. The blank cassette was the ultimate *cool* medium. Less than low resolution, it was no resolution. A blank tape was stone cold dead. It demanded deep engagement to bring it to life. It took effort to craft, and, if you received one, you took time to listen to it. The mixtape converted mass culture into a personal gesture. It disconnected music from the profit motive. It unified content and medium, meaning and mode. If the digital playlist is everything everywhere all at once, the mixtape was this thing, at this place, in this moment. Resonant and present. All senses engaged in low resolution: the auditory sense, of course, but the other senses, too, as we dubbed songs verse by verse, doodled on J-cards, and felt the anticipation of the tape's delivery. It was life itself—a tactile inscription motivated by the flesh-space reality of love and friendship.

ACKNOWLEDGMENTS

This book would not exist without the support of Kyle Wagner at the University of Chicago Press. His belief in the project and guidance along the way have put me in his debt. Many thanks also to Kristin Rawlings and the University of Chicago Press's entire editorial team.

I am indebted to Grammy-nominated sound archivist Patrick Feaster, whose readiness to talk about early twentieth-century music curation assured me this project was worth pursuing; his willingness to sift through his own collection for examples of personalized music mixes assured me the project was worth finishing. Without his 1949 mix-disc, I would not have maintained my excitement about mixtape-making as an important touchstone for understanding America's collective shift from physical to streaming music. I am also deeply grateful for Patrick's help with transcribing the most muddled seconds of that 1949 recording.

The book was greatly improved by the generosity of Bob Purse. His R2R tape collection, his willingness to make the collection public, and his willingness to speak with me made the book's first chapter come alive. Without the commitment of collectors like Mr. Purse, media history would be impossible. More importantly, Mr. Purse's dedication to physical media makes me confident that his invaluable recordings will outlast the fickle internet.

Many thanks to Josh Shepperd and Jason Luther, who provided me with helpful suggestions, potential sources, and general camaraderie as fellow music fans struggling to make sense of what has happened to music—for better or worse—in the digital millennium. Dr. Shepperd made time for an interview with me in a busy year that saw the release of his award-winning book on public broadcasting; I was very grateful for his time.

Thanks to my ever-supportive parents, without whom I would be nowhere. Thanks to my son, Dominic, for being a hilarious three-year-old while I wrote this book. And thanks to my wife, Tina Marie (like the Perry Como song), for putting up with my late bedtimes while I went down rabbit holes of audio archives and old *Billboard* issues. And *credit where credit is due*: one night, while both of us were hunched over laptops searching through newspaper archives on Ancestry.com, Tina is the one who found the 1973 mixtape reference in the *Kingsport Times*. This book is as much hers as mine.

NOTES

INTRODUCTION

1. "CBS, Kenwood, Join in Audiophile Tape Promo," 72.
2. Helopaltio, "From the Music Capitals of the World," 54.
3. Winthrop-Young, *Kittler and the Media*, 64.
4. Packard, *The Waste Makers*, 55–56.
5. Skallas popularized the Lindy Effect, whose cultural resonance has grown strong enough that it earned Skallas a profile in the *New York Times* in 2021 (Marcus, "The Lindy Way of Living").
6. New media's influence on cultural *production* is a different issue from their impact on cultural *consumption*.
7. Skallas, "Culture Is Stuck."
8. It is possible that the smartphone has simply returned us to something like, but not exactly like, the pre-twentieth-century media architecture. The twentieth century's mass media were after all, a historical anomaly. Like the medieval peasant, we are all now plugged in to our little corner of the universe and don't often come into contact with other corners.
9. See Chapekis et al., "When Online Content Disappears"
10. As argued persuasively in Dmitri Brereton's viral article "Google Search Is Dying."
11. Hodgson and MacLeod, *Representing Sound*, 5.
12. Hawk, "Sound: Resonance as Rhetorical," 317.
13. See Mithen, *The Singing Neanderthals*.
14. The reference here is to Plato, *Phaedrus*, 274d–277e, just after Plato's famous description of the invention of writing. Plato of course would not suffer storytelling in either book form or oratorical form or sophistic speechmaking of any kind. Plato's ideal was not only flesh-space speech but flesh-space dialectic as the proper format for discovering truths.
15. Carr, "Is Google Making Us Stupid?"
16. Moore, *Mix Tape*, 43.
17. Recording Industry Association of America, *Year-End 2022*.

CHAPTER ONE

1. Burns, *Mixtape Nostalgia*, 9.
2. Moore, *Mix Tape*, 18.

3. Moore, 9.
4. Moore, 20.
5. Olsen, letter to "Hints from Heloise."
6. Heidelbaugh, "Vietnam-War Audio Correspondence." Also see American Red Cross, "Vietnam War and the American Red Cross," 4.
7. Lynn, "Family records."
8. Portraitsofwar, "A Voice from the Past."
9. For a nice sampling of audio letters, including an audio valentine, listen to Radio Diaries, "Voice in the Mail."
10. "El Presidente Diaz al Señor Edison," Thomas Edison National Historical Park.
11. "A Sailor's Message to His Family—May 7, 1945," Internet Archive.
12. Purse, "Pantywaist!"
13. "Drunk Singing and Talking 1940s?," Internet Archive.
14. Purse, "The 1954 Indianapolis 500."
15. Sawyer and family, "Brown Wax Home Recording."
16. Keillor, "Black Wax Home Recording."
17. Tinkcom, "USO phonograph recording."
18. Bijsterveld, "What Do I Do with My Tape Recorder?," 616.
19. "Manufacturer Profiles—RCA," Museum of Magnetic Sound Recording, https://museumofmagneticsoundrecording.org/ManufacturersRCA.html.
20. Philips, "First-Hand."
21. Purse, "Vintage R&B Radio."
22. Purse, "Recordings from the Very Dawn of Home Reel to Reel Recorders." Side 1 of this R2R tape features home recordings that provide the date range; however, the Lanza/Grayson duets, which date from 1951, could have been dubbed later. A wrinkle with dating these things is that just because a tape or disc contains a song released in the twenties, thirties, or forties, doesn't mean the thing itself was dubbed that early on. Dated labels or contextual clues in the recording are better chronological evidence than song titles.
23. Purse, "Your Hit Parade."
24. Bijsterveld, "What Do I Do with My Tape Recorder?," 620.
25. "The Messiah and Longines Symphonette Radio Recordings," Internet Archive; "1958 Various Recordings," Internet Archive.
26. For example, an audio letter from Ernie Miller, circa 1967, includes Vietnamese radio music, recorded via a microphone. See Miller, "Ernie Miller's Personal Letters to Home."
27. Baronowski, "Lost & Found Sound."
28. Dating an audio letter relies on one of the following: a labeled sleeve or package, a reference to the full date by one of the recording's speakers, tape or disc technical specifications that can help pinpoint a range of production years, or circumstantial evidence (such is the case with this recording). This reel-to-reel tape is undated, and the sailor never mentions a year. He does reference dates, however, that tell us Easter fell on March 26 during the year of his audio letter. Easter fell on March 26 in 1967 and 1978, so this recording most likely hails from the 1960s rather than the late 1970s, by which time reel-to-reel formats had become obsolete; Purse, "An Audio Letter from a Sailor."
29. Lynn, "Recovered."
30. Aslanian, "Reporter's Notebook."

31. Snead, "Gary Snead 22 (28 Aug 1968)."
32. A 1967 audio letter from the same archive references a custom compilation tape, but said tape is not extant. See Livingston, "Audio Letter from Lee Livingston to his parents."
33. Snead, "Gary Snead 01 (11 August 1968)."
34. One audio letter from the Gary Snead collection mentions a man helping Kay Surber with the recordings. See Snead, "Gary Snead 01 (11 August 1968)."
35. Snead, "Gary Snead 22 (28 Aug 1968)."
36. Purse, "A Homemade Radio Show."
37. Miller, "Ernie Miller's Personal Letters to Home."
38. From Jack Horntip's amazing online collection of military song books: "Military."
39. For a good overview of Lansdale's collections and the role of soldiers' "folksongs," see Fish, "General Edward G. Lansdale," 390.
40. Cleveland, "Songs of the Vietnam War."
41. Veterans of the UTT sell a "Songs of UTT" cassette online as a fundraising tool—these cassettes presumably being media grandchildren of the UTT's master recording on R2R.
42. Purse, "Greetings from Germany, 1960"; Purse, "What's 'In the Bag'?"; Purse, "The 1950's on the Radio."
43. Cameron, *On the Farm*, 8.
44. "20 Greatest Duos of All Time," *Rolling Stone*.
45. Purse, "Blowout Post #5."
46. Dating this tape—like many others—relies on contextual clues such as the style of packaging or offhand remarks made by someone on the tape. In this case, the release date of most of the songs cluster between 1959 and 1962, with none after 1962. Of course, that doesn't mean anything by itself, this couple may have just liked older music. But Talmadge, the sender, at 11:15 remarks, "I just picked that up yesterday," referring to the Four Aces' "I Love Paris," which was released in 1959. Again, not a smoking gun, but it's enough evidence, I think, to claim that this tape is from the early 1960s.
47. Purse, "Bob Hope's Murder."
48. Purse, "Bob Hope's Murder."
49. Patrick Feaster, interview with author, October 10, 2023.
50. Thompson, "Remix Redux."
51. "An Important Accessory," *The Talking Machine World*, 6.

CHAPTER TWO

1. Horowitz, "'Illegit' Disco Tapes," 1.
2. Melanson, "Illicit Disco Tapes Surge," 65.
3. Coates, *X-Ray Audio*.
4. Logan, "The Development of Jazz in the Former Soviet Union," 229.
5. "What Is the Private Copy Levy?," Government of the Netherlands.
6. Eggertsen, "SoundExchange Expanding."
7. Harrington, "The [Record] Industry."
8. Harrington, "The [Record] Industry."
9. Fantel, "An Era Ends."
10. Galloway, *The Interface Effect*, 120.

11. A caveat to this framing is that Japanese and German media manufacturers were not the same corporate entities as Anglophone musicians and music publishers, so there was no reason for the former to consider the latter's economic concerns. Producing goods that allowed consumers to create mixtapes was in the economic interest of Philips, Maxell, Sony, and so on, even if it wasn't in the interest of Virgin Records.

12. The *Association for Recorded Sound Collections (ARSC) Journal* contains excellent details about the Mapleson cylinders; members of the ARSC were at the forefront of collecting the cylinders and migrating their contents to modern media. See, for example, Owen, "Electrical Reproduction of Acoustically Recorded Cylinders and Disks," 11–12.

13. Founded in 1894 and rebranded in 1897, *Billboard* is one of the world's oldest trade magazines. It began life as an advertising industry rag but grew into a weekly behind-the-scenes magazine for all things entertainment, from vaudeville to film to early music recording. Its archive is a treasure for anyone interested in the evolution of American media.

14. "Romantic Lands," *Billboard*, 13.

15. "Fox's Suit," *Billboard*, 20.

16. "Highlights of AFM-Radio Talks," *Billboard*, 7.

17. Humphrey, "Air Briefs: Chicago," 9.

18. Bach v. Longman, (1777) 98 Eng. Rep. 1274–75. For an excellent overview of this and other early musical copyright disputes, see Cronin, "I Hear America Suing."

19. I've simplified the story here. For more details, see "The Productions," University of Rochester River Campus Libraries.

20. Hornby, *About a Boy*, chap. 8, e-book.

21. McCartney and Lennon only received a 15% stake in Northern Songs Ltd. when it became a public company in 1965. See Rys, "A Brief History."

22. Portis, "That New Sound from Nashville," 79.

23. Portis, 79.

24. Martin, "Disklegger," 1, 11.

25. Martin, 11.

26. "LP Industry Warned," *Billboard*, 20.

27. Miller v. Goody, 139 F. Supp. 176 (S.D.N.Y. 1956).

28. Miller v. Goody.

29. Miller v. Goody.

30. Dryer, "Writing Is Not Natural," 28.

31. *Prohibiting Piracy of Sound Recordings* (statement of Stanley M. Gortikov on behalf of the Recording Industry Association of America, Inc.).

32. *Prohibiting Piracy of Sound Recordings* (statement of Jack Grossman, president of the National Association of Record Merchandisers, Inc.).

33. Weber, "NARM Urges Action," 14.

34. Copyright Act of 1976.

35. "FBI Raids L.A. Tape Assembler," *Billboard*, 14.

36. Moore, *Mix Tape*, 9.

37. Horrell, "Eight Reasons Why."

38. Smith, "The Sport Compact Nostalgia."

39. McLuhan, *Understanding Media*, 5.

40. Lewis, *An Experiment in Criticism*, 105.

41. Lizardi, *Mediated Nostalgia*, chap. 1, e-book.

42. Pruchnic and Lacey, "The Future of Forgetting," 475.

43. Spicer2, "Hollywood's Vanishing Creativity?"
44. Gioia, "Is Old Music Killing New Music?"
45. Ingham, "Why Superstar Artists Are Clamoring." Also see Rys, "A Brief History."
46. Lynch, "Unwinding."
47. Lewis, "On Three Ways of Writing for Children," 46.
48. Michael Washington quoted in Barrett, "Old-School Ties."

CHAPTER THREE

1. Komurki and Bendandi, *Cassette Cultures*, 61.
2. Komurki and Bendandi, 25.
3. Burns, *Mixtape Nostalgia*, 19.
4. McLuhan and Fiore, *Medium Is the Massage*, 49.
5. Bob Purse, interview with author, October 14, 2023.
6. Hosokawa, "The Walkman Effect," 170.
7. McLuhan and Fiore, *Medium Is the Massage*, 41.
8. The Polaroid picture, Kate Eichhorn notes, was a one-off piece of ephemera. If the Polaroid camera anticipated the smartphone, the picture itself did not anticipate social media circulation. The Polaroid picture was not meant to be "duplicated and shared." It was a "one of a kind document [that] circulated as intimate and singular prints" and in some sense had more in common with mixtapes than the camera itself had. See Eichhorn, *The End of Forgetting*, 40.
9. Reeve, "Andy Warhol's Deaths," 662.
10. Matias Viegener in Moore, *Mix Tape*, 35.
11. Luther, "DIY Delivery Systems."
12. Kurlinkus, "Nostalgic Design," 423.
13. Goodman, "Mr. Jaws."
14. The neighbor kid was the son of a radio producer, so I don't expect as many readers will recall creating break-in cassettes as will remember making mixtapes.
15. See the Museum of Magnetic Sound Recording's wonderful collection of midcentury audio advertising: https://museumofmagneticsoundrecording.org/ManufacturersRCA.html.
16. Burns, *Mixtape Nostalgia*, 99.
17. Kittler, *Gramophone, Film, Typewriter*, 22.
18. Charles Cros quoted in Kittler, *Gramophone, Film, Typewriter*, 22.
19. Kittler, 27-28.
20. Because this is a book about mixtapes, not a precise audio history, I'm going to punt on the 4-track and 8-track question. Both the 8-track and the cassette are fairly categorized as magnetic tape cartridges, so the 8-track can be described as a finnicky, bulky iteration of the Compact Cassette.
21. For a theoretical exploration of the VHS vs. Betamax standards war, see Liebowitz and Margolis, "Path Dependence, Lock-in, and History," 208-209.
22. Conan, "The Mix Tape."
23. See all comments at "First a Vinyl Revival."
24. Knopper, "Cassettes Are Making a Comeback."
25. Bershidsky, "Cassette Tapes."
26. Knopper, "Cassettes Are Making a Comeback."

27. Moore, "Who the Hell."
28. Norwood, "Why 2019 Will Be the Year of the Cassette (Again)."
29. Bershidsky, "Cassette Tapes."
30. Moore, *Mix Tape*, 68.
31. Olsen, letter to "Hints from Heloise."
32. Lili Dwight quoted in Moore, *Mix Tape*, 36.
33. Harley, "Music against Fascism," 145.
34. Bolin, "Media Generations," 124.
35. Bolin, 125.
36. Bolin, 126.
37. Bolin, 125.
38. Moore, *Mix Tape*, 12.
39. Josh Sheppard, interview with author, June 28, 2023.
40. See Reeve, "Andy Warhol's Deaths."
41. Vlach, "Properly Speaking," 19.
42. Prinz, *The Vinyl Princess*, 182.
43. Cianfrance, "Mike Patton/Derek Cianfrance."
44. Komurki and Bendandi, *Cassette Cultures*, 113.
45. Johnson, *Stray City*, part 3, e-book.
46. Moore, *Mix Tape*, 65.
47. Valéry, "The Conquest of Ubiquity," 225.
48. Faithfull, "Dust Down Your Sony Walkman."
49. Komurki and Bendandi, *Cassette Cultures*, 114.
50. Biron, "Vinyl Sales Surpassed."
51. Sisario, "Vinyl Is Selling."

CHAPTER FOUR

1. King, *The Stand*, 3.
2. Fantel, "An Era Ends."
3. Mitchell, "Choosing Tape," 41-42.
4. Maxell UD advertisement, 1984, https://archive.org/details/maxell-ud-90-1984.
5. Stark, "Tape Equipment," 44.
6. Ranada, "The Basics of Noise Reduction," 49.
7. "Merchandising Is Key," *Billboard*, 4.
8. Stark, "Tape Equipment," 44.
9. That such a cycle relied on offshored, mechanized labor was lost on the youth. They simply came to rely on cheap items, taking the market ecosystem for granted. The ecosystem itself took cheap, abundant media staples for granted.
10. Thomas Schelling developed the idea in *The Strategy of Conflict*, 57-59.
11. See chapter 5, "A Rhetoric and Poetics of the Mixtape," for a discussion of the meaning of *metonym*.
12. See, again, Liebowitz and Margolis, "Path Dependence," 208-209.
13. Stephen Witt quoted in Lynskey, "How the Compact Disc."
14. Warhol's quote about the sameness of Coca Colas appears in Warhol, *The Philosophy of Andy Warhol*, 100-101.
15. McLuhan, *Understanding Media*, 184.

16. Taleb, *Antifragile*, 318.
17. Christman, "The Final Countdown,"174.
18. EMV stands for "Europay, Mastercard, Visa," the companies that initiated the new standard for point-of-sale credit cards. EMV chips are produced with glass and circuitry not magnetized tape.
19. Maxell still produces Type I cassettes for the Japanese market.
20. Knopper, "Cassettes Are Making a Comeback."
21. Gregurich, "Unspooling the Cassette Tape."
22. Moore, "Who the Hell."
23. Tanashin was the last company standing in the cassette-deck market, producing cheap tape-player equipment until 2020, a miraculously long time after Sony, Panasonic, Pioneer, and Nakamichi (whose Nakamichi 1000 impressed Craig Stark back in 1972) had exited the market. High-end tape players disappeared first, as early adopter audiophiles switched to compact discs in the eighties and nineties. I recall being able to purchase cheap Pioneer cassette players in the early 2000s, but they made no pretense to high-fidelity audio quality. By 2010, only Tanashin remained. When Lexus installed the last factory-spec cassette stereo into the SC 340 (see Williams, "For Car Cassette Decks"), they likely installed a Tanashin player. After Tanashin exited the market in 2020, its design quickly reemerged, however, from those unlicensed Chinese shops. Today, cheap Walkman clones, expensive retro decks, and all-in-one music integration decks (the kind that offer tape player, CD player, and Bluetooth) are all presumably manufactured by a small number of Chinese factories. If the cassette revival gains steam, these shops may reap the benefits.
24. Gregurich, "Unspooling the Cassette Tape."
25. National Audio Company, "Cassette Manufacture."
26. Del Mastro, "Swipe and Play."
27. Gregurich, "Unspooling the Cassette Tape."
28. Schroeder, "2013 Mac Pro."
29. Nicas, "A Tiny Screw Shows."
30. Cox, "Technics Explains."
31. Horaczek, "New US Environmental Regulations."
32. Madison, "Does This Chart Reveal."
33. Del Mastro, "The Shape of Metal."
34. Del Mastro, "The Shape of Metal."
35. Del Mastro, "The Economic Secret."
36. Del Mastro, "The Shape of Metal."
37. Sisario, "Vinyl Is Selling So Well."
38. Blistein, "This is Disastrous."
39. Gregurich, "Unspooling the Cassette Tape."
40. Walton, "Last Known VCR Maker."
41. Navarro, "Trapped on VHS."
42. Eichhorn, *The End of Forgetting*, 55–56.
43. Kleinman, "MySpace Admits."
44. Chapekis et al., "When Online Content Disappears."
45. In the best-case scenario, a dead link such as ellegirl.com/lastguy may be accessible at a new URL, but even then, there's no way to know if the link has been updated in the intervening decades. The Wayback Machine relies on a steady URL to document such updates.

46. Kricheli, "Updating Our Inactive Account Policy."
47. Imgur, "Imgur Terms of Service Update."
48. Whitney, "Twitter Says."
49. Skallas, "The Internet."
50. McCall, "Google Search Is Dying."
51. Lizardi, *Mediated Nostalgia*, chap. 2, e-book.
52. Lizardi, chap. 2., e-book. *The Wedding Singer*—a box office hit in 1998—proved that audiences were in the mood for 1980s nostalgia by the end of the nineties.
53. Judd Apatow quoted in Lizardi, *Mediated Nostalgia*, chap. 2, e-book.
54. The *Mandela effect* refers to a culture collectively misremembering an event from the past; its name is taken from Nelson Mandela, whom many Americans believed had died in prison.
55. Quintilian, *Institutio Oratoria*, 11.2.

CHAPTER FIVE

1. Burns, *Mixtape Nostalgia*, 77.
2. Carman, "CBS Lineup."
3. Chbosky, *The Perks of Being a Wallflower*, 10.
4. Dean Wareham quoted in Moore, *Mix Tape*, 28.
5. Moore, *Mix Tape*, 43.
6. Hornby, *High Fidelity*, 323.
7. Hornby, 266.
8. Hornby, 56.
9. Hornby, 3.
10. Hornby, 233, 235.
11. Hornby, 252–253.
12. Hornby, 261–262.
13. Hornby, 45.
14. Adorno, "The Curves of the Needle," 54.
15. Hornby, *High Fidelity*, 114, 116.
16. Burns, *Mixtape Nostalgia*, 88.
17. Burns, 107.
18. Sheffield, *Love Is a Mix Tape*, 218.
19. Burns, *Mixtape Nostalgia*, 99.
20. Lewis, "Dante's Similes," 66.
21. Landau, "Using Metaphor," 65.
22. Landau, 65.
23. Johnson, *Stray City*, part 3, e-book.
24. Johnson, part 3, e-book.
25. Synecdoche is a particular kind of metonymy that makes use of part/whole relationships (e.g., referring to workers as "hands"). The relationship invoked by metonymy needn't be part/whole in any strict sense.
26. Yvonne Prinz quoted in Burns, *Mixtape Nostalgia*, 123.
27. Prinz, *The Vinyl Princess*, 200.
28. Smith, *Record Collecting for Girls*, 151–152.
29. Meno, *Hairstyles of the Damned*, 4–5.
30. Sanderson, *Mix Tape*, back cover.

31. Valéry, "The Conquest of Ubiquity."
32. Valéry, "The Conquest of Ubiquity."
33. Hornby, *High Fidelity*, 323.
34. Hawk, "Sound," 315.

CHAPTER SIX

1. Richter, "Vinyl Sales Surpass CDs."
2. Terry, "The Year in the Music Business," YE-46.
3. Riding the Media Bits, https://ride.chiariglione.org/.
4. Lynskey, "How the Compact Disc."
5. Jon Webster quoted in Lynskey, "How the Compact Disc."
6. Strauss, "Pennies That Add Up."
7. Stephen Witt quoted in Lynskey, "How the Compact Disc."
8. Jon Webster quoted in Lynskey, "How the Compact Disc."
9. Sony released a variety of "anti-skip" portable CD players, but to my recollection, none of them worked very well.
10. Spilker and Hoier, "Technologies of Piracy?," 2072.
11. Witt, *How Music Got Free*, 8.
12. Sterne, *MP3*, 3.
13. Witt, *How Music Got Free*, 8.
14. To my knowledge, no one has put together a comprehensive, detailed overview of car-audio turnover. One is left to compare sales brochures of individual makes. The Ford Thunderbird (my first car, or, rather, my dad's car that he let me drive on occasion) provides a representative anecdote. The T-Bird first offered an optional factory-installed cassette player in 1966 and continued to offer it until the T-Bird's demise in 1997; it became the standard option in the mid-1980s. In 1989, the T-Bird began to offer an optional factory-installed CD player, which it continued to offer as an option until 1997. However, when Ford rereleased the T-Bird from 2002 to 2005, despite the retro styling, it came equipped with a six-disc CD changer, with no option for a cassette player. Most car manufacturers seem likewise to have phased out cassette players during the same period. The last holdout was Lexus, who offered a cassette deck option on its SC 430 until 2010. See Williams, "For Car Cassette Decks."
15. Sterne, *MP3*, 140.
16. Sterne, 201.
17. Spilker and Hoier, "Technologies of Piracy?," 2073.
18. Spilker and Hoier, 2073.
19. Sterne, *MP3*, 206.
20. Dunn, "The Rise and Fall." Prior to the invention of the smartphone, MP3 players never did get cheap enough to be adopted as widely as the Walkman or Discman. And after the invention of the smartphone, why would anyone buy an MP3 player?
21. Annual sales of these devices have dropped from nearly $3 billion in 2013 to $700 million in 2018, economically healthier than the cassette's sales, but at least the cassette is trending in an upward direction. In the 2020s, consumers who want a "retro" music experience will reach for physical media, because a physically inscribed *thing* is what people usually mean by "retro" music. The MP3 player fails to offer a thing other than itself.
22. Michaels, "Timeline."
23. Richter, "Farewell iPod."

24. Richter, "The Losers of the Smartphone Boom."
25. Recording Industry Association of America, *Year-End 2022*.
26. Laricchia, "Global Smartphone Sales to End Users 2007–2023."
27. Laricchia, "Apple's iPhone Sales Revenue 2007–2024."
28. Recording Industry Association of America v. Diamond Multimedia Sys., Inc., 180 F.3d 1072 (9th Cir. 1999).
29. Jeffrey, "Downloading Songs," 3.
30. Anderson, "Napster Expelled."
31. Mann, "The Heavenly Jukebox."
32. Josh Sheppard, interview with author, June 28, 2023.
33. MGM Studios v. Grokster, 545 US 913 (2005).
34. Capitol Records Inc. v. Jammie Thomas-Rasset, Case No. 06-cv-1497 (MJD/RLE) (D. Minn. June 2009).
35. Kravets, "RIAA Wants Infamous File-Sharer."
36. Capitol Records, Inc. v. Noor Alaujan, Civ. Act. No. 03-cv-11661-NG (D. Minn. Oct. 2008).
37. Capitol Records, Inc. v. Noor Alaujan, 593 F. Supp. 2d 319 (D. Mass. 2009).
38. "How to Not Get Sued," Electronic Frontier Foundation.
39. Harrington, "The [Record] Industry."
40. Rosen, "For the Record."
41. Laricchia, "Apple iPhone Sales Worldwide 2007–2022."
42. Recording Industry Association of America, "U.S. Music Revenue Database," infographic.
43. "Last Guy Standing," *Elle Girl*, 150–151.
44. "Last Guy Standing," 150–151.

CHAPTER SEVEN

1. McLuhan, *Understanding Media*, 13.
2. McLuhan, 14.
3. Johnson, *User-Centered Technology*, 88.
4. McLuhan and Fiore, *Medium Is the Massage*, 45.
5. "Ampex Brochure."
6. This more accurately describes the personal computer. The pocket-sized computer simply allowed the desktop's nascent effects to burst out of the office and into everyday life.
7. Webster, "Travis Scott's First Fortnite Concert."
8. Winthrop-Young, *Kittler and the Media*, 101.
9. Skallas, "Culture Is Stuck."
10. Gioia, "Is Old Music Killing New Music?"
11. Ingham, "New Music Drops Every Minute."
12. Gioia, "Is Old Music Killing New Music?"
13. Skallas, "Culture Is Stuck."
14. "Tubi Rabbit Hole: Super Bowl," Tubi.
15. Halperin, "It's the End of the World Famous KROQ."
16. For a discussion of the lifecycles of literary genres and how they relate to economic and generational turnover, see Moretti, *Graphs, Maps, Trees*, 67–92, and Underwood, "The Life Cycles of Genres."

17. Aisch and Giratikanon, "Charting the Rise of Twitch"; Key, "Why Twitch Is Giving Network TV Real Competition."
18. Goldstone, "Follow These Best Fashion Influencers."
19. Smith, "Disney Stock"; Mullin, "Quibi Is Shutting Down."
20. Chevrolet, "Chevrolet TV Spot."
21. Manovich, *The Language of New Media*, 73.
22. Wang, "The Eternal Revenue Stream."
23. Josh Sheppard, interview with author, June 28, 2023.
24. Jovanovich, "The Universal Xerox," 249.
25. Portis, "That New Sound from Nashville."
26. Combs, "Disney and Spectrum."
27. Grady, "Why Taylor Swift."
28. Maddaus, "'South Park' Lawsuit."
29. Recording Industry Association of America, *Year-End 2022*.
30. Skallas, "The Internet."
31. Harmon, *The Annotated Mixtape*.
32. Roger Caillois quoted in Foster, *The Return of the Real*, 165.
33. Reeve, "Andy Warhol's Deaths," 664.
34. Jameson, "Postmodernism."
35. Stimson, *Citizen Warhol*, 177.
36. McLuhan, *Understanding Media*, 15. McLuhan points to Siegfried Giedion's *Mechanization Takes Command*, published in 1948, as an example of the industrial revolution already being appreciated as an artistic process.
37. Eichhorn, *Content*, 3.
38. Some confusion about McLuhan's distinction arises because he categorizes TV as a cool medium. This categorization is its own media effect: in the 1960s, TV was quite literally low resolution compared to both midcentury cinema as well as our current cable and streaming television; also, the popularity of game shows and live audiences influenced McLuhan's idea that television invited audience participation in a way that cinema did not. A more recent example of television as a "cool medium" would be *American Idol* and other call-in voting shows.
39. McLuhan, *Understanding Media*, 114.
40. McLuhan, 12.
41. Jon Caramanica quoted in Cruz, "Love Music."
42. Eichhorn, *Content*, 74.
43. McLuhan, *Understanding Media*, 76.
44. Eichhorn, *Content*, 5.
45. Powell, *A Passion for Books*, 19.
46. Friedrich Nietzsche quoted in Young, *Friedrich Nietzsche*, 37.
47. Boswell, *Boswell's Life of Johnson*, 352.
48. Recording Industry Association of America, *Year-End 2022*.
49. Winthrop-Young, *Kittler and the Media*, 65.
50. Kittler, *Optical Media*, 67.
51. Winthrop-Young, *Kittler and the Media*, 65.
52. McLuhan and Fiore, *Medium Is the Massage*, 45.
53. Johnson, *User-Centered Technology*, 88.

BIBLIOGRAPHY

"1958 Various Recordings." Internet Archive. Uploaded by Oldradios90, May 6, 2021. MP3 audio, 1:24:36. https://archive.org/details/1958-various-recordings.

"20 Greatest Duos of All Time." *Rolling Stone*, December 17, 2015. https://www.rollingstone.com/music/music-lists/20-greatest-duos-of-all-time-16272/.

Adorno, Theodor E. "The Curves of the Needle." Translated by Thomas Y. Levin. *October* 55 (Winter 1990): 48–55.

Aisch, Gregor, and Tom Giratikanon. "Charting the Rise of Twitch." *The New York Times*, August 27, 2014. https://www.nytimes.com/interactive/2014/08/26/technology/charting-the-rise-of-twitch.html.

American Red Cross. "Vietnam War and the American Red Cross." Accessed May 1, 2024. https://www.redcross.org/content/dam/redcross/National/history-vietnam-war.pdf.

"Ampex Brochure." 1950. https://museumofmagneticsoundrecording.org/images/R2R/vinAd50AmpexBro13.jpg.

Anderson, Kevin. "Napster Expelled by Universities." *BBC News*, September 26, 2000. http://news.bbc.co.uk/2/hi/business/942090.stm.

Aslanian, Sasha. "Reporter's Notebook: Tapes Take Us inside History." *Minnesota Public Radio News*, July 1, 2008. https://www.mprnews.org/story/2008/06/27/vietnamnotebook.

Bach v. Longman. (1777) 98 Eng. Rep. 1274–75.

Baronowski, Michael. "Lost & Found Sound: Recordings of Lance Corporal Michael Baronowski." *All Things Considered*, April 21, 2005. MP4 audio, 21:41. https://www.npr.org/2005/04/21/3207115/vietnam-tapes.

Barret, Jonathan. "Old-School Ties." *Civilization: The Magazine of the Library of Congress* 5, no. 4 (August/September 1998): 28.

Bershidsky, Leonid. "Cassette Tapes Are Making a Comeback. But It's about the Culture, Not the Sound." *Los Angeles Times*, August 6, 2019. https://www.latimes.com/business/story/2019-08-05/column-cassette-tapes-are-back-but-its-not-about-the-music.

Bijsterveld, Karin. "'What Do I Do with My Tape Recorder?': Sound Hunting and the Sounds of Everyday Dutch Life in the 1950s and 1960s." *Historical Journal of Film, Radio, and Television* 24, no. 4 (2004): 613–34.

Biron, Bethany. "Vinyl Sales Surpassed CDs for the First Time in 35 Years as Records Make 'Remarkable Resurgence.'" *Business Insider*, March 9, 2023. https://www.businessinsider.com/vinyl-sales-surpass-cds-first-time-since-1987-record-resurgence-2023-3.

Blistein, Joe. "'This is Disastrous': How the Vinyl Industry Is Responding to the Apollo Masters Fire." *Rolling Stone*, February 18, 2020. https://www.rollingstone.com/pro/news/vinyl-industry-apollo-masters-fire-951903/.

Bolin, Göran. "Media Generations: Objective and Subjective Media Landscapes and Nostalgia among Generations of Media Users." *Participations: Journal of Audience and Reception Studies* 11, no. 2 (November 2014): 108–131.

Boswell, James. *Boswell's Life of Johnson*. New York, NY: Charles Scriber's Sons, 1917.

Brereton, Dmitri. "Google Search Is Dying." *DKB Blog* (blog), February 15, 2022. https://dkb.blog/p/google-search-is-dying.

Brown, Jake. *50 Cent: No Holds Barred*. Phoenix: Amber Communications Group, 2005.

Burns, Jehnie I. *Mixtape Nostalgia*. London: Lexington Books, 2021.

Cameron, Stevie. *On the Farm: Robert William Pickton and the Tragic Story of Vancouver's Missing Women*. Toronto: Alfred A. Knopf Canada, 2010.

Capitol Records Inc. v. Jammie Thomas-Rasset, Case No. 06-cv-1497 (MJD/RLE) (D. Minn. June 2009). https://beckermanlegal.com/Lawyer_Copyright_Internet_Law/virgin_thomas_090618SpecialVerdict.pdf.

Capitol Records, Inc. v. Noor Alaujan, 593 F. Supp. 2d 319 (D. Mass. 2009). https://web.archive.org/web/20120522123800/http://beckermanlegal.com/pdf/?file=%2FLawyer_Copyright_Internet_Law%2Flondonsire_does_080617TranscriptConference.pdf.

Capitol Records, Inc. v. Noor Alaujan, Civ. Act. No. 03-cv-11661-NG (D. Minn. Oct. 2008). https://www.scribd.com/doc/17299117/Plaintiffs-Supplemental-Disclosure-Statement-10-28-08.

Carman, John. "CBS Lineup Isn't Exactly Scintillating." SFGATE, May 18, 2000. https://www.sfgate.com/entertainment/article/CBS-Lineup-Isn-t-Exactly-Scintillating-2759327.php.

Carr, Nicholas. "Is Google Making Us Stupid? What the Internet Is Doing to Our Brains." *The Atlantic*, July/August 2008. https://www.theatlantic.com/magazine/archive/2008/07/is-google-making-us-stupid/306868/.

"CBS, Kenwood, Join in Audiophile Tape Promo." *Billboard*, November 20, 1982.

Chapekis, Athena, Samuel Bestvater, Emma Remy, and Gonzalo Rivero. "When Online Content Disappears." *Pew Research Center*, May 17, 2024. https://www.pewresearch.org/data-labs/2024/05/17/when-online-content-disappears/.

Chbosky, Stephen. *The Perks of Being a Wallflower*. New York: MTV Books, 1999.

Chevrolet. "Chevrolet TV Spot, 'EVs for Everyone' Song by Fleetwood Mac." iSpot, February 9, 2023. Video, 0:30. https://www.ispot.tv/ad/29NH/chevrolet-evs-for-everyone-song-by-fleetwood-mac-t1.

Christman, Ed. "The Final Countdown." *Billboard*, December 19, 2009.

Cianfrance, Derek. "Mike Patton/Derek Cianfrance." By Lindsay Zoladz. *Pitchfork*, March 22, 2013. https://pitchfork.com/features/interview/9089-mike-pattonderek-cianfrance/.

Cleveland, Les. "Songs of the Vietnam War: An Occupational Folk Tradition." *New Directions in Folklore* 7 (August 2015). Indiana University ScholarWorks Journals.

Coates, Stephen, ed. *X-Ray Audio: The Strange Story of Soviet Music on the Bone*. London: Strange Attractor Press, 2015.
Combs, Mary-Elisabeth. "Disney and Spectrum Clash Leaves Millions without ESPN Access." CNET, September 9, 2023. https://www.cnet.com/tech/home-entertainment/disney-and-spectrum-clash-leaves-millions-without-espn-access/.
Conan, Neil. "The Mix Tape: Art and Artifact." *Talk of the Nation*, July 14, 2005. MP3 audio, 12:46. https://www.npr.org/transcripts/4701169.
Copyright Act of 1976, 17 U.S.C. § 101.
Cox, Joe. "Technics Explains SL-1200G Price and Hints at Cheaper Turntables." *What Hi-Fi?*, February 28, 2016. https://www.whathifi.com/news/technics-explains-sl-1200g-price-and-hints-cheaper-turntable.
Cronin, Charles. "I Hear America Suing: Music Copyright Infringement in the Era of Electronic Sound." *Hastings Law Journal* 66, no. 5 (2015): 1187–1255.
Cruz, Gilbert. "Love Music to Surprise You? Jon Caramanica Recommends TikTok Dives." *The New York Times*, January 1, 2021. https://www.nytimes.com/2021/01/01/arts/music/best-albums-tiktok.html.
Del Mastro, Addison. "The Economic Secret Hidden in a Tiny, Discontinued Pasta." *The Bulwark*, January 13, 2023. https://www.thebulwark.com/the-economic-secret-hidden-in-a-tiny-discontinued-pasta.
———. "The Shape of Metal." *The Deleted Scenes* (blog). Substack, January 19, 2023. https://thedeletedscenes.substack.com/p/the-shape-of-metal.
———. "Swipe and Play," *The Deleted Scenes* (blog). Substack, February 28, 2023. https://thedeletedscenes.substack.com/p/swipe-and-play.
"Drunk Singing and Talking 1940s? Acetate." Internet Archive. Uploaded by Oldradios90. MP3 audio, 6:04. https://archive.org/details/acetate-01.-drunk-singing-and-talking.
Dryer, Dylan B. "Writing Is Not Natural." In *Naming What We Know: Threshold Concepts of Writing Studies*, edited by Linda Adler-Kassner and Elizabeth Wardle, 27–29. Logan: Utah State University Press, 2015.
Dunn, Jeff. "The Rise and Fall of Apple's iPod, in One Chart." *Business Insider*, July 28, 2017. https://www.businessinsider.com/apple-ipod-rise-fall-chart-2017-7.
Eggertsen, Chris. "SoundExchange Expanding into Private Copy Royalty Collection in the U.S." *Billboard Pro*, July 13, 2021. https://www.billboard.com/pro/soundexchange-private-copy-royalty-collection-us/.
Eichhorn, Kate. *Content*. Cambridge, MA: MIT Press, 2022.
———. *The End of Forgetting: Growing Up with Social Media*. Cambridge, MA: Harvard University Press, 2019.
"El Presidente Diaz al Señor Edison." Thomas Edison National Historical Park, NPS object catalog number: EDIS 39847. MP3 audio, 1:56. http://www.nps.gov/edis/photosmultimedia/upload/EDIS-SRP-0190-06.mp3.
Erdrich, Heid E. "Autobiography as Mix Tape for Lady Mon de Green." In *Curator of Ephemera at the New Museum for Archaic Media*. East Lansing: Michigan State University Press, 2017.
Faithfull, Mark. "Dust Down Your Sony Walkman, Cassette Sales Are Soaring Again." *Forbes*, April 20, 2023. https://www.forbes.com/sites/markfaithfull/2023/04/20/dust-down-your-sony-walkman-cassette-sales-are-soaring-again.

Fantel, Hans. "An Era Ends as Cassettes Surpass Disks in Popularity." *The New York Times*, November 21, 1982. https://www.nytimes.com/1982/11/21/arts/sound-an-era-ends-as-cassettes-surpass-disks-in-popularity.html.

"FBI Raids L.A. Tape Assembler." *Billboard*, May 31, 1975.

"First a Vinyl Revival, Now a Cassette Comeback." *What Hi-Fi?* Forums, April 19, 2023. https://forums.whathifi.com/threads/first-a-vinyl-revival-now-a-cassette-comeback.128453/.

Fish, Lydia M. "General Edward G. Lansdale and the Folksongs of Americans in the Vietnam War." *The Journal of American Folklore* 102, no. 406 (October–December 1989): 390–411.

Foster, Hal. *The Return of the Real*. Cambridge: MIT Press, 1996.

"Fox's Suit against MPPA Is Settled Out of Court." *Billboard*, January 16, 1932.

Galloway, Alexander R. *The Interface Effect*. Malden, MA: Polity Press, 2012.

Gioia, Ted. "Is Old Music Killing New Music?" *The Atlantic*, January 23, 2022. https://www.theatlantic.com/ideas/archive/2022/01/old-music-killing-new-music/621339/.

Goldstone, Penny. "Follow These Best Fashion Influencers ASAP for All the Sartorial Inspo." *Marie Claire*, February 13, 2024. https://www.marieclaire.co.uk/fashion/the-best-fashion-blogs-ever-69888.

Goodman, Dickie. "Mr. Jaws." Track A1 on *Mr. Jaws and Other Fables*. Cash Records CR 6000, 1975, LP.

Grady, Constance. "Why Taylor Swift Is Recording All Her Old Songs." *Vox*, August 10, 2023. https://www.vox.com/culture/22278732/taylor-swift-re-recording-1989-speak-now-enchanted-mine-master-rights-scooter-braun.

Gregurich, Avery. "Unspooling the Cassette Tape in Springfield, Missouri." *Belt Magazine*, January 11, 2023. https://beltmag.com/unspooling-the-cassette-tape-in-springfield-missouri/.

Halperin, Shirley. "It's the End of the World Famous KROQ as We Know It." *Variety*, May 19, 2020. https://variety.com/2020/music/news/kroq-kevin-bean-music-ratings-post-malone-1234609654/.

Harley, Ben. "Music against Fascism: DIY versus the Right Wing Safety Squad." *Rhetoric Society Quarterly* 51, no. 2 (2021): 138–151.

Harmon, Joshua. *The Annotated Mixtape*. Ann Arbor, MI: Dzanc Books, 2014.

Harrington, Richard. "The [Record] Industry Goes to War on Home Taping." *The Washington Post*, June 15, 1980. https://www.washingtonpost.com/archive/lifestyle/1980/06/15/the-reocrd-industry-goes-to-war-on-home-taping/80be4100-3fa2-4f73-8999-1efb6dd282d9/.

Hawk, Byron. "Sound: Resonance as Rhetorical." *Rhetoric Society Quarterly* 48, no. 3 (2018): 315–323.

Heidelbaugh, Lynn. "Vietnam-War Audio Correspondence." Smithsonian National Postal Museum. Accessed May 1, 2024. https://postalmuseum.si.edu/collections/object-spotlight/vietnam-war-audio-correspondence.

Helopaltio, Kari. "From the Music Capitals of the World." *Billboard*, July 27, 1974.

"Highlights of AFM-Radio Talks." *Billboard*, August 7, 1937.

"Hodgepodge Tape 1971." Internet Archive. Uploaded by Oldradios90. MP3 audio, 21:04. https://archive.org/details/cassette-01.-sharp-sampler-tape-oct-1971.

Hodgson, Jay, and Steve MacLeod. *Representing Sound*. Waterloo, ON: Wilfrid Laurier University Press, 2013.

Horaczek, Stan. "New US Environmental Regulations Killed Fujifilm Velvia 100 Slide Film." *PopPhoto*, July 7, 2021. https://www.popphoto.com/news/fujifilm-velvia-100-slide-film-discontinued/.

Hornby, Nick. *About a Boy*. New York: Riverhead Books, 1998. E-book.

———. *High Fidelity*. New York: Riverhead Books, 1995.

Horrell, Paul. "Eight Reasons Why the Old Toyota Supra Was So Cool." *BBC Top Gear*. Accessed May 1, 2024. https://www.topgear.com/car-news/retro/eight-reasons-why-old-toyota-supra-was-so-cool.

Horntip, Jack. "Military: 1967 497th TFS Night Owls Song Book." The Jack Horntip Collection. Last modified March 30, 2020. https://www.horntip.com/html/songs_sorted_by_informant/military_songbooks/index.htm.

Horowitz, I. S. "'Illegit' Disco Tapes Peddled by Jockeys." *Billboard*, October 12, 1974.

Hosokawa, Shuhei. "The Walkman Effect." *Popular Music* 4 (1984): 165–180.

"How to Not Get Sued for File Sharing." Electronic Frontier Foundation, July 1, 2006. https://www.eff.org/wp/how-not-get-sued-file-sharing.

Humphrey, Harold. "Air Briefs: Chicago." *Billboard*, August 27, 1938.

Imgur. "Imgur Terms of Service Update." Safety and Standards Policies. https://help.imgur.com/hc/en-us/articles/26479362527771-Imgur-Terms-of-Service-Update.

"An Important Accessory—Albums for Filing Disc Records." *The Talking Machine World*, February 15, 1920, 6.

Ingham, Tim. "New Music Drops Every Minute. But Back-Catalogs Are Driving the Industry's Transformation." *Rolling Stone*, September 8, 2020. https://www.rollingstone.com/pro/features/music-catalogs-value-keeps-rising-could-it-change-the-face-of-the-entire-industry-1056229/.

———. "Why Superstar Artists Are Clamoring to Sell Their Music Rights." *Rolling Stone*, January 15, 2021. https://www.rollingstone.com/pro/features/famous-musicians-selling-catalog-music-rights-1114580/.

Jameson, Frederic "Postmodernism, or The Logic of Late Capitalism," *New Left Review* 146 (July-August 1984): 54–92.

Jeffrey, Don. "Downloading Songs Subject of RIAA Suit." *Billboard*, June 21, 1997.

Jesperson, Otto. "The Fall from Poetry." *New England Review* 25, no. 1/2 (Winter–Spring 2004): 320–329.

Johnson, Chelsey. *Stray City*. New York: Custom House, 2018. E-book.

Johnson, Nathan. *Architects of Memory: Information and Rhetoric in a Networked Archival Age*. Tuscaloosa: University of Alabama Press, 2020.

Johnson, Robert R. *User-Centered Technology: A Rhetorical Theory for Computers and Other Mundane Artifacts*. Albany, NY: SUNY Press, 1998.

Jovanovich, William. "The Universal Xerox Life Compiler Machine." *American Scholar* 40, no. 2 (Spring 1971): 249–255.

Keillor, Mr. "Black Wax Home Recording of Irish Immigrant Song by Mr. Keillor." UCSB Cylinder Audio Archive. MP3 audio, 2:11. https://library.ucsb.edu/OBJID/Cylinder12809.

Key, Kimberly. "Why Twitch Is Giving Network TV Real Competition." *Screen Rant*, July 1, 2020. https://screenrant.com/twitch-stream-viewer-numbers-television-ratings-higher-2020/.

King, Stephen. *The Stand*. New York: Doubleday, 1978.
Kittler, Friedrich A. *Gramophone, Film, Typewriter*. Translated by Geoffrey Winthrop-Young and Michael Wutz. Stanford: Stanford University Press, 1999.
———. *Optical Media: Berlin Lectures 1999*. Translated by Anthony Enns. Cambridge: Polity Press, 2010.
Kleinman, Zoe. "MySpace Admits Losing 12 Years' Worth of Music Uploads." *BBC*, March 18, 2019. https://www.bbc.com/news/technology-47610936.
Knopper, Steve. "Cassettes Are Making a Comeback, But Can Production Keep Up?" *Billboard Pro*, February 1, 2023. https://www.billboard.com/pro/cassette-tapes-comeback-taylor-swift-artists/.
Komurki, John Z., and Luca Bendandi. *Cassette Cultures: Past and Present of a Musical Icon*. Salenstein, Switzerland: Benteli, 2019.
Kravets, David. "RIAA Wants Infamous File-Sharer to Campaign against Piracy." *Wired*, July 11, 2013. https://www.wired.com/2013/07/riaa-asks-infamous-file-sharer/.
Kricheli, Ruth. "Updating Our Inactive Account Policy." Safety & Security, Google, May 16, 2023. https://blog.google/technology/safety-security/updating-our-inactive-account-policies/.
Kurlinkus, William C. "Nostalgic Design: Making Memories in the Rhetoric Classroom." *Rhetoric Society Quarterly* 51, no. 5 (2021): 422–438.
Lakoff, George, and Mark Johnson. *Metaphors We Live By*. Chicago: University of Chicago Press, 1981.
Landau, Mark J. "Using Metaphor to Find Meaning in Life." *Review of General Psychology* 22, no. 1 (March 2018): 62–72.
Laricchia, Federica. "Apple's iPhone Sales Revenue 2007–2024." *Statista*. Accessed January 2024. https://www.statista.com/statistics/263402/apples-iphone-revenue-since-3rd-quarter-2007/.
———. "Apple iPhone Sales Worldwide 2007–2022." *Statista*. Accessed November 2023. https://www.statista.com/statistics/276306/global-apple-iphone-sales-since-fiscal-year-2007/.
———. "Global Smartphone Sales to End Users 2007–2023." *Statista*. Accessed February 2024. https://www.statista.com/statistics/263437/global-smartphone-sales-to-end-users-since-2007/.
"Last Guy Standing." *Elle Girl*, July 3, 2006.
Lewis, C. S. "Dante's Similes." In *Studies in Medieval and Renaissance Literature*, edited by Walter Hooper, 64–77. Cambridge: Cambridge University Press, 2013.
———. *An Experiment in Criticism*. Cambridge: Cambridge University Press, 2013.
———. "On Three Ways of Writing for Children." In *Of Other Worlds*, edited by Walter Hooper, 43–57. New York: Fount, 1982.
———. *The Pilgrim's Regress*. New York: Bantam, 1981.
Liebowitz, S. J., and Stephen E. Margolis. "Path Dependence, Lock-In, and History." *Journal of Law, Economics, and Organization* 11, no. 1 (April 1995): 205–226.
Livingston, Lee. "Audio Letter from Lee Livingston to His Parents, #6, 30 January 1967." 2212AU2489, Lee Livingston Collection, Vietnam Center and Sam Johnson Vietnam Archive, Texas Technical University. https://www.vietnam.ttu.edu/virtualarchive/items.php?item=2212AU2489.
Lizardi, Ryan. *Mediated Nostalgia: Memory and Contemporary Mass Media*. Lanham, MD: Lexington Books, 2015. E-book.

Logan, Wendell. "The Development of Jazz in the Former Soviet Union: An Interview with Victor Lebedev." Translated by Satrina Yrina. *Black Music Research Journal* 12, no. 2 (Autumn, 1992): 227–232.

Long, Seth. *Excavating the Memory Palace: Arts of Visualization from the Agora to the Computer*. Chicago, IL: University of Chicago Press, 2020.

"LP Industry Warned against Handling Pirated Miller Disks." *Billboard*, February 23, 1952.

Luther, Jason. "DIY Delivery Systems: The Extracurriculum in the Age of Neoliberalism." PhD diss., Syracuse University, 2017.

Lynch, Joe. "Unwinding the Birth, Rise, Fall, and Return of the Cassette Tape." *Billboard*, February 27, 2023. https://www.billboard.com/business/tech/cassette-tape-comeback-birth-sales-1235260347/.

Lynn, Capi. "Recovered: MIA Army Pilot from Salem Who Crashed during Vietnam War." *Statesman Journal*, May 23, 2018. https://www.statesmanjournal.com/story/news/2018/05/23/mia-army-pilot-salem-recovered-identified-vietnam-war/621013002/.

Lynn, Linda. "Family Records 'Voices from Home' in 1966 for Sailor in Vietnam." *The Oklahoman*, November 24, 2022. https://www.oklahoman.com/story/news/2022/11/24/throwbackthursday-family-records-message-in-1966-for-husband-father/69661040007/.

Lynskey, Dorian. "How the Compact Disc Lost Its Shine." *The Guardian*, May 28, 2015. https://www.theguardian.com/music/2015/may/28/how-the-compact-disc-lost-its-shine.

Maddaus, Gene. "'South Park' Lawsuit: Warner Bros. Discovery Sues Paramount Global Over Licensing Dispute." *Variety*, February 24, 2023. https://variety.com/2023/tv/news/south-park-lawsuit-hbo-max-sues-paramount-1235534780/.

Madison, Madison. "Does This Chart Reveal Kodak Self-Imploding Again? Are Other Film Manufacturers Following Their Lead?" Fstoppers, February 16, 2022. https://fstoppers.com/film/does-chart-reveal-kodak-self-imploding-again-are-other-film-manufacturers-595687.

Maher, Natalie. "50 Cent Says Listening to Jay-Z's '4:44' Makes Him Feel Like Carlton Banks." *Billboard*, January 17, 2018. https://www.billboard.com/music/music-news/50-cent-jay-z-444-carlton-banks-8094765/.

Mann, Charles C. "The Heavenly Jukebox." *The Atlantic*, September 2000. https://www.theatlantic.com/magazine/archive/2000/09/the-heavenly-jukebox/305141/.

Manovich, Lev. *The Language of New Media*. Cambridge, MA: MIT Press, 2001.

Marcus, Ezra. "The Lindy Way of Living." *The New York Times*, June 17, 2021. https://www.nytimes.com/2021/06/17/style/lindy.html.

Martin, Joe. "'Disklegger,' Riding High, Floods Phony Label Widely." *Billboard*, September 1, 1951.

McCall, Isaiah. "Google Search Is Dying, Something New Is Coming." Medium, March 3, 2023. https://medium.com/yardcouch-com/google-search-is-dying-something-new-is-coming-1c7b1bb1b213.

McLuhan, Marshall. *Understanding Media: The Extensions of Man, Critical Edition*. Berkeley, CA: Gingko Press, 2011.

McLuhan, Marshall, and Quentin Fiore. *The Medium Is the Massage*. New York: Random House, 1967.

Melanson, Jim. "Illicit Disco Tapes Surge." *Billboard*, September 6, 1975.
Meno, Joe. *Hairstyles of the Damned*. New York: Akashic Books, 2004.
"Merchandising Is Key to Increased Audiophile Sales." *Billboard*, May 8, 1982.
"The Messiah and Longines Symphonette Radio Recordings." Internet Archive. Uploaded by Oldradios90. MP3 audio, 1:03:25. https://archive.org/details/reel-to-reel-01.-the-messiah-and-longines-symphonette-monomix.
MGM Studios v. Grokster. 545 U.S. 913 (2005).
Michaels, Philip. "Timeline: iPodding through the Years." *Macworld*, October 22, 2006. https://www.macworld.com/article/182065/ipodtimeline.html.
Miller, Ernie. "Ernie Miller's Personal Letters to Home, 1966–1967 (Reel 5)." 1857AU2255, 1967, Ernie Miller Collection, Vietnam Center and Sam Johnson Vietnam Archive, Texas Tech University. https://www.vietnam.ttu.edu/virtualarchive/items.php?item=1857AU2255.
Miller v. Goody. 139 F. Supp. 176 (S.D.N.Y. 1956).
Mitchell, Peter W. "Choosing Tape." *Stereo Review*, March 1984: 41–43. https://www.americanradiohistory.com/Archive-All-Audio/Archive-HiFI-Stereo/80s/HiFi-Stereo-Review-1984-03.pdf.
Mithen, Steven. *The Singing Neanderthals*. Cambridge, MA: Harvard University Press, 2007.
Moore, Sam. "Who the Hell Is Buying Cassettes in 2020? NME Investigates." *NME Blogs*, July 21, 2020. https://www.nme.com/blogs/nme-blogs/cassettes-resurgence-103-percent-increase-2711548.
Moore, Thurston, ed. *Mix Tape: The Art of Cassette Culture*. New York: Universe Publishing, 2004.
Moretti, Franco. *Graphs, Maps, Trees*. New York: Verso Books, 2005.
Mullin, Benjamin. "Quibi Is Shutting Down Barely Six Months after Going Live." *The Wall Street Journal*, October 22, 2020. https://www.wsj.com/articles/quibi-weighs-shutting-down-as-problems-mount-11603301946.
National Audio Company. "Cassette Manufacture." Accessed May 1, 2024. https://www.nationalaudiocompany.com/cassette-manufacture/.
Navarro, Megan. "Trapped on VHS: 10 Fun Horror Movies Only Available on Tape." *Bloody Disgusting*, July 16, 2019. https://bloody-disgusting.com/editorials/3570660/trapped-vhs-10-horror-movies-available-tape/.
Nicas, Jack. "A Tiny Screw Shows Why iPhones Won't Be 'Assembled in U.S.A.'" *The New York Times*, January 28, 2019. https://www.nytimes.com/2019/01/28/technology/iphones-apple-china-made.html.
Norwood, Aubrey. "Why 2019 Will Be the Year of the Cassette (Again)." Medium, December 30, 2018. https://medium.com/@georgefrancislee/why-2019-will-be-the-year-of-the-cassette-7f9fb91859a3.
Olsen, Margie B. Letter to "Hints from Heloise." *Kingsport Times*, May 16, 1973.
Owen, Tom. "Electrical Reproduction of Acoustically Recorded Cylinders and Disks." *ARSC Journal* 14, no. 1 (1982): 11–18.
Packard, Vance. *The Waste Makers*. New York: David McCay Company, 1960.
Philips, Robert R. "First-Hand: Bing Crosby and the Recording Revolution." Engineering History and Technology Wiki, September 15, 2022. https://ethw.org/First-Hand:Bing_Crosby_and_the_Recording_Revolution.

Plato. *Phaedrus*. Translated by Alexander Nehamas and Paul Woodruff. In *Plato: Complete Works*, edited by John M. Cooper, 506–577. Indianapolis: Hackett Publishing Company, 1997.

Portis, Charles. "That New Sound from Nashville." In *Escape Velocity*, edited by Jay Jennings, 70–86. New York: Overlook Press, 2013.

Portraitsofwar. "A Voice from the Past—WWII 'Letter on a Record' Digitized!" *Portraits of War* (blog), June 13, 2013. https://portraitofwar.com/2013/06/13/a-voice-from-the-past-wwii-letter-on-a-record-digitized/.

Powell, Lawrence. *A Passion for Books*. Westport, CT: Greenwood Press, 1973.

Prinz, Yvonne. *The Vinyl Princess*. New York: Harper Collins, 2009.

"The Productions: Mikado in America." University of Rochester River Campus Libraries. Accessed December 10, 2023. https://rbscpexhibits.lib.rochester.edu/exhibits/show/gilbert-sullivan/americamikado.

Prohibiting Piracy of Sound Recordings: Hearings on S. 646 and H.R. 6927, before Subcommittee No. 3, Committee on the Judiciary, House of Representatives. 92nd Cong. (1971).

Pruchnic, Jeff, and Kim Lacey. "The Future of Forgetting: Rhetoric, Memory, Affect." *Rhetoric Society Quarterly* 41, no. 5 (2011): 472–494

Purse, Bob. "The 1950's on the Radio and at Home with the Coughlin's, Charlie Louvin Fandom, More Shortwave, and the Reasons People Buy Cars." *Inches per Second* (blog), April 16, 2022. https://inches-per-second.blogspot.com/2022/04/the-1950s-on-radio-and-at-home-with.html.

———. "The 1954 Indianapolis 500, the Hits of 1952, More from Germany, Some Pizza, and Then Some!" *Inches per Second* (blog), May 31, 2021. https://inches-per-second.blogspot.com/2021/05/the-1954-indianapolis-500-hits-of-1952.html.

———. "An Audio Letter from a Sailor." *Inches per Second* (blog), April 30, 2017. https://inches-per-second.blogspot.com/2017/04/an-audio-letter-from-sailor.html.

———. "Blowout Post #5." *Inches per Second* (blog), July 4, 2023. https://inches-per-second.blogspot.com/2023/07/blowout-post-5.html.

———. "Bob Hope's Murder, a 75 Year Old Mix Tape, a Lot More Jack Eigen, the Irish in America, 1970's Folkies, Cheesiness from a Night Club and 'Whatever Happened'?" *Inches per Second* (blog), May 31, 2024. https://inches-per-second.blogspot.com/2024/05/bob-hopes-murder-75-year-old-mix-tape.html

———. "Greetings from Germany, 1960." *Inches per Second* (blog), July 28, 2016. https://inches-per-second.blogspot.com/2016/07/greetings-from-germany-1960.html.

———. "A Homemade Radio Show, for a Friend Out at Sea." *Inches per Second* (blog), October 30, 2019. https://inches-per-second.blogspot.com/2019/10/a-homemade-radio-show-for-friend-out-at.html.

———. "'Pantywaist!', a Nostalgic Grandpa, More from Japan, a Short Reunion, and . . . SUNDAY SUNDAY SUNDAY!!!!" *Inches per Second* (blog), February 15, 2022. https://inches-per-second.blogspot.com/2022/02/pantywaist-nostalgic-grandpa-more-from.html.

———. "Recordings from the Very Dawn of Home Reel to Reel Recorders." *Inches per Second* (blog), December 30, 2019. https://inches-per-second.blogspot.com/2019/12/recordings-from-very-dawn-of-home-reel.html.

———. "Vintage R&B Radio, Some Religiosity, Savings Bonds, a Letter to Carole, a REALLY Short Reel, and the Oldest Tape I've Ever Owned." *Inches per Second* (blog),

May 18, 2023. https://inches-per-second.blogspot.com/2023/05/vintage-r-b-radio-some-religiosity.html.

———. "What's 'In the Bag'?, Greetings from Germany, a Few Moments on WLS, and More." *Inches per Second* (blog), June 30, 2021. https://inches-per-second.blogspot.com/2021/06/whats-in-bag-greetings-from-germany-few.html.

———. "Your Hit Parade, Local Basketball, the Newest in Stereo Sound and Much More!" *Inches per Second* (blog), March 30, 2022. https://inches-per-second.blogspot.com/2022/03/your-hit-parade-local-basketball-newest.html.

Quintilian. *Institutio Oratoria (The Orator's Education, Books 11–12)*. Translated by Donald A. Russell. Cambridge, MA: Harvard University Press, 2001.

Radio Diaries. "Voice in the Mail: Audio Love Letters Were Hot in the 1930s and '40s." *All Things Considered*, February 14, 2018. MP4 audio, 5:09. https://www.npr.org/2018/02/14/585776715/voice-in-the-mail-audio-love-letters-were-hot-in-the-1930s-and-40s.

Ranada, David. "The Basics of Noise Reduction." *Stereo Review*, March 1984: 49–51. https://www.americanradiohistory.com/Archive-All-Audio/Archive-HiFI-Stereo/80s/HiFi-Stereo-Review-1984-03.pdf.

Recording Industry Association of America. "U.S. Music Revenue Database." Infographic. Accessed May 1, 2024. https://www.riaa.com/u-s-sales-database/.

Recording Industry Association of America. *Year-End 2022 RIAA Revenue Statistics*. Accessed May 1, 2024. https://www.riaa.com/wp-content/uploads/2023/03/2022-Year-End-Music-Industry-Revenue-Report.pdf.

Recording Industry Association of America v. Diamond Multimedia Sys., Inc., 180 F.3d 1072 (9th Cir. 1999).

Reeve, Charles. "Andy Warhol's Deaths and the Assembly-Line Autobiography." *Biography* 34, no. 4 (2011): 657–675.

Richter, Felix. "Farewell iPod: The Rise and Fall of an Icon." *Statista*, May 11, 2022. https://www.statista.com/chart/10469/apple-ipod-sales/.

———. "The Losers of the Smartphone Boom." *Statista*, June 29, 2017. https://www.statista.com/chart/10066/losers-of-the-smartphone-boom/.

———. "Vinyl Sales Surpass CDs for the First Time Since 1987." *Statista*, April 21, 2023. https://www.statista.com/chart/29781/cd-and-vinyl-album-sales-in-the-united-states/.

"Romantic Lands a Song Sheet Bootlegger's Idea of Heaven." *Billboard*, December 17, 1938.

Rosen, Hilary. "For the Record, for What It's Worth." *The Huffington Post*, June 4, 2006. https://web.archive.org/web/20070218180330/http://www.huffingtonpost.com/hilary-rosen/for-the-record-for-what-_b_22177.html.

Rys, Dan. "A Brief History of the Ownership of the Beatles Catalog." *Billboard*, January 20, 2017. https://www.billboard.com/music/rock/beatles-catalog-paul-mccartney-brief-history-ownership-7662519/.

"A Sailor's Message to His Family—May 7, 1945." Internet Archive. Uploaded by Oldradios90. MP3 audio, 6:18. https://archive.org/details/acetate-01.-a-sailors-message-5-7-1945.

Sanderson, Jane. *Mix Tape*. London, UK: Black Swan, 2020.

Sawyer, Joseph, and family. "Brown Wax Home Recording of Birthday Speeches and Singing of Hymns by Joseph Sawyer and Family, October 22, 1894." UCSB Cylinder Audio Archive. MP3 audio, 3:55. https://library.ucsb.edu/OBJID/Cylinder13303.

Schelling, Thomas. *The Strategy of Conflict*. Cambridge, MA: Harvard University Press, 1960.

Schroeder, Stan. "2013 Mac Pro Wasn't Built in the U.S. Because Apple Couldn't Get Enough Screws, Report Says." *Mashable*, January 28, 2019. https://mashable.com/article/apple-mac-pro-screw.

Sharf, Zach. "Christopher Nolan Says Streaming-Only Content Is a 'Danger' and Can 'Get Taken Down,' Guillermo del Toro Calls Owning Physical Media a 'Responsibility'" *Variety*, November 20, 2023. https://variety.com/2023/film/news/christopher-nolan-streaming-films-danger-risk-pulled-1235802476/.

Sheffield, Rob. *Love Is a Mix Tape*. New York: Crown Publishing, 2007.

Sisario, Ben. "Vinyl Is Selling So Well That It's Getting Hard to Sell Vinyl." *The New York Times*, June 23, 2023. https://www.nytimes.com/2021/10/21/arts/music/vinyl-records-delays.html.

Skallas, Paul. "Culture Is Stuck." *The Lindy Newsletter* (blog), December 31, 2022. https://lindynewsletter.beehiiv.com/p/culture-stuck.

———. "The Internet Is Not Forever." *The Lindy Newsletter* (blog). May 23, 2023. https://lindynewsletter.beehiiv.com/p/internet-not-forever.

Smith, Connor. "Disney Stock Hits Lowest Close of 2023. It's Nearing a 52-Week Low." *Barron's*, July 17, 2023. https://www.barrons.com/articles/disney-stock-loss-52-week-low-a748427e.

Smith, Courtney E. *Record Collecting for Girls: Unleashing Your Inner Music Nerd, One Album at a Time*. Boston: Mariner Books, 2011.

Smith, Fred. "The Sport Compact Nostalgia Cycle Is Finally Here." *Road & Track*, October 29, 2023. https://www.roadandtrack.com/news/g45654193/tokyo-auto-show-2023-sports-car-roundup/.

Snead, Gary. "Gary Snead 01 (11 August 1968)." 1393AU1387, Gary Snead Collection, Vietnam Center and Sam Johnson Vietnam Archive, Texas Tech University. https://www.vietnam.ttu.edu/virtualarchive/items.php?item=1393AU1387.

———. "Gary Snead 22 (28 Aug 1968)." 1393AU1408, Gary Snead Collection, Vietnam Center and Sam Johnson Vietnam Archive, Texas Tech University. https://www.vietnam.ttu.edu/virtualarchive/items.php?item=1393AU1408.

Sparks, Nicholas. *The Notebook*. New York: Grand Central Publishing, 1996.

Spicer2. "Hollywood's Vanishing Creativity? Proportion of Original Films in the Worldwide Top 50 Grossing Films, 1978–2019." Infographic. Reddit r/DataIsBeautiful, September 7, 2020. https://www.reddit.com/r/dataisbeautiful/comments/io3x6l/oc_hollywoods_vanishing_creativity_proportion_of/.

Spilker, Hendrik Storstein, and Svein Hoier. "Technologies of Piracy? Exploring the Interplay Between Commercialism and Idealism in the Development of MP3 and DivX." *International Journal of Communication* 7 (2013): 2067–2086.

Stark, Craig. "Tape Equipment." *Stereo Review*, March 1984: 44–48. https://www.americanradiohistory.com/Archive-All-Audio/Archive-HiFI-Stereo/80s/HiFi-Stereo-Review-1984-03.pdf.

Sterne, Jonathan. *MP3: The Meaning of a Format*. Durham, NC: Duke University Press, 2012.

Stimson, Blake. *Citizen Warhol*. London: Reaktion Books, 2014.

Strauss, Neil. "Pennies That Add Up to $16.98: Why CDs Cost So Much." *The New York Times*, July 5, 1995. https://www.nytimes.com/1995/07/05/arts/pennies-that-add-up-to-16.98-why-cd-s-cost-so-much.html.

Taleb, Nassim Nicholas. *Antifragile: Things That Gain from Disorder*. New York: Random House, 2012.

Terry, Ken. "The Year in the Music Business." *Billboard*, December 21, 1991.

Thompson, Emily. "Remix Redux." *Cabinet Magazine* 35 (Fall 2009). https://www.cabinetmagazine.org/issues/35/thompson.php.

Tinkcom, Harry Marlin. "USO Phonograph Recording Made by Harry Tinkcom [Thursday June 10, 1943]." Harry Marlin Tinkcom Collection (AFC/2001/001/19728). Veterans History Project, American Folklife Center, Library of Congress. MP3 audio, 1:45. https://www.loc.gov/item/afc2001001.19728/.

"Tubi Rabbit Hole: Super Bowl." Tubi. February 12, 2023. YouTube video, 1:00. https://www.youtube.com/watch?v=GtyxWvifru8.

Underwood, Ted. "The Life Cycles of Genres." *Journal of Cultural Analytics* 2, no. 2 (2017). https://culturalanalytics.org/article/11061-the-life-cycles-of-genres.

Valéry, Paul. "The Conquest of Ubiquity." Translated by Ralph Mannheim. In *The Collected Works of Paul Valéry: Aesthetics*, edited by Jackson Mathews, 225–226. New York: Pantheon Books, 1964.

Vlach, John Michael. "Properly Speaking: The Need for Plain Talk about Folk Art." In *Folk Art and Art Worlds*, edited by John Michael Vlach and Simon Bronner, 13–26. Logan: Utah State University Press, 1986.

Walton, Mark. "Last Known VCR Maker Stops Production, 40 Years after VHS Format Launch." *Ars Technica*, July 21, 2016. https://arstechnica.com/gadgets/2016/07/vcr-vhs-production-ends.

Wang, Amy X. "The Eternal Revenue Stream of Led Zeppelin." *Rolling Stone*, May 14, 2019. https://www.rollingstone.com/pro/features/revenue-stream-led-zeppelin-826933/.

Warhol, Andy. *The Philosophy of Andy Warhol*. New York: Harcourt Brace, 1975.

Weber, Bruce. "NARM Urges Action vs. Pirates; Warn of Ruin." *Billboard*, October 3, 1970.

Webster, Andrew. "Travis Scott's First Fortnite Concert Was Surreal and Spectacular." *The Verge*, April 23, 2020. https://www.theverge.com/2020/4/23/21233637/travis-scott-fortnite-concert-astronomical-live-report.

"What Is the Private Copy Levy?" Government of the Netherlands. Accessed May 1, 2024. https://www.government.nl/topics/intellectual-property/question-and-answer/what-is-the-private-copy-levy.

Whitney, Lance. "Twitter Says It's Purging Inactive Accounts: What You Need to Know." *ZDNet*, May 10, 2023. https://www.zdnet.com/article/twitter-says-its-purging-inactive-accounts-what-you-need-to-know/.

Williams, Stephen. "For Car Cassette Decks, Playtime Is Over." *The New York Times*, February 4, 2011. https://www.nytimes.com/2011/02/06/automobiles/06AUDIO.html.

Winthrop-Young, Geoffrey. *Kittler and the Media*. Malden, MA: Polity Press, 2011.

Witt, Stephen. *How Music Got Free*. New York: Viking, 2015.

Young, Julian. *Friedrich Nietzsche: A Philosophical Biography*. Cambridge, UK: Cambridge University Press, 2010.

INDEX

Page numbers in italics refer to figures.

Adorno, Theodor E., 107
AFRN (Armed Forces Radio Network), 17, 50, 51
American Red Cross, 16–17
Ampex, 21, 143
Apollo Masters Corporation fire, 93
Aslanian, Sasha, 26
audio letters, 16–20, 33, 44, 81, 168n28

Bach v. Longman, 47
back catalogs, 58, 145
Baronowski, Michael, 24
Bendandi, Luca, 9, 62, 80, 89
Bershidsky, Leonid, 71
Betamax, 68–69, 85, 124
Bijsterveld, Karin, 20, 22
Blu-ray, 84, 124, 152
Bolin, Göran, 72, 73, 76, 90, 160
bone records, 43
boombox, 61–62
bootleg, 5, 45–46, 49
Boswell, James, 161
Brandenburg, Karlheinz, 122–24
break-in record, 66, 171n14
Brereton, Dmitri, 167n10
Burns, Jehnie I., 2, 14, 67, 102, 108

Capitol Records, Inc. v. Noor Alaujan, 132
Capitol Records Inc. v. Jammie Thomas-Rasset, 132
Carman, John, 103

Carr, Nicholas, 7, 161
cassette: industrial production, 88–91; revival, 69–70, 78, 89, 173n23; technical details, 81–84
Chbosky, Stephen, 102
Cianfrance, Derek, 75
Coates, Stephen, 43
Conan, Neil, 69
Copyright Act: of 1909, 51–52; of 1976, 55–56
Cros, Charles, 68

Dead Kennedys, 61
Del Mastro, Addison, 90, 92, 93, 94
Discman, 120, 127, 128
disco tapes, 42, 44, 45, 56
diskleggers, 49, 54
Dolby, 82–83
Dryer, Dylan B., 52

Edison, Thomas, 17, 67
Eichhorn, Kate, 95, 156, 159, 160, 171n8
8-tracks, 3, 15, 42, 89, 120
Elle Girl, 96, 136–38

file sharing, 11, 77, 125, 128–35
first-sale doctrine, 43, 61, 152
Fish, Lydia M., 30
Foster, Hal, 155
4-tracks, 3, 15, 89
Fraunhofer-Gesellschaft, 123–25, 129, 131

Galloway, Alexander R., 45
GeoCities, 96, 154
Gioia, Ted, 145, 146
Goodman, Dickie, 66
Gregurich, Avery, 90
Guardians of the Galaxy, 89, 102

Harley, Ben, 72
Harmon, Joshua, 154
Hawk, Byron, 6, 115
HD-DVD, 84, 124, 152
headphones, 6, 7, 62, 63, 64, 115, 126
High Fidelity, 34, 48, 102–8, 116, 117
hip-hop, 1, 10
Hodgson, Jay, 6
Hoier, Svein, 125
Home Audio Recording Act of 1992, 43, 44, 130, 134
home recordings, 8, 16–20, 44, 81
Hornby, Nick, 48, 102–8
Horntip, Jack, *31*
Hosokawa, Shuhei, 64

internet: dial-up, 77, 122, 129; and longevity, 95–98, 154

Jameson, Fredric, 155
J-card, 9, 76, 114, 119, 158
Johnson, Chelsey, 75, 111–12
Johnson, Robert R., 142, 163
Jovanovich, William, 150

King, Stephen, 80
Kingsport Times, 15, *16*, 42, 71
Kittler, Friedrich, 68, 162
Komurki, John Z., 9, 62, 80, 89
KROQ, 147, 148
Krug, Joseph, 50–51, 52, 53
Kurlinkus, William C., 65

Lacey, Kim, 57–58
Landau, Mark J., 110
Lewis, C. S., 57, 59, 110
Lindy effect, 3, 86–87, 167n5
Lizardi, Ryan, 57–59, 98–99
Luther, Jason, 9, 65, 66

MacLeod, Steve, 6
Mann, Charles C., 130
Manovich, Lev, 148
Mapleson, Lionel, 46, 142
Mapleson cylinders, 46, 170n12
McCall, Isaiah, 98
McLuhan, Marshall, 2, 4, 57, 62, 64, 141, 142, 156–59, 162, 177n36
media: monoculture, 12, 146–51, 160; physical ownership of, 151–62
MGM Studios v. Grokster, 131
Miller, Ernie, 29–32
Miller v. Goody, 50–52
mixtapes: on compact discs, 77–78, 125–28; as DIY culture, 9, 53, 66–67, 74–78, 147; as figure of arrangement, 108–10; as metaphor, 110–12; as metonymy, 112; on reel-to-reel tape, 20–23, 27, 28, 29, 32–34, 35; on 78 rpm, 36–40; in Vietnam, 23–32
Moore, Thurston, 10, 14, 69, 71, 73, 104
MP2, 121, 123, 124
MP3: encoders, 124–25; players, 103, 125–28, 130
MPEG (Moving Pictures Expert Group), 118, 123
multiturntable machines, 37
music: digital algorithms, 146–51; licensing and publishing, 46–48, 119, 145, 152–53, 159, 170n21; live concerts, 5–8; sheet, 46–49, 51, 52, 134, 142; virtual concerts, 143
MySpace, 96, 97, 98, 154

NAC (National Audio Company), 88–91
Norelco, 16, 64, 82
nostalgic cycles, 56–59, 98–101, 138–39

Oldradios90, 23
Olsen, Margie B., 15–16, 42, 56, 71, 76, 102

P2P (peer-to-peer) sharing, 11, 77, 125, 128–35
Packard, Vance, 2
Philips, 15, 20, 25, 43, 82, 83, 102, 117, 119, 123, 131, 134, 135

phono-post booths, 17, 53
Plato, 7, 167n14
player pianos, 49, 142
Polaroid, 58, 64, 114, 144, 171n8
Portis, Charles, 48, 51, 150
Powell, Lawrence, 161
Pruchnic, Jeff, 57–58
psychoacoustic research, 121, 122
Purse, Bob, 18, 21, 22, 28, 29, 32, 35, 36, 63

Quintilian, 101

Ranada, David, 83
rap, 1, 102, 139, 150, 151
RCA (Radio Corporation of America), 15, 20, 34, 37
Recording Industry Association of America v. Diamond Multimedia Sys., Inc., 129–30, 134
Reeve, Charles, 155
RIAA (Recording Industry Association of America), 43, 55–56, 128–34, 136, 153
Rosen, Hilary, 134, 135

Sanderson, Jane, 113
Schelling point, 84–86, 93, 120, 128, 129, 152, 162
Scotch, 20, 21, 22, 25
Seitzer, Dieter, 121–23, 135, 153
Sheffield, Rob, 102, 109–10
Skallas, Paul, 3, 4, 86, 97, 145, 146, 147, 154, 167n5
Smith, Courtney E., 113
Snead, Gary and Kay, 27–28
sonic rhetoric, 6, 72
Sony BMG v. Tenenbaum, 132–33

Spilker, Hendrik Storstein, 125
Stark, Craig, 82, 84, 173n23
Sterne, Jonathan, 118, 123
Stimson, Blake, 155
stuck culture, 4, 12, 59, 144–51, 153
Sullivan, Arthur, 47, 48, 134, 142
Surber, Kay. *See* Snead, Gary and Kay

Taleb, Nassim Nicholas, 87
technological determinism, 142, 163
Thompson, Emily, 37
3M, 17, 25
turntables, 34, 37, 75, 91, 160

Urban Outfitters, 89, 90

Valéry, Paul, 77, 114–15, 122, 141
VCR, 84, 94, 95, 162
VHS, 85, 94, 95, 120, 124, 140, 152, 162
Vietnam unit song books, 29–32
Virgin Records, 118, 119, 160
Vlach, John Michael, 75
"Voices from Home," 16, 25, 34

Walkman, 3, 61–64, 71, 90, 120, 144, 157, 160
Wang, Amy X., 148, 149
Warhol, Andy, 64, 74, 86, 155
wax cylinders, 17, 19, 38, 46, 143, 164
Webster, Jon, 118, 119
Westinghouse, 62, 63
What Hi-Fi?, 69–70
Wilcox-Gay Recordio, 21, 38, 164
Winthrop-Young, Geoffrey, 2, 3, 144, 162
Witt, Stephen, 86, 118, 119, 122, 124

www.ingramcontent.com/pod-product-compliance
Lightning Source LLC
Chambersburg PA
CBHW022011290426
44109CB00015B/1140